STEPHEN   RAIA

JANNER'S COMPLETE PRODUCT LIABILITY

GREVILLE JANNER QC MP

*J*ANNER'S COMPLETE PRODUCT LIABILITY

Incorporating Peter Madge
on Product Liability Insurance

Gower

Published by
Gower Publishing Company Limited,
Gower House,
Croft Road,
Aldershot,
Hants GU11 3HR,
England

Gower Publishing Company,
Old Post Road,
Brookfield,
Vermont 05036,
U.S.A.

The authors and Gower Publishing Company Limited have used their best efforts in collecting and preparing material for inclusion in *Janner's Complete Product Liability*. They do not assume, and hereby disclaim, any liability to any party for any loss or damage caused by errors or omissions in *Janner's Complete Product Liability*, whether such errors or omissions result from negligence, accident or any other cause.

British Library Cataloguing in Publication Data

Janner, Greville
    Janner's complete product liability,
    incorporating Peter Madge on product
    liability insurance.
    1. Products liability——Great Britain
    I. Title   II. Madge, Peter
    344.1063'82   KD1987

    ISBN 0–566–02747–X

Printed and bound in Great Britain by
Biddles Ltd, Guildford and King's Lynn

To
Davide Sala and Sami Shamoon
with my thanks for their friendship and kindness
and with great affection

Contents

PART II LIABILITY IN NEGLIGENCE

PART III THE CONSUMER PROTECTION ACT 1987: CIVIL LIABILITY

Contents

directors and employees – costs and expenses of criminal
proceedings – cross-liabilities – retrospective cover –
excess of loss policies – residual product liability

Acknowledgements

My thanks are due to Willis, Faber and Dumas for sponsoring this work and contributing its insurance sections; to Christopher Newdick of Reading University for his assistance with the research and writing, in particular in updating parts which appeared in my previous book on this subject; to my partner, Paul Secher, and to our colleague, Leslie Benson, for their work in revising and proofreading the text; and to Pat Garner, Margaret Lancaster, Hermione Winters and Mandy Brooks, who between them have typed and retyped it.

GJ

Introduction

The Thalidomide disaster sparked off that angry demand for legal change which, in the UK, has culminated in the 'product liability' rules contained in the Consumer Protection Act 1987. This book sets out and explains those rules, in the context of the general law of contract, negligence and crime, without which they can be neither understood nor applied. And with the valued contribution from Peter Madge of Willis, Faber and Dumas, we explain the insurance consequences and how to cope with them to the best effect and at the least cost.

In ordinary English, the words 'product liability' mean: liability of those who produce a product or put it into circulation, where that product is defective and the defect causes death, injury or damage. In the jargon of both law and commerce, it has come to mean: 'strict' or 'without fault' liability for the effects of such defects. Broadly, where such defects cause damage the sufferer does not have to prove negligence; instead, the producer, the importer into the EEC or the 'own-brander' is presumed to have been negligent. The burden of proof shifts on to him.

Liability is not 'absolute'. The defendant may establish one of a number of defences. But the task of the sufferer becomes vastly lighter; the burden on the defendant increases; and so will the premiums charged by his insurers.

Where the sufferer is the direct purchaser of the product, the situation remains largely unchanged. Liability under the law of contract never did depend upon fault. If the goods you buy are defective, you are not in the least concerned as to why the defect occurred or whether the supplier has some reasonable excuse for the default. He is in breach of contract; you are entitled to your remedy – his liability is 'strict'.

This book explains the basic rules of contract law, with the minimum of jargon and the maximum of clarity. Whether you are dealing with contract law in your business or in private life (as a 'consumer'), we offer you the essential rules, in readable and digestible form.

Unfortunately, 'no fault' liability contract law applies (in general) only to those who are parties to the contract. The Thalidomide parents and children (for instance) could not bring actions in contract against the manufacturers of the disaster drug because they had no contract with them. They had to sue in the 'tort' (or civil wrong) of negligence. They had to prove positively that the manufacturers were careless – that they had acted without proper care or that they had failed to take such steps as a reasonable, skilful manufacturer would have done, whether by testing or otherwise, to avoid marketing a defective product.

This burden was so heavy that the UK plaintiffs, without exception, settled their cases. They accepted sums far smaller than courts would have awarded, had they won their cases. Manufacturers pleaded that they had taken such steps as were reasonably practicable, having regard to the current state of medical and scientific knowledge (the 'state of the art' defence). Recognizing that this defence could well have succeeded, the unhappy plaintiffs felt forced to settle their cases. Had the burden of proving innocence rested on the manufacturers, the plaintiffs' prospect of success would have been excellent. As it was, justice (most people felt) had emphatically not been done.

The English and Welsh Law Commission, the Scottish Law Commission and, above all, the Royal Commission on Civil Liability, chaired by the late Lord Pearson (the Pearson Commission) unanimously recommended that the principle of strict, no fault liability for defective products should be introduced into UK law. It had already crept into US law, largely through court decisions; and (by statute) into the laws of France and West Germany.

The EEC introduced a draft directive on product liability, and then a revised draft. Largely due to opposition from the UK, this directive was blocked. In July 1986, the UK government withdrew its opposition; Parliament approved the directive, which then came into force; all members of the EEC were required to introduce product liability legislation by August 1988. The UK legislation is in the Consumer Protection Act 1987.

Like the law of contract, that of negligence remains in force. It is strengthened, not replaced, by the new rules. So this book explains the law of negligence, as it does those of contract.

In one sphere only, UK law already operated the 'strict liability' principle. If an employee suffers death or personal injury due to a defect in plant or equipment supplied at work, his employers are deemed to have been negligent. The Employers' Liability (Defective Equipment) Act 1969 shifts the burden of proof from the suffering employee or (if killed) from his dependants. Negligence is presumed against the employers.

In employment cases, as in all others, even if the defendants are liable to the plaintiffs, they may still seek contribution or indemnity from those who are really responsible. For instance: I am your employee and am injured by defective equipment which you supplied to me; you will be liable to pay my damages. But if you can show (for instance) that the true fault lay with (say) those who supplied the defective equipment to you – or who installed or maintained it – or even those who designed it – you can bring them into the legal proceedings and seek your remedy against them. The same principles apply to product liability litigation, brought under the 1987 Act, as we shall explain.

The law of contract, of negligence and the strict 'product liability' rules are all part of the civil law. They are designed to give remedies to people who are affected or afflicted by the wrongful acts of others. Actions are brought in civil courts, claiming civil remedies.

The criminal law runs alongside, imposing rules designed to protect the community as a whole – to set up, maintain and enforce minimum standards of conduct. If your products are defective and cause injury, the sufferer may sue. And whether or not he does so, you may also be prosecuted – taken before a criminal court, charged with a criminal offence.

The Health and Safety at Work Act 1974 is the Crown's most

likely vehicle for attack. But other sections of the Consumer
Protection Act 1987, or the Trade Descriptions Act 1968, or the
Factories Acts – or many other criminal statutes, sometimes
specific to the particular equipment or circumstances – may be
wheeled into action.

As the streams of the civil and criminal law flow alongside and
so often intermingle, proper consideration of product liability
involves an understanding of both. The civil law is bad enough for
the businessman, especially if product liability rules apply. But at
least you can insure against civil liability.

The criminal law is worse. No insurer can (or is legally permitted
to) stand in your place in the dock or even to pay your fine. The
criminal conviction and record will be yours, either personally or
through your company. These rules, too, this book expounds and
explains. Its object, like that of any good lawyer, is not so much to
help you to be acquitted, or to win your legal action; it is rather to
keep you as far away from courts, tribunals and other avoidable
miseries as a full understanding of the law can achieve.

After all, it is lawyers who (rightly and necessarily) win cases.
Litigants lose. Indeed, as a judge pointed out long ago, our courts
are like the Waldorf Hotel – open to all.

If you are rich, the best lawyers are available to you. If you are
sufficiently poor and have a reasonable prospect of success in your
action, then (with exceptions, such as defamation) you should get
legal aid and the prospect of justice. But if you are a person of
average income and limited means, the luxury of litigation is not
for you. You cannot afford the risk of losing or, perhaps (because
of the peculiar rules on legal costs), even the expense of winning.

This obvious lack of universally available justice provided yet
another reason for the product liability law. If you are almost sure
to win your case, you will rarely be forced to bring it. The
defendants or their insurers will pay.

So while on the one hand we must await interpretation of the
1987 Act by the courts, and while lawyers in the field of product
liability need not be too anxious about their sustenance drying up,
at the same time it is earnestly to be hoped that more sufferers will
be compensated, more readily and generously, and that the need
for litigation in this area will be reduced.

British business people are made anxious by American precedent.
Their fears are not justified. Our lawyers are (rightly or wrongly)

forbidden to accept work on a 'contingency' basis, taking a share of any winnings and themselves bearing any loss. So litigation remains discouraged. And awards of damages by our courts are at much lower levels than their transatlantic equivalents.

Still, the scene created by the 1987 Act is a changed one, in crucial respects. This book presents the new law in the context of the old. And the crucial insurance aspect – its main, allied and unavoidable practicality – is most ably dealt with by our insurance broker colleagues.

And so, on to the book. Just as you cannot set a jewel into a crown without first building its structure, so we start with the laws of (especially) contract and negligence. With these firmly in position, then (and only then) we put into place the new rules on product liability, fully and understandably explained.

PART I
LIABILITY IN CONTRACT

1 Statements made before the contract is formed

Manufacturers' advertisements

Manufacturers' advertisements are normally called 'trade puffs'. They are vague statements of opinion that cannot be described as promises. So if you say that your product is 'the best value for money', 'the bargain of the century' or that it washes 'brightest', 'bluest' or 'cleanest', that does not give the purchaser any rights. These are acceptable ways of promoting a product without legal consequences.

But if the terms of your advertisement are precise and make specific promises, you may be bound by them. In the famous case of *Carlill* v. *Carbolic Smoke Ball Co*, the defendants sold a cure for influenza and promised that they would pay £100 to any person who inhaled the remedy in the prescribed way and then contracted flu. It was held that it was the clear intention of both the manufacturer and the buyer that the promise in the advertisement should be binding. So when Mrs Carlill caught flu, she was entitled to her £100.

The test adopted by the courts depends on the broad intention of advertiser and purchaser, but it is most unlikely that your advertisements will have any legal consequences unless they make specific claims of fact.

Warnings

As a manufacturer, you will often include information about your product with your goods. This might say how the product should be used, what dangers it could present to the user and how it should be assembled. Can you be made liable, not so much for your product, as for your failure to provide adequate information about it?

The law of negligence requires you to take 'reasonable care' to see that those who are likely to come into contact with your products are kept reasonably safe. The word 'reasonable' means that you are not responsible merely because loss is caused by your goods. The buyer must use the product in a normal and careful way. So far as obvious dangers are concerned, no particular notice is required. You need not tell users of knives, razor blades or circular saws that they are sharp. All depends on the nature and extent of the warning and of the hazard, and the likelihood that the person who sees or hears it will take sufficient heed.

Whether or not a warning will free the seller from liability will depend on all the circumstances of the particular case.

The sad saga of Mr Devilez, who spilled Boots' corn solvent on to his genitals, shows that a warning may be important. Neither the fact that no one appears to have suffered the same fate previously, nor Boots' plea that 'surely you don't have to tell someone to be careful not to pour corn solvent over his private parts', availed the unfortunate defendants. A stern warning should have been placed on the bottle, such as (presumably): 'Handle with care ... keep away from all personal projections ...'!

If you know or ought to know of the danger, you should take reasonable care to ensure that others are warned. Manufacturers owe a duty to distributors; distributors to retailers; retailers to customers; and, doing the legal leap-frog, manufacturers to 'ultimate consumers'.

Barnes Ltd delivered a container of nitric acid to carriers Russell Ltd. They gave no warning of the dangers of the contents, although they knew or ought to have known of them. The container exploded and one of the carriers' employees (Mr Farrant) was injured. Barnes were held liable for the dangerous product. They should have given due warning.

The Army & Navy Co-operative Store sold a tin of chlorinated lime to Mrs Clarke, as a disinfectant powder. They knew of accidents caused by the substance so they should have realized that the tin might cause danger. When Mrs Clarke was injured by the substance, she won damages because she was given no warning.

Jeffrey Ltd manufactured a cleaning fluid which they modestly dubbed the 'pluperfect liquid'. Unfortunately, when it came into contact with cast iron, it emitted fumes of highly inflammable gas. Anglo-Celtic Shipping Company Ltd employed Elliott Ltd to repair one of their ships and instructed them to use the 'pluperfect' wonder liquid to clean a condenser. The workman came towards the condenser carrying a naked flame. Anglo-Celtic sued both Elliott and Jeffrey for the damage arising out of the resultant explosion.

Neither the plaintiffs nor Elliott knew of the special danger from the 'pluperfect liquid'. The manufacturers either knew or ought to have known. The article was dangerous in itself and the instructions failed to give any adequate warning to the users. So they were liable to compensate the sufferers.

Some dangerous substances are dealt with by statute or regulations. If you are concerned with the manufacture of pharmaceuticals, medicines, foods or drugs, you should know the various Acts, rules and regulations. These cover not only labelling and warning, but in some cases also packaging.

Section 6 of the Health and Safety at Work Act 1974 places a further criminal responsibility on manufacturers to give adequate information to enable their products to be properly used. Manufacturers of a substance containing a small quantity of cadmium marketed it in sticks, bundled together with a warning around the outside. A chandler separated a bundle and sold the sticks separately. A plumber used a brazing alloy on one, inhaled cadmium fumes, and died. The company's insurers duly paid. The company and its officers should have been grateful that the Health and Safety at Work Act was not yet in force, as *they* could have been prosecuted.

Harrods Ltd defended an action brought by a Mrs Fisher. They supplied a fluid for cleaning jewellery in a plastic bottle with a plastic bung and screw top. The fluid contained components which could damage eyesight. Mrs Fisher squeezed the bottle; the bung burst out and fluid shot into and damaged her eye. The court held that Harrods should have warned that the fluid must be kept away from eyes.

The more obvious the danger, the less the need to warn. Conversely, the less obvious the danger, the more obvious the need to warn against it.

Too many people are poisoned by household bleaches. Adults read warnings; children are poisoned.

Some kitchen cleansing substances are not only marketed in tubs like those used for margarine but actually look like that delectable substance. Both may be on the same shelf in the same kitchen at the same time. Common sense requires the cleanser to be marked with a warning.

In the old case of *British Chartered Company of South Africa* v. *Lennon Ltd*, Lennon dispatched cattle dip marked with labels intended for smaller tins. The British Chartered Company used the substance in accordance with the incorrect instructions. They had realized there was something wrong with the quantities marked but presumed that the substance and not the label had been altered. The court held the manufacturers negligent and liable.

Mrs Watson's scalp was damaged by hair-dye made by Buckley, Osborne, Garrett & Company Ltd. Preliminary 'patch testing' would have revealed the plaintiff's sensitivity but the defendants had advertised that no testing was needed. So they and not the hairdressers were negligent and liable to compensate the customer.

Rapidol Ltd supplied hairdressers with a dye of their own manufacture. The bottles and accompanying brochures warned that the dye might be dangerous to certain skins and that patch tests were necessary. A hairdresser named Ashford thought that she knew better. Ignoring the warning, she applied the dye to Mrs Holmes' hair, without testing. Result: dermatitis. Mrs Holmes sued both the hairdresser and the manufacturer.

The Court of Appeal held that the warning given by the manufacturers was sufficient to alert a hairdresser to the potential dangers of the substance; that more could not be expected of the manufacturers; and that it would be 'unreasonable and impossible' to expect them to give a warning in such form that 'it must come to the knowledge of the particular customer who was going to be treated'. The hairdresser was in breach of contract with her customer and was also liable in negligence. The manufacturers discharged their duty to 'the ultimate consumer' by giving the warning to the hairdresser.

In some cases the use of warning pictures or symbols can convey as much information as words. Many products incorporate them. Make sure your warnings are at least as striking as your competitors'.

In broad terms, where common sense requires warnings, so does the law. If in doubt, warn, and ensure that the warning is itself correct and adequate, within the bounds of reasonable practicability.

Manufacturers' guarantees and collateral warranties

Manufacturers often include 'guarantees' with their products. Sometimes the guarantees are contained in general advertisements (as discussed earlier in this chapter), or they may be included as a written promise in the product itself. Alternatively, the manufacturer may make a specific guarantee about his goods, to a particular purchaser. What, then, is the legal status of a guarantee?

If the product fails to live up to the guarantee, you may have remedies in contract or tort. Be sure, however, that the guarantee can be given some concrete meaning. The phrase 'our reputation is your guarantee' is meaningless in law. To have any legal effect, the guarantee must be seen as a promise which gives rise to specific expectations of performance from the product or its manufacturer.

Your remedies in contract depend on being able to establish a direct connection between you and the manufacturer.

The concept of 'privity of contract' means that only those who are party (or 'privy') to a contract may obtain a legal remedy against those who break it (see Chapter 2). Strangers may have rights in tort, but only parties have rights in contract. There is, though, one major exception, where the stranger can rely on a so-called 'collateral warranty' – a promise given by someone who was not a party to the contract, in order to induce the plaintiff to enter into an agreement.

The collateral warranty is generally a statement made by a manufacturer or other person who stands to benefit by the sale of a product to someone else to induce that other person to purchase.

The manufacturer (or other beneficiary) says, in effect, 'If you purchase my product from X, I will give you the following warranties about the goods . . .'

Normally, either a warranty or a condition is a term of the contract in question – a specific part of the contract itself. A 'collateral warranty', though, is one which does not form part of the contract made between those who are 'privy' to the agreement. It is only 'collateral' to it – but may nevertheless be dragged into the centre of a legal battle, as it has been in the leading cases on the subject.

Motor dealers represented that a car was 'in perfect condition'. The purchaser paid a deposit to the dealer and then entered into a hire-purchase agreement with a finance company. The contract for the purchase of the vehicle was thus made between the buyer and the finance house; the dealers were strangers to the transaction. The buyer paid all instalments due, plus the usual option-to-purchase fee. The car became his.

Unfortunately, the car turned out to be in poor and unroadworthy condition and the buyer had to spend a large amount on repairs. He sued the dealers for damages for breach of warranty. They retorted that they were not parties to the bargain. The judge held that the dealers had

> given a warranty as to the condition of the car; that the plaintiff was induced by the warranty to enter into the hire-purchase agreement; that the warranty was broken; and that the plaintiff suffered damage through the breach as he paid a larger sum under the hire-purchase agreement for the car than it was worth and than he would have paid had the warranty not been given.

The plaintiff was awarded damages – the difference between the value of the car at the date of the hire-purchase agreement and the value it would have had if it had matched up to the warranty. For the first time, a defendant had been made liable in an action founded in contract, even though he was not a party to that contract.

Under the Consumer Credit Act 1974, both the finance company (which sells the car) and the dealer (who supplies it) are jointly liable to the consumer under the sale. Furthermore, any statements the dealer makes in the course of negotiations are deemed to be made on behalf of the actual seller. The consumer has a remedy – and the dealer and the finance company can sort out between themselves who will bear the cost of the defect.

The decision in the car case was followed in a manufacturer's case, on typical lines. Paint manufacturers (Detel Products Ltd) represented to the owners of the Shanklin Pier that their paint would be suitable for repainting the pier and 'would give a surface impervious to dampness, would prevent corrosion and the creeping of rust and would have a life of 7–10 years'. In reliance on this statement, the pier authorities specified that their contractors should use Detel paint. Unfortunately, the paint was not suitable for the protection of the pier and its life was 'of a very short duration'. Result: massive additional expense for the pier company and a claim for damages against Detel Products, who were not a party to the contract.

The court held that 'the consideration for the warranty in the usual case was the entering into of the main contract in relation to which the warranty was given'. The warranty was collateral to the main contract. There was a separate arrangement between the manufacturers and the purchaser: 'Specify that our paint is to be used ... ensure that the contractor purchases our product ... and we will warrant that it will do the job required by your ...' The Shanklin Pier authorities were entitled to rely on that collateral warranty. They won their case.

Next came *Yeoman Credit Limited* v. *Odgers & Others*, decided by the Court of Appeal. Briefly, a car dealer warranted that a vehicle was 'in perfect condition', as a result of which the purchaser entered into a contract with a finance company. The vehicle 'almost immediately proved unroadworthy because of persistent defects in the brakes', so the purchaser stopped paying the instalments.

The Court of Appeal held that 'the hire-purchase agreement was the purpose and the product of the warranty'. The damage suffered by the hirer was the 'loss directly and naturally resulting from the breach of warranty' and included 'the wasted instalments' and other amounts paid under the hire-purchase agreement. The hirer was entitled to rely upon the collateral warranty given by the dealer, who was not a party to the contract with the finance house.

This decision was followed in the case of *Wells (Merstham) Ltd* v. *Buckland Sand and Silica Company Ltd*. Buckland Sand warranted that their product conformed to a specified analysis and would be suitable for use in the growing of crysanthemums – the purpose for which (as Buckland well knew) Wells were buying the sand. The product did not conform to the warranty.

The judge held that there are

> two ingredients and two only ... required in order to bring about a collateral contract containing a warranty: (a) the promise or assertion by A as to the nature, quality or quantity of the goods which B may reasonably regard as being made with the intention that it be relied upon and (b) acquisition by B of the goods in reliance on that promise or assertion.

Lord Wedderburn said: 'The consideration given to the promise is no more than the act of entering into the main contract. Going ahead with that bargain is a sufficient price of the promise, without which it would not have gone ahead at all.'

It followed that those who had purchased the sand on the basis of the product maker's warranty were entitled to rely upon the promise or assertion given to them. The promise was broken; the assertion was incorrect; the manufacturers had to pay damages.

In another case a claim was brought by a Mr Watson, who had his hair dyed by Mrs Buckley in her salon. He arranged to have it tinted 'to an auburn shade' and Mrs Buckley had recommended a new dye called 'Melereon'. She showed him the trade journal advertisement, which read: "Make your next hair dye order "Melereon" – the safe, harmless hair dye ... no ifs or buts; it is a hair dye that will not harm the most sensitive skin; the hair dye which positively needs no preliminary tests.'

Accepting the assurance that the new dye was safe and harmless, Mr Watson put his head into Mrs Buckley's hands – whence it emerged, itchy and ridden with dermatitis. Mrs Buckley had been in no way negligent and had applied the solution entirely in accordance with the maker's directions. Unfortunately, the dye contained a 4 per cent solution of acid, to be diluted to a 2 per cent solution before it was applied to the head. It was unsafe.

Following the principle in the famous 'snail' case of *Donoghue* v. *Stevenson* (see Chapter 7), Mr Watson could have sued the manufacturers. But (as, alas, is not unusual) their company dissolved even more effectively than their products. So he sued the hairdresser and the distributor.

The court held that the hairdresser had impliedly warranted that the solution was 'a merchantable hair dye' and she was therefore liable to him in damages for breach of contract. However, the distributors had been negligent and by their advertisements had 'intentionally excluded interference with, or examination of, the article by the consumer'. They had therefore brought themselves into a direct relationship with Mr Watson, to whom they were duly liable on their collateral warranty. Indeed, the judge went further. The product was itself a dangerous one; 'an unusual standard or care was required'; and on this ground the distributors even 'owed a duty to take care towards the plaintiff'. As they were in breach of that duty, they were liable to pay damages.

Finally, let us consider the case of *Andrews* v. *Hopkinson*. The manager of a secondhand car showroom described a saloon vehicle as 'a good little bus. I would stake my life on it.' He added: 'You will have no trouble with it.' Mr Andrews paid his deposit and entered into an agreement with a finance company.

About a week later, Mr Andrews was driving the car when it collided with a lorry. He was seriously injured. When the car was examined it was found that a joint in the steering mechanism had failed. The car was neither safe nor fit for use on the highway and the defect was 'long standing'. Although the fault was probably 'not discoverable by an ordinary owner-driver', it could easily have been spotted 'by any competent mechanic'. Once again, the hirer sued the dealer, rather than the finance company. This time he claimed not merely the difference between the value of the car as warranted and its value as delivered, but also damages for his personal injury.

The court held that Mr Andrews' injuries were indeed 'a direct and natural result of the breach of warranty' – so he had a good claim against the dealer in contract. In addition, he was entitled to damages for the tort of negligence. The dealer had failed to use 'reasonable diligence' either to examine the car or to warn Mr Andrews that there had been no such examination.

So finally the two streams of the law – in contract and in tort – flowed together, reaching the same legal outlet. The dealer was a stranger to the contract, but had formed a direct relationship through the 'collateral warranty'. As the 'ultimate consumer' of the dangerous product, the injured Mr Andrews could leap over the contractual buyer and bring a successful claim under the law of negligence.

Statements made before contract

So far we have looked at the manufacturers' statements, advertisements and guarantees and when they are bound to honour them. A different question arises if the sellers make a statement to you which entices you into making a contract with them, but you then discover the statement was wrong. What can you do?

Your position depends on a number of factors. Did the statement become incorporated as a term of the contract? If so, see Chapter 3.

If the statement did not form part of the contract but was nevertheless incorrect, you may have an action under the Misrepresentation Act 1967. Was the statement incorrect but made innocently and in good faith, or was it made negligently and without proper care?

Innocent misrepresentation

Before a contract is made, you may have spent time adjusting the terms on which the agreement is to be made. Statements may be made which are incorrect, but which are made responsibly and were never intended to mislead. They are an innocent mistake for which no blame can be attached. Nevertheless, they are still responsible for tempting the other party into the contract. This is an innocent misrepresentation. Such a mistake might occur, for example, where you reasonably rely on a set of statistics provided by an independent party, which were either wrong or incorrectly formulated.

In cases like this, the Misrepresentation Act provides you with a limited form of remedy if you can show that the statement induced you to enter into the contract. In the first place you may simply refuse to perform your side of the bargain. If the other side were to sue you for breach of contract, the court (provided it was satisfied a misrepresentation had been made) would refuse to award damages or order the contract to be performed.

This is a suitable remedy, however, only if you have not suffered a loss under the contract. But if you have invested time and money on your side of the bargain before discovery of the mistake, you may want compensation. The 1967 Act provides that you are entitled to the remedy of 'rescission', i.e. to be put back into the position you were in before the contract was made. It must be possible, broadly, for you both to give back to each other any money or property which has been transferred. This remedy of cancelling the contract and restoring you both to your original positions has rarely been considered by the courts.

But what is the position if the victim of the innocent misrepresentation has sold the product in question, or it has been destroyed or been incorporated into other products so as to make its return impossible?

Again, a remedy is available, but it is not very generous. The 1967 Act gives you the right to 'damages in lieu of rescission'. You are probably entitled to the amount of expenditure directly and necessarily incurred by entering the contract. This may be the purchase price of the goods. This limited amount does not seem to extend to the additional losses suffered due to the failure of the product to work in the anticipated way and, for example, failing to create the expected profit or causing damage to other property.

Clearly, where you are both free from fault, a careful balance has to be struck in awarding damages. But the losses which could be suffered because of an innocent misrepresentation may far exceed the damages which the courts are entitled to award.

Negligent misrepresentation

Where a statement is made without proper care, so that a person can be said to be at fault for making it, better remedies are available. Damages may be awarded in two broad sets of circumstances:

(1) (as in the case of innocent misrepresentations) when the statement has been made to induce you to enter into contract with the person who made it; and
(2) when the misrepresentation has not led to the creation of a contract with the person who made it.

Contract induced with person who made careless statement

The remedy for this situation arises either under the Misrepresentation Act or the law of negligence. In both cases it is essentially the same. The statement must have been made when there was no reasonable ground to believe that it was correct.

Once liability has been established, you are entitled to damages to cover all loss foreseeably arising from the misstatement. In

Howard Marine and Dredging Co Ltd v. *Ogden & Sons (Excavations)* an incorrect statement was made relating to the carrying capacity of barges. It was stated to be greater than was the case and, as a result, the hirers of the barges lost money by having to make alternative arrangements for the work which was not completed. The statement ought not to have been made without being checked and the Court of Appeal held that the hirers could recover the extra expense incurred in hiring other barges.

Negligent statement made by person who is not a party to the contract

When you seek independent advice before entering into a contract with another party, the independent adviser may be liable if he gives inaccurate advice. In many cases, of course, you will have paid the independent adviser for his services, in which case a contract will exist. In such case an additional action may lie for breach of contract (see Chapter 3). But there are cases where specialist advice has been given without a contract between the parties. In this case your remedy may lie in negligence.

For the remedy to be available an important requirement must be satisfied: the parties must be in what has been called 'a special relationship'. This term means that one party, by his expertise and specialist knowledge, must have given the other party to believe that his advice was so reliable that it could be acted on without question. The other must have acted reasonably in reliance upon it and have suffered loss as a result.

A 'special relationship', therefore, has arisen because of the advice of a bank to someone who wanted advice about the financial position of a client of the bank before lending money; an accountant for the preparation of accounts prior to the sale of a business; an insurance broker for inaccurately advising as to the extent of obligations undertaken; a surveyor for a negligent survey of a house prior to its sale; and a solicitor for failing to advise the witness of a will that he would be barred from benefiting under the will.

Although the special relationship is most likely to arise in the context of professional advisers, the mere fact that their advice is wrong and leads to loss does not necessarily mean they were negligent. In one case the advice of a stockbroker led to loss but it was held that, given the vagaries and unpredictability of the stock market, the loss had not arisen as a result of negligent advice but, rather, through bad luck.

2 Liability in contract

A contract is a legally binding agreement between two or more parties. Liability of the parties under the contract normally depends upon the terms of the agreement. These may be either express or implied.

An *express* term is one which has been explicitly agreed, such as the price, the quantity, the nature or quality of the goods and the delivery date. Additional terms are *implied*, sometimes as a result of court decisions, sometimes by the Sale of Goods Act 1979.

The first place to look to discover whether or not one contracting party can hold the other liable under the agreement is the agreement itself – which may be oral or in writing, or partly oral and partly written. There is no legal requirement that, to be binding, a contract involving a product must be in writing. Only in rare cases will the law not enforce a contract because of the absence of writing. The main terms of a contract for the transfer of an interest in land, or of a contract of guarantee, or hire purchase or insurance, must be in writing. In most other cases, an oral deal is as binding as a written one.

In practice, the trouble with an oral contract, of course, arises when the parties disagree on its terms. Can they prove an express agreement? What implications should be drawn from the words used – and what were they? So, wise contractors put the terms in writing or later confirm the important terms, in written form. Where liability depends upon the contract, look for writing; and then see whether there are further terms to be implied.

As we have seen (in connection with manufacturers' guarantees), normally only those who are party (or 'privy') to a contract can acquire rights under it. With the exception of collateral warranties (representations made usually by manufacturers but sometimes by dealers, to induce customers to enter into contracts with others – see Chapter 1), where there is no 'privity of contract' there can be no good contractual claim.

A duty may be owed to strangers under the rules on negligence. But liability for a product is generally owed in contract only to other parties to the deal. In this chapter we examine contractual liability for products; the nature of 'privity of contract', and exceptions to it; and we look especially at implied terms concerning the quality and fitness of products (under the Sale of Goods Act 1979) and at the limits placed on the power of contracting parties to reduce or exclude contractual liability through contractual terms, notices or disclaimers. The Supply of Goods (Implied Terms) Act 1973 and the Unfair Contract Terms Act 1977 have brought about massive changes in this field.

So also has the famous *Romalpa* decision. This established that the seller of goods may not only retain ownership until he has been paid for them but even trace the proceeds of sale of those goods, when the goods have passed into the hands of third parties. We shall look at the *Romalpa* rules generally, but with specific reference to defective products.

Remember, though, that a claim arising on a contract due to a defect in a product depends upon proof of an express or implied term, of breach of that term, and of damage flowing from the breach. Once again, no default under the contract means no right to damage. In contract law, strict liability only arises from the agreement of the parties.

Before you can understand how contractual obligations may be enforced you must know the basic essentials of a valid, binding contract. Where those essentials are present, the contract is binding. Subject to restrictions on exclusions, all parties to the agreement are bound by it. Conversely, if any essential of the contract is missing, either party may refuse to proceed.

Suppose, then, that you are a supplier of products. You

recognize that the risks involved in the sale are greater than its potential profits? You are worried at the rights which the buyer will have if the product is defective? Or are you a purchaser who has acquired a good deal? You wish to know whether you can force the unwilling supplier to honour his obligations? Once again, consider whether your contract contains all the essential terms. The absence of even one will destroy the entire deal.

Offers, acceptances, counter-offers and invitations to treat

The first stage in making a binding contract is the 'offer'. 'I offer to produce these goods for you ...' 'I offer to buy these products from you ...' 'We will distribute these items on your behalf ...' An offer is a clear and unqualified statement that you are willing to be bound in law by your promise.

If you advertise goods in a catalogue or exhibit them in a trade fair or in a shop window, you are not making an 'offer' but only inviting others to offer to purchase from you. You are issuing a so-called 'invitation to treat'. Therefore, when your customer says 'I'll take those goods ... I'll buy that machinery ... I accept your offer ...', he is in law himself making the offer. At this stage, you may reject that offer or accept it on different terms. That is why in civil law no one is forced to sell goods at the price marked, to any particular customer or at all. Provided that the seller does not discriminate against customers on grounds of sex or race, he may contract or not, as he sees fit.

In criminal law, the rules are different. The Trade Descriptions Act 1968 makes it an offence to advertise or to offer goods for sale at a price lower than that at which you are prepared to supply them (see Chapter 22). Most wrongful acts (including, frequently, the marketing of a dangerous or defective product) produce both potential civil and criminal consequences (see the manufacturer's liability under section 6 of the Health and Safety at Work Act). In this case, though, the supplier is generally in the clear in civil law but at risk under the Trade Descriptions Act.

To be capable of acceptance, an offer must also be unconditional. 'I can supply you these goods at your price, if I can get the board to agree ...' is not an 'offer' which the customer can accept. 'I offer you this job subject to references ...' or 'We will gladly

supply this product, if we can obtain the necessary materials ...'
are both statements of intent, not offers which are capable of being
accepted.

Note, though, the vital distinction between a 'conditional offer'
and an 'offer subject to conditions'. 'We offer to supply these
goods subject to our usual terms of trading, printed on the back
hereof ...' is a firm, acceptable and 'unconditional' offer to supply
the goods on the terms stated. Every offer is made 'on conditions'.
But no acceptable offer is 'conditional'.

Similar rules apply to 'acceptances'. To be effective, an acceptance must be both 'unconditional' and on the other party's terms.
You cannot accept the other's offer by agreeing to only part of his
proposal. If you do that you are making a new offer and rejecting
his suggestion. It is now for him to accept your offer if he wishes. If
you write: 'We thank you for your order which we accept, subject
to ...', you are almost certainly giving a 'conditional acceptance',
which has no legal effect whatsoever. You are not bound to satisfy
the condition; meanwhile, the other contracting party may revoke
his offer – for any reason or for none, but probably because he can
do a better deal elsewhere.

More subtly, you are likely to send an 'acceptance' which
is 'subject to our standard terms of trading'. If these differ
substantially from the terms in the offer, you are not 'accepting'
the offer made by the customer but (in law) making a 'counter-
offer' – which he, in his turn, may accept or reject.

Suppose, for instance, that you are a supplier of products.
Your customer's 'acceptance' includes a clause which poses new
responsibilities on you for research or testing, or includes exclusion clauses which may have some legal effect. Or suppose that
you offer to supply goods on a certain date, specifying that 'while
every effort will be made to deliver on the stated date, no
responsibility can be accepted for delay, howsoever caused'. Your
customer 'accepts' on the basis that 'time of delivery shall be an
essential term of this contract'. In all these cases, your customer is
in reality saying 'I do not agree to purchase your products on your
terms. I will only do so on mine – which are different.' He is trying
to substitute his terms for yours. He is offering to buy, not
accepting *your* offer to sell.

Note that the names of the documents are irrelevant. You
may call your 'offer' an 'order', 'acknowledgement', 'quotation',

'estimate' or any other name that suits your current fancy or that of your lawyers. Equally, your customer may put his terms into an 'acceptance', 'acknowledgement of order', 'confirmation' or any other document. 'The law looks at the reality and not at the form' – at the situation created by the document, not at the name conferred upon it.

So what happens in practice? The supplier makes his offer perhaps in a firm estimate, a quote or even in a letter. The customer sends his 'counter-offer'. If the supplier spots the differences and rejects them, he makes a 'counter-counter-offer'. We thank you for your "acceptance" but we regret that we cannot guarantee the delivery date as you ask . . . that we are not prepared to undertake the additional research and testing which would be required by your clause . . . that we are not prepared to contract other than on the basis that we retain title in the goods until payment is made.'

At this stage, there is still no deal. Negotiations are proceeding – or, perhaps, have come to an abrupt end. There is no contract. Either party may break away.

Now suppose that the supplier does not spot the differences in the customer's terms and simply delivers the goods. By delivering, he impliedly accepts the terms in the counter-offer. So far as any exclusion clause is contained in that counter-offer (for example) and is binding, the customer is in luck. Generally, he who contracts last contracts best. It is the last document in the chain that contains the 'agreed' terms. It is irrelevant that the agreement is implied rather than expressed.

Alternatively, maybe the supplier gets the last written word. Perhaps he puts in a counter-counter-offer and then delivers the goods, which the customer accepts. In that case, when the customer accepted the goods, he also accepted the supplier's counter-counter-offer. The supplier's terms prevail.

Other essentials of a binding contract

If an unconditional offer has been unconditionally accepted, what other ingredients are essential for a binding contract?

First, some contracts must be either made in writing or evidenced by some note or memorandum in writing, if they are to be legally binding. In the past, writing was required for most contracts of any importance.

As discussed at the beginning of this chapter, the requirement for writing is almost solely limited to: contracts for the transfer of an interest in land; contracts of hire purchase, insurance or for the transfer of shares; and contracts of guarantee.

The expression 'There was nothing in writing, so I hereby cancel' should be expunged from the business vocabulary. The absence of writing makes the terms of the deal harder to prove . . . and makes dispute and litigation much more likely in origin and unpredictable in outcome . . . but it does not normally affect the validity of the bargain. In cases for the supply, sale or distribution of products, writing is legally irrelevant.

Most deals may effectively be made by telephone. However, wise contractors confirm terms in writing, for the avoidance of dispute. Equally, if you receive someone else's purported confirmation of (perhaps) a telephone order or agreement to supply, check it with care. Failure to challenge an incorrect statement in a letter of confirmation is almost always fatal to denial of accuracy at a later stage.

Next, in England and Wales (but not in Scotland), a contract will not be binding unless there is some 'consideration'. Each party must give something in return for what he receives – if only one promise in return for another. 'In consideration of your agreeing to supply this product at that price, I undertake to pay that price . . .'

In practice, 'consideration' generally becomes a live problem where you seek an option. 'Will you keep that offer open until tomorrow?' 'Can I have time to consult my board?' A simple agreement to give the option is not binding in law. 'Consideration' in such a case is normally called a deposit.

If you put down a deposit on goods and then decide not to proceed with the deal, the deposit is usually forfeited, although there is nothing to prevent you from coming to some other arrangement, like agreeing that the deposit money will be put on one side, as credit towards a future purchase. Conversely, if the deal goes off through the fault of the party who takes the deposit, it will be returnable.

Deposits on the sale of property are invariably paid 'subject to contract'. If no contract is made, the deposit is repayable. Equally, the party who takes the deposit on that basis is not bound to grant an option. It is merely 'an earnest of good faith' on the part of the proposed purchaser.

Suppose, then, that there is an unconditional offer, unconditionally accepted; that there is no need for writing and that the parties have exchanged promises so that there is 'consideration' for the deal. That leaves 'illegality' and 'capacity to contract'.

An illegal contract is void. Anyone who makes an agreement (for instance) to evade VAT or tax or customs duty is not bound by his wrongful act. Or suppose that you engage someone to work on a defence contract but you cannot get clearance for him. You may not be allowed to tell him why you are not prepared to honour your word, but the continuation of the contract of employment may be in grave peril.

Finally, parties must have 'contractual capacity'. A 'minor' – that is, someone under the age of eighteen – cannot be held to a business contract, neither can he be forced to repay a loan. Only contracts for 'goods or services reasonably necessary for him at the time when he made the contract' will be binding. A business deal is never one for a 'necessary'. So do not give credit to youngsters or make advances on pay to young employees – unless you recognize that the law will not be able to help you if they dishonour their obligations.

A company may make an effective contract within the limits laid down in the objects clause of its memorandum of association. Any contract which goes outside those powers is said to be *ultra vires*. However, thanks to EEC legislation with which we have had to comply, even an *ultra vires* contract may now be enforced by the innocent, unwitting third party.

Privity of contract

Only parties to contracts may take advantage of their terms. A 'third party' – that is, one who has no contractual arrangements with the others – may directly or indirectly benefit from the contract or lose if that contract is broken, but he cannot enforce it. One of the parties involved may take steps to protect his interest – but the third party is powerless. 'In the law of England, certain principles are fundamental. One is that only a person who is party to a contract can sue on it . . .'

Dew entered into a contract with Dunlop to buy tyres and other goods from them at list prices, Dunlop having agreed to give them certain discounts. As part of the deal, Dew undertook not to sell to certain classes of customers at prices below the current list prices of Dunlop. However, they were entitled to sell to a class of customer that included Selfridges at a discount substantially less than they were themselves to receive from Dunlop. In the case of any such sale, they undertook to obtain a written undertaking from the customer that he would observe those terms which they had themselves undertaken.

Selfridges agreed to buy Dunlop's goods from Dew and gave the required undertaking not to cut prices. They broke that agreement and Dunlop sued.

So Dew bought from Dunlop and sold to Selfridges. There was no contractual relationship between Selfridges and Dunlop and therefore (said the House of Lords) they could not sue on the deal. Even though they had been wronged, they had no rights against Selfridges, who were strangers. They might possibly have sued their customers (Dew) for not enforcing the resale price maintenance agreement. They could not leap over their customer and on to those who had no contractual relationship with them. There was no 'privity of contract' between Dunlop and Selfridges.

Now suppose that Dunlop had sold defective tyres to Dew who had sold them on to Selfridges. In the absence of some collateral warranty (perhaps contained in a 'guarantee' or 'warranty') from the manufacturer (see Chapter 1) Selfridges would have had no contractual rights against Dunlop. The product was defective? Then their remedy in contract would lie against their supplier – Dew. If by some mischance Dew had gone out of business or into liquidation, Selfridges would have been left without remedy in contract.

The same principle would have applied down the line – Selfridges' customer would sue them; they would bring Dew into the action as 'third party', and Dew could seek an indemnity from the manufacturer of the defective product as a fourth party.

If someone had suffered personal injury as a result of the defective tyre, that sufferer (as the 'ultimate consumer' of the product) could have jumped the queue and, like the lady who swallowed the soft drink polluted by the decomposing snail, he could have gone straight for the negligent manufacturer (see Chapter 7 and the case of *Donoghue* v. *Stevenson*).

So the principle in the *Dunlop* case goes far beyond the facts which, in any event, have been largely superseded by rules banning resale price maintenance. In the realm of liability for defective products, the principle of claims being restricted to those with whom the plaintiff has a contractual relationship remains supreme.

A curious variant on this theme appeared in the well-known case of *Daniels & Daniels* v. *R. White & Sons Ltd and Tarbard*. Mr Daniels was a street trader, dealing in secondhand clothing and furniture. He sued R. White & Sons, manufacturers and bottlers of (amongst other things) lemonade. Mr Daniel's wife joined him in the action, both alleging that Whites had supplied 'a bottle of lemonade which in fact contained carbolic acid'. They included as a defendant a Mrs Tarbard, licensee of the Falcon Arms pub.

The plaintiffs alleged that Whites 'did not exercise reasonable care as manufacturers to prevent injury being done to the consumers or purchasers of their wares'. Mr Daniels also alleged that Mrs Tarbard was in breach of the warranty implied (then as now) by the Sale of Goods Act, that the lemonade would be 'reasonably fit for the purpose of drinking, and that it contained no deleterious or noxious matter and/or that it was of merchantable quality'.

'A perfectly sober gentleman', Mr Daniels not only drank the polluted lemonade himself but gave some to his wife. Both of them 'immediately realized that there was something burning in the liquid . . . and at once thought that they had been poisoned . . .'

Whites were acquitted of any liability. Unlike the case of *Donoghue* v. *Stevenson*, in which the manufacturer had clearly failed to clean out the offending bottle, Whites (said the judge) had taken 'reasonable care'. There was 'quite adequate supervision' at the factory. The method of cleansing the bottles was 'described as foolproof'. So the manufacturers walked out of court, freed from blame and responsibility.

What, then, of the licensee who had retailed the defective goods? There was a sale by description; a breach of the implied condition that the goods should be of merchantable quality; therefore Mr Daniels – but not his wife – had a good claim against Mrs Tarbard.

So Mrs Daniels lost her case. She had no contractual relationship with the retailer or (still less) with the manufacturer. So there
was none of the 'no fault liability' which the Sale of Goods Act in
effect imposes on most sellers of goods. Those who retail are
bound (in general) to supply goods which are 'of merchantable
quality' and 'reasonably fit for the purpose supplied'. The fact that
they may have taken all reasonable and proper care is irrelevant.
They are in breach of contract.

As Mrs Daniels had no contract with the licensee, she had to
show that her position was the same as that of the plaintiff in
Donoghue v. *Stevenson*. She had to establish that they owed a duty
of care; that they were in breach of that duty; and that damage
flowed. *Donoghue* v. *Stevenson* ensured no difficulty in proving a
'duty of care', as Mrs Daniels was the 'ultimate consumer' of the
liquid. She fell ill and therefore suffered damage. But there was no
negligence . . . no breach of duty . . . no fault . . . and therefore no
liability in negligence.

Can pre-contractual statements become terms?

Before you enter into a contract, time may have been spent in
negotiations discussing your requirements and limitations. You
may have given undertakings or made statements which were not
included in the written terms of the contract. There may then be a
dispute as to whether those statements have become binding as
part of the contract.

One solution to a potential problem of this sort has already been
examined, namely, the action for misrepresentation (see Chapter
1). In that case the allegation is that the statement was not
included in the contract, it merely *induced* its creation. But there is
a different question: was the statement actually incorporated into
the body of the contract?

There used to be a rule that when parties had made an
agreement and committed it to writing, it was impossible to argue
afterwards that there were other terms of the contract which had
been agreed orally, but had not been written down. But this rule
has not been used for a long time. Recent cases have expressly
added oral promises to the written terms of the contract. A
contract may be formed both in words and writing.

The matter is decided according to the overall intentions of the parties. If you both intended the contract to comprise written and oral terms, the law will respect your wishes.

How are your intentions to be assessed? The more important the statement in question, the more likely it is that it should be regarded as a term, rather than a mere pre-contractual flourish which was intended to have no effect. If the maker of the statement does not claim any particular expertise or knowledge about the matter, the law is reluctant to attach great weight to his undertaking. But if he holds himself out to be a specialist in a particular field, it is more likely that you will be allowed to say 'he was the expert, he invited me to rely on his word and I did so as a result'. Conversely, if he deliberately advises you not to rely on his word but to check the information for yourself, it is unlikely to be regarded as a term.

These are guidelines as to the sort of factors that a court would consider when asking 'what did the parties intend?'.

Types of term in the contract

It is, of course, essential to know where and to what extent the contract has created obligations. You are obliged to do no more than the contract requires, but a breach of contract may make you liable to pay damages. You may include as a term of the contract any provision you wish, provided it is not illegal.

You can only sue for breach of a 'term' of the contract. The courts have laid down rules about when a term is to be regarded as a part of the contract. Parties may include terms in their agreement either expressly, in writing or orally, or by implication.

Express terms

The easiest and most obvious way of including a provision is by signature. If you put your name to a set of terms, or one party indicates that he is accepting the terms suggested by the other, it is most probable that he will be bound by those terms. This is the case even if you have never bothered to read the terms, provided the other party has not misled or deceived as to their significance. On the other hand, if your signature was induced by deceit or misrepresentation, you may be able to withdraw from the deal and cancel the contract.

There may be a number of instances, however, when you agree to contract without putting your name to a document. In some cases the terms of the agreement may be available in writing elsewhere. In others there may be no written terms at all, the contract being created orally.

In cases like this, the general rule is that a term will be included provided you give reasonable notice of it to the other party and he agrees to it before the contract is made. For example, if you reserve a hotel room through the receptionist and then enter your room to find a notice on the door excluding the liability of the hotel for loss or damage to your property, the notice will be ineffective. The contract was made at the reception desk with no mention of such an exclusion. After that time, variations depend on mutual agreement between the parties. But if you have had a series of dealings with the hotel in the past and have, in that way, become familiar with the terms of the contract, this could constitute reasonable notice to you of those terms. For a term to be included in this way there must have been a consistent history of previous contracts between the parties. If the previous undertakings have been on different terms, it cannot be said that you ought to know on what basis the present agreement has been made.

Terms in general professional or trade usage may also be incorporated simply by reference to the relevant standard form, for example, the 'JCT' (Joint Council of Tribunals) or 'ICE' (Institution of Civil Engineers) forms of contract.

Implied terms

In two important respects, terms which were not specifically raised or discussed by the parties may be implied into a contract.

Terms implied by unspoken agreement

Inevitably, whether or not a contract is put into writing, matters are likely to arise which were not specifically discussed between you and the other party. What is the position where you either did not provide for, or did not foresee, a particular eventuality? On what basis should a court decide whether or not the contract covers the circumstances in question?

Generally the courts imply a term into the contract if it is necessary to give the contract practical effect. It asks itself the question: 'What would the parties have said at the outset if they were asked about the particular question at issue?' Would they have answered: 'Yes of course, we intend the contract to cover those circumstances.'? But it will not do so just because it thinks it would be fair and reasonable to do so, or if it believes that one of the parties would not have agreed to it being included.

On this basis, terms have been implied into contracts for the mooring of a ship, that the mooring should be free from hidden dangers which might damage the boat, and have also been implied into contracts for leases, that the landlords should take reasonable steps to keep the stairways and corridors of a high-rise block free from obstruction. Without such an implication, the contracts, would, for practical purposes, be unworkable.

But in a contract between the vendor of a house and an estate agent no term has been implied that the vendor would not take independent steps to sell his house; or, in a contract between large-scale manufacturers of goods and their retailers, that the manufacturers would not discriminate against one such retailer by selling to him at higher prices than the others. In these cases the contracts could take effect without such an implication.

Terms implied by statute

Terms may also be impliedly included in contracts by Acts of Parliament. In the law of product liability the most important of these are the Sale of Goods Act 1979, the Supply of Goods (Implied Terms) Act 1973 and the Supply of Goods and Services Act 1982. Details of these are given in Chapter 3.

Relative importance of terms

Not all the terms of a contract have the same significance; some are more important than others. This difference in status is recognized by the law so that, if you wish, you may indicate which terms are to be of central importance, and which are to be secondary. This distinction is given effect by referring to the terms of a contract as either 'conditions' or 'warranties'.

Sometimes, of course, the terms of the contract may not say

which are to be regarded as conditions and which as warranties. In this case the court uses its own judgment in deciding how they are to be labelled. They do so on the following basis. 'Conditions' contain the central purpose of the contract: were they not to be performed the whole commercial purpose of the agreement would be lost. By contrast, 'warranties' are peripheral to the main intentions of the parties. Their non-performance may cause inconvenience, but the commercial purpose of the agreement still remains intact.

In contracts concerning the sale or hire of goods, the Sale of Goods Act 1979, the Supply of Goods (Implied Terms) Act 1973 and the Supply of Goods and Services Act 1982 say which of the obligations are to be considered as conditions, and which as warranties. Hence, unless you have agreed otherwise, the following terms are implied into the contract, with the status of conditions: the goods correspond with their description; they are of merchantable quality; they are reasonably fit for their purpose; and when a sale is made on the basis of a sample, the bulk will correspond with the sample in quality. On the other hand, unless a different intention appears, stipulations as to time (for example of delivery) are warranties only.

The distinction affects your remedies when one or more of the contractual terms is not performed. If the term has the status of a condition it can give rise to serious consequences. The innocent party is given a choice. He can terminate all the future obligations arising under the contract and claim his reasonable loss in damages. As a result the parties' legal obligations to perform cease and are replaced by an obligation on the party in the wrong to pay damages. Alternatively, the innocent party can decide to press on with the contract, despite the breach, and claim for any losses outstanding at the end of the day. The choice may depend, amongst other things, on the degree of faith he has in the ability of the other party to complete the contract.

But if the term broken is only a warranty, all that can be done is to claim damages. There is no right to get out of the contract. You both must complete your contractual obligations and let money settle the dispute afterwards.

Occasionally, a term is expressed in such a broad fashion that it is capable of giving rise to both serious breaches, affecting the very foundation of the contract, and peripheral breaches of less importance. How should a breach of such term be dealt with? A term of this sort is known as an 'intermediate (or innominate) term'. The law adopts a wait-and-see approach. If the breach of the term turns out to be very serious, it will have the same consequences as if it were a breach of a condition. But if it happens to be a relatively trivial matter, it will give a right to damages alone.

3 Performance of the contract

You must comply exactly with the terms of the contract. In theory, any departure from the requirements of the contract entitles the injured party to damages. In practice, of course, where the extent of the loss is very small, the cost of attempting to claim damages for the breach would make a nonsense of pursuing the claim.

As already explained, you are free to agree any terms you wish, provided that they are not illegal. You are entitled to the benefit of the clauses inserted in your favour and must honour those to your detriment.

Contracts for the sale of goods

Contracts for the sale of goods are governed by the general rules already outlined, and by the Sale of Goods Act 1979. The Act does not apply to goods supplied on hire purchase, or to the provision of services (see below).

The most important requirements of the Act are for goods supplied in the course of business. In general, these must be fit for their purpose and of merchantable quality.

'In the course of a business'

The contracts you make as part of a domestic or private arrangement and not as part of a business are not covered by the 1979 Act. They are controlled by the general rules as to the incorporation and status of terms discussed above. In these informal contracts, the principle 'let the buyer beware' applies to put the buyer on warning that it is up to him to ensure that he gets what he wants.

The 1979 Act applies in its full force to business transactions. Clearly it will govern goods of the type normally supplied by a business.

Merchantable quality

It is an implied condition in sale of goods contracts that the goods supplied must be of merchantable quality. This includes the containers the goods are supplied in and any dangerous ingredient they might inadvertently contain. This duty is strict. It arises without any fault on the part of the seller. It is most important if you are a wholesaler or retailer who has sold goods without any particular knowledge as to their quality (especially when those goods have been pre-packed and are not open to inspection by the supplier). The seller promises merchantable goods. He is obliged to provide them.

'Merchantability' means that the goods should be as fit for the purpose for which goods of that kind are commonly bought as it is reasonable to expect. So, underwear must be free from chemicals which make it unsuitable for wearing next to the skin; coal must be delivered free from explosive material; and fizzy drinks must be put into bottles adequate to contain them without exploding and causing damage.

It is not necessary that the goods should cause damage. Goods which simply fail to work in the manner reasonably anticipated are unmerchantable. The failure may arise from a missing part, from faulty manufacture or assembly or, perhaps, through their failure to conform to the good quality generally expected of goods sold at a particular price.

This provision does not apply to defects which you specifically draw to the buyer's attention, or where the buyer has actually examined the defective goods in a way which ought to have revealed the defect and he has purchased them nevertheless.

Reasonable fitness for buyer's purpose

The goods you sell must be reasonably fit for the buyer's purpose. This condition applies when the buyer has expressly or impliedly made known what he wants to use the goods for. In many cases, if you fail to comply with the condition of merchantability, you will also be in breach of this condition, particularly when the goods are normally used for one purpose only.

This is not always so. Your goods may be suitable for a variety of purposes but the buyer says he wants them for one particular purpose. In this case, if the buyer indicates why he wants the goods and relies on your advice on their suitability, they must be fit for that purpose. It does not matter whether or not they also happen to be suitable for other purposes.

Contracts for the hire of goods

There is a difference between hire contracts and sale of goods contracts. The distinction lies in the fact that after the sale of goods, ownership passes from the seller to the buyer. But under a contract for hire, the person who hires out the goods does not give up ownership. He merely gives the other party the right to possess and use them for a period of time, on the understanding that they will be returned.

Terms are implied into hire contracts by the Supply of Goods and Services Act 1982. The terms are almost identical to those implied by the Sale of Goods Act 1979. The hired goods must comply with their description, be of merchantable quality and be fit for their intended purpose. Subject to that, of course, they must be returned at the end of the period of hire.

The Reed family hired a motor launch from Dean & Co for a river holiday. Two hours after their happy departure, a fire broke out. They grabbed the extinguisher thoughtfully provided by Deans. It was out of order. The blazing launch sank with the Reed family's possessions, and the hirers also suffered from burns and shock.

Ruling that a term is implied into a contract of hire that the goods hired should be 'as fit for the purpose as reasonable care and skill can make them', the judge awarded the plaintiffs the damages they sought.

Those who hire out goods owe a duty of care not only to those with whom they contract but also to the 'ultimate consumer' whom they ought reasonably to contemplate would suffer through a defect in the product. After all, if your equipment explodes or collapses, it is far more likely that a stranger to the contract will be hurt than your clients themselves.

Contracts for hire purchase

Contracts of hire purchase contain the same implied terms as contracts for hire. Their essential difference lies in the fact that in hire-purchase agreements the consumer is entitled to keep the goods, to have the ownership in them transferred to himself once the hire-purchase payments are completed.

When you give credit to the consumer so that he can buy on hire purchase, the transaction is regulated by the Consumer Credit Act 1974. The Act controls the way in which businesses are able to offer credit to the consumer, the information they must provide to him and his rights to withdraw from a credit agreement after it has been made.

Any business which provides credit to its customers as a matter of course should be aware of the general rights and obligations created by the Act.

Contracts for the supply of services

The Supply of Goods and Services Act 1982 requires contracts for services to be carried out with reasonable care and skill.

If you are in the business of giving advice you supply a service. Likewise, if you have a contract to service goods but do not yourself sell goods. The Act requires that these contracts for services be performed competently and without negligence. The standard of care required is the standard of the reasonable supplier exercising skill in his trade or profession. But it does not demand from the supplier a duty of strict liability, such that you will always be made liable for a failure to provide satisfaction irrespective of fault. You will not be liable unless you have done the job negligently.

Contracts for the supply of services alone are therefore governed by a less strict rule than contracts for the supply of goods. In the latter case, as we have seen, the supplier will be liable for any failure of the goods relating to their description or merchantability whether at fault or not.

Contracts for the supply of goods and services

As soon as a contract to supply services includes a significant element of providing goods, the Supply of Goods and Services Act 1982 requires strict compliance with the terms of the contract. If you fail to perform the agreement properly, it is no defence for you to say that you were not at fault and, therefore, not responsible. Liability is 'strict'.

Examples of this type of contract are the 'design and build' agreements undertaken by some firms of builders, or contracts to make false teeth. In contracts to service motor cars, in the course of which parts are supplied, the repairers make themselves responsible for the parts (even if those parts have been supplied by a third party). They have promised that, by their skill, they will provide goods that are satisfactory.

The time for performance

Many contracts make provision for the time of performance. Once time has the force of a contractual term, the consequences of late performance depend on the status of the term. If the term takes the form of a 'condition', or it provides that time is to be of the essence of the contract, the breach of the term will give the innocent party the right, if he wishes, to terminate the future obligations (if any) under the contract.

If no particular status has been given to the term, the matter will be determined by the court, looking at all the circumstances of the case. The trend is to treat time clauses in large-scale commercial contracts (for example shipping contracts) as crucial conditions. But as the scale of the agreement diminishes, so the court is more likely to treat the term as a mere warranty. In the majority of cases, therefore, the failure of one party to honour the time when performance should have occurred will give rise only to the right to damages. The guilty party will then have a reasonable time to perform his side of the bargain, after which the other can withdraw completely.

If no particular time for performance has been expressed, the Sale of Goods Act inserts an implied term into the contract that performance must take place within a 'reasonable time'. As always, 'reasonableness' depends on all the circumstances of the case.

Responsibility for subcontracted work

You may promise to supply goods or services to a buyer on the understanding that part of the contract will be performed on your behalf by a subcontractor. What is the position where, through no fault of yours, the subcontractor provides defective goods or services?

If there is no contract between buyer and subcontractor, the buyer has no contractual remedies against the subcontractor. The only person the buyer can turn to in this case is you, the seller. Your obligation to see that the work is done properly is strict. It is no defence for you to say 'I was not at fault, blame my subcontractor'. If the subcontractor provides defective work, you are responsible for it. But if you suffer loss as a result, you in turn may recover from the subcontractor the cost of making good the defective work. You may effectively claim an indemnity from the subcontractor.

4 Responsibility for damaged goods: buyer or seller?

There is a time in every contract when the ownership of the goods passes from seller to buyer. It is important for the law to be able to identify precisely when the transfer takes place. For example, the property may be damaged for reasons unconnected with the conduct of the parties. Is the seller or the buyer the owner of the goods at the time in question, so as to be responsible for making good the damage? Equally, the value of the goods may be subject to fluctuation. If the buyer of the goods is himself offered a good price for them, are they his to sell?

The answer depends on whether the goods are 'specific' or 'unascertained'.

Ownership of specific goods

The Sale of Goods Act describes 'specific goods' as those which have been identified and agreed upon before the sale is made. It is not good enough that your contract refers to a particular class of goods if the specific goods which will be delivered have not yet been selected from that class. To be 'specific', you must have identified the very goods to be sold.

The rule is: 'Where there is a contract for the sale of specific or ascertained goods the property in them is transferred to the buyer at such time as the parties to the contract intend it to be transferred.'

You may agree, for example, that the property in the goods will not pass until all the payments to be made by the buyer have been made. Until that time, the seller is entitled to recover the goods if the buyer defaults on the payments. A clause of this type is known as a 'reservation of title' (or *Romalpa*) clause. If the relevant goods are both identifiable and available, it may be very effective. But once the goods have been sold by the buyer, or subjected to a process of manufacture or mixed with other goods, it may be impossible to say exactly which goods belong to the seller and, therefore, impossible to give the clause effect.

Once again, the courts seek to give effect to the intentions of the parties. If you have not foreseen a particular problem and, therefore, not included terms providing for it, the law may be asked to provide a solution. The rest of this section shows how the Sale of Goods Act deals with these problems. Remember, these rules apply when you have not made your own arrangements. If you regard them as unsuitable, then make alternative plans before the contract of sale is finalized.

The following rules are paraphrased from Section 18 of the Sale of Goods Act 1979.

(a) *Rule 1*: When specific goods are in a deliverable state, the property in the goods passes to the buyer when the contract is made, and it is immaterial whether the time of payment or the time of delivery, or both, be postponed.

Under this rule, the goods become the buyer's when the contract is made, provided they are in a 'deliverable state'.

Goods are in a deliverable state when they are in the condition in which the buyer has agreed to accept them. If the contract requires further work to be performed before delivery, they are not in a deliverable state.

What if the goods are ready for delivery, but contain a defect? It could be argued that the buyer would generally not agree to accept defective goods and, therefore, that defective goods are generally not in a deliverable state. But, if the buyer has not discovered the defect and has actually accepted the goods as they stand, they may have been accepted in their deliverable state. The answer will probably depend on the nature of the contract and the extent of the defect. In a case like this you should seek specialist advice.

It is open to the parties to abandon this rule by agreeing that ownership should not pass until delivery takes place, or until all the instalments are paid, or whatever time they decide.

(b) *Rule 2*: In a contract for the sale of specific goods in which the seller is bound to do something to the goods for the purpose of putting them into a deliverable state, the property does not pass until the thing is done and the buyer has notice that it has been done.

It is up to the seller to inform the buyer when the required work has been performed. The risk does not pass to the buyer until that time. Until then, the seller remains responsible for them.

(c) *Rule 3*: In a contract for the sale of specific goods in a deliverable state in which the seller is bound to weigh, measure, test or do some other act with reference to the goods in order to ascertain the price, the property does not pass until that act is done and the buyer has notice that it has been done.

Again, if it is for the seller to do something to the goods in question, they stay his until those things are done and he informs the buyer of that fact.

(d) *Rule 4*: When goods are delivered to the buyer on approval, or on sale or return, or other similar terms, the property in the goods passes to the buyer:

(1) when he signifies his approval or acceptance to the seller or does any other act adopting the transaction;
(2) if he does not signify his approval or acceptance to the seller but retains the goods without notice of rejection, then, if a time has been fixed for the return of the goods, at the expiration of that time, or, if no such time has been fixed, at the expiration of a reasonable time.

Notice that this rule applies before any contract is made. It explains when an agreement to allow a purchaser time to inspect the goods will become a contract. Normally, the seller will fix a specific time during which the goods may be inspected, after which they will be regarded as sold. Alternatively, if during that time the prospective buyer uses the goods for his own purposes or damages them, that may constitute an act 'adopting the transaction'. Then they become his.

This rule does not apply to goods delivered to a prospective buyer without his prior request. The Unsolicited Goods and Services Act 1971 provides that uninvited deliveries of this nature may ultimately become the property of the recipient without his having to pay for them.

Ownership of unascertained goods

'Unascertained goods' are those which have yet to be identified by buyer and seller. They may be goods which are to be manu-factured at a future date, crops to be grown or goods to be chosen from a bigger sample.

In this case there is an absolute rule: 'Where there is a contract for the sale of unascertained goods, no property in the goods is transferred to the buyer unless and until the property is ascertained.' So, if goods are shipped in bulk by a supplier to a number of buyers without having first been separated and the various items identified by reference to their particular buyers, they are not yet ascertained. If they are damaged in transit, the risk lies with the supplier. You cannot by-pass this rule. However, once the goods have been ascertained, transfer depends on your intentions.

Where the intentions of the parties have not already been made clear, Section 18 of the Sale of Goods Act says:

(a) *Rule 5(i)*: In a contract for the sale of unascertained goods, when goods of that description in a deliverable state are unconditionally appropriated to the contract, either by the seller with the assent of the buyer, or by the buyer with the assent of the seller, the property in the goods then passes to the buyer; and the assent may be express or implied, and may be given either before or after the appropriation is made.

This means that property will pass to the buyer when two things have happened: the goods have been separated in order to be sold; and you have both agreed that those goods should form the basis of the contract. The first part of this requirement is straightforward, the second less so. In one case there was an 'unconditional appropriation' of the goods because the seller had packed them in containers supplied by the buyer. But the opposite result was achieved when the seller had earmarked the goods himself. He was entitled to change his mind and supply them to another buyer (the original buyer having gone bankrupt). But even if the goods are not intended to be delivered for some time, for example because they are in the process of being manufactured, the fact that they have been partially assembled solely for the buyer's purposes could show that they have been unconditionally appropriated to the contract.

> (b) *Rule 5(ii)*: Where, in pursuance of the contract, the seller delivers the goods to the buyer or to a carrier or other bailee (whether named by the buyer or not) for the purpose of transmission to the buyer, and he does not reserve the right of disposal, he is to be taken to have unconditionally appropriated the goods to the contract.

A 'bailee' is a person who has been given responsibility for goods for a period of time, but who is not the owner of them.

So, once the goods have been given to a carrier for delivery, provided they have been ascertained, property in them passes to the buyer.

The distinction between ownership and risk

What happens when the goods are damaged before delivery to the buyer?

So far we have assumed the risk of damage passes to the buyer when ownership is transferred to him, even if the goods have not yet been delivered. This is the rule that usually applies to businesses. The Sale of Goods Act provides that '*unless otherwise agreed*, the goods remain at the seller's risk until the property in them is transferred to the buyer, but when the property in them is transferred to the buyer the goods are at the buyer's risk *whether delivery has been made or not'*. Be sure, then, to arrange insurance when the goods are legally yours. Do not wait until they have arrived.

In contracts with consumers, the passing of ownership and risk may not coincide.

A customer agrees to buy furniture from a shop. The furniture is left with the shop before delivery. The furniture is 'specific goods in a deliverable state'. Under the rules discussed above, the ownership in them could pass, unless you have agreed otherwise. What if, before delivery, the shop is flooded and they are damaged?

Though the buyer now owns the goods, the risk of damage to the goods probably remains with the seller until delivery. The customer is unlikely to have arranged insurance to cover these circumstances and the rule applicable to businesses may not have effect because the parties may be deemed to have *intended* the risk to pass at a later time.

Finally, if damage has been caused because of someone's fault, risk will be his. If goods perish in transit because the buyer gave the wrong address for delivery, or the seller's lorry broke down, the responsibility for it belongs to the person at fault.

5 Excluding liability for breach

Until 1977 the law relating to exclusion clauses in contracts for the provision of services was in a mess. Whilst the general effect of the contract is to undertake to provide goods or services, an exclusion clause claims to restrict or exclude liability if the obligation is not honoured. In recent times the judges took a dim view of this form of clause and they devised ways of avoiding them or interpreting them in a way which favoured the party they were to be used against. This led to fair decisions, but not to the simplification of the law.

Fortunately, that simplification took place under the Unfair Contract Terms Act 1977. This Act controls most of the exemption clauses in contracts for the provision of services, but it does not apply to contracts of insurance or overseas contracts, which are specifically excluded. Its general effect is to invalidate some attempts to exempt liability altogether, whilst in others the clause will only survive if it passes the test of 'reasonableness'.

When does the Unfair Contract Terms Act apply?

The Act applies to clauses in contracts which attempt to avoid 'liability for breach of obligations or duties arising from things done

42

or to be done, in the course of a business'.

The Act applies to contracts either between businesses or between a business and a consumer. It does not apply to contracts between consumers unless one party tries to deny liability for having no right to sell goods.

Liability for negligence

The Act distinguishes between attempts to exclude liability for causing death or personal injury by negligence, and other damage caused by negligence.

The Act applies both to contractual terms which attempt to exclude liability for negligence and non-contractual notices, directed to persons generally or to a particular person. Non-contractual notices may be found (for example) at the entrance to fairgrounds where the public have been given access, and claim to exclude liability for damage whilst they are on the property.

Negligence means the breach of the common law duty of care (see Chapter 7) or the breach of an express or implied term of a contract to exercise reasonable care and skill in the performance of it.

Death and personal injury

Under the 1977 Act you cannot exclude or restrict your liability for causing death or personal injury by negligence. Any such attempt is automatically invalid. If you cause injury or death by negligence in the course of your business, you cannot limit your liability.

Other damage

'Other damage' means damage to property, or the damage resulting from the negligent performance of a contract. In this case a clause restricting or excluding liability may be valid provided it is reasonable.

So far there have been few cases dealing with the meaning of 'reasonable', but factors to be considered include: the circumstances leading to the damage (had they occurred before and should particular care have been taken to avoid them?); the extent of the damage caused (was it so great as to suggest that the party responsible for it should bear the cost of compensation, for example by means of his insurance cover?); whether the other party should have his own insurance cover (should he have been equally aware of the possibility of damage and have taken out his own cover?).

Liability for breach of contract

The Act controls attempts to exclude liability for breach provided one of two circumstances exists. Either:

(1) one of the parties must have entered into the contract as a consumer (the other being a business); or

(2) if both parties are businesses, one must have entered into the contract on the other's 'standard written terms' of business.

A 'consumer' is a person who does not make the contract in the course of business and who enters into it with the other party whose purpose is to deal in the course of business and, in the case of contracts concerning goods, they are of a type ordinarily supplied for private use or consumption.

'Standard written terms of business', or standard form contracts, are contracts where one party signs an agreement which includes a substantial number of terms which are used, without significant variation, with other contractors as well. In other words, they are ready-drafted, do not require significant alteration and are generally used by one of the parties to the contract.

In either of these cases all attempts to exclude liability will be subject to control by the Act.

The Act provides that when you deal with a consumer you cannot either restrict or exclude your liability for breach or render a contractual performance substantially different from that which was reasonably expected of you, or render no performance at all; except in so far as any such term satisfies the requirement of reasonableness.

'Reasonableness' in this context depends on a number of factors. For example:

(1) Were the parties of unequal bargaining strength?
(2) Could the plaintiff have found more suitable contracts else-where, or were his options effectively limited to the contract of the type in question?
(3) Was it reasonable to expect you to have taken insurance cover for the loss in question?
(4) Could you have been expected to offer the plaintiff the opportunity of taking out his own insurance cover?
(5) Did the breach of contract arise out of your negligence?

Exclusions in sale of goods contracts

In any event, in the case of contracts for the sale of goods or of hire purchase, you can *never* contract out of the condition (implied by the Sale of Goods Act 1979, the Consumer Credit Act 1974 and the Supply of Goods and Services Act 1982) that the seller has the right to sell or (in the case of hire or hire purchase) that the user will remain entitled to use the goods without interference from others.

The conditions listed below may never be excluded when one of the parties is a consumer. Where both are businesses, the test of reasonableness applies before any exclusion is allowed:

(1) the implied condition that the goods are reasonably fit for their purpose;
(2) the implied condition of merchantable quality;
(3) the implied condition that the goods will correspond with their description; and
(4) the implied condition that the goods will correspond with their sample.

Therefore, consumers are always entitled to these conditions. But businessmen may exclude them from their contracts with other businesses provided it is reasonable to do so.

Excluding liability by a 'guarantee'

Guarantees may serve to confer rights on the consumer which he might not otherwise have. But all too often manufacturers and suppliers have tried to use guarantees to restrict or exclude liability for defects. Such guarantees have generally guaranteed nothing but trouble for the consumer; they are now outlawed.

The Act applies to the guarantees given to the consumer by the manufacturers. The situation it regulates arises when the manufacturer stipulates in the guarantee that, for example, it will be effective only if returned within a set period of time after purchase, or that complaint must be submitted within so many days of discovery of the defect.

Guarantees of this type are ineffective if they exclude or restrict liability for loss or damage caused by the negligence of the manufacturer or distributor of the goods. The ordinary remedies in negligence are available to the consumer who has been injured by defective goods.

Note that this measure of protection is available only with respect to damage caused by the goods in consumer use. It does not, therefore, extend to guarantees of this nature which are attached to goods used by a business.

6 Remedies for breach of contract

The remedies available against the party in breach depend on the circumstances in which the breach has arisen.

Party in breach refuses to perform the contract

If a party simply refuses to carry on with the agreement he is said to renounce the contract. Renunciation will often be obvious from his express intentions. He may say 'I've found a more attractive bargain with someone else, I shall abandon my present obligations'. Alternatively, he may simply be unable to perform his side of the bargain, perhaps for lack of funds. Alternatively, the defaulting party may be willing to continue with the arrangement, but under such altered terms that, in effect, it is not the same contract at all. If he were to refuse to perform an essential element of the bargain in these circumstances, he will have renounced his obligations.

The only remedy to the injured party in this case is to claim damages. Although the court has power to compel the party in breach to perform the contract, in practice it will not do so unless the contract is so unique that it would not be possible for someone else to fulfil the requirement. In most cases, once damages have

been awarded, the injured party is compensated for having had to
get someone else to do the work required.

Breach of condition, warranty or innominate term

Breach of a condition gives you the right to terminate the future
obligations under the contract and claim damages instead. Breach
of a warranty does not give the option to cancel the contract, but
does entitle you to damages for your loss. You may identify terms
as conditions or warranties as you both wish and the courts will
give effect to your intentions. If you make no specific provision for
the status of the terms of the contract the court will decide for
you on the basis that crucial and central terms which lie at the
very foundation and purpose of the contract will be said to be
conditions, and the remainder will be held to be warranties or
innominate terms.

'Innominate terms' are those which are so broadly drafted that
they are capable of covering a wide variety of breaches. Some may
be central to the contract, others peripheral. In this case, the
remedy depends on the seriousness of the breach relative to the
contract as a whole. If the breach of the term can be said to have
affected matters central to the contract, the remedy will be as for a
breach of condition. But if it is not, it will be as for a breach of
warranty.

The position here is unlike that where one of you refuses to
perform. If there has been a breach of a condition, or of an
innominate term going to the foundation of the contract, the
injured party has a choice. He may terminate the contract and
claim the full extent of his loss from the other party, or he can
affirm its continuance and insist that the other performs the
remaining obligations. The possibility arises because the guilty
party may well be willing to carry on and repair the breach as well
as he can. Provided he is willing to do so, the choice is given to the
injured party to terminate or affirm.

If the contract is affirmed and the breach nevertheless causes
loss, damages may be recovered as compensation.

Special remedies of the seller following non-payment by the buyer

The remedies discussed above have been based on the principle that money is the best means of repairing the damage. In some cases, however, you may prefer to have your goods back.

Your right to take action directly against the goods themselves arises despite the fact that the ownership in the goods has passed to the buyer (see Chapter 4). For this remedy to be available, however, a number of circumstances must exist.

First, the right can be exercised only if you are an 'unpaid seller', that is one to whom the whole of the price has not been paid. Once you have been paid, you lose your right to retain the goods. The right may be exercised over part of the goods only, for example when there has been delivery by instalments. Of course, you are not obliged to insist on full payment at the time of sale. You may give credit facilities to the buyer, in which case you cannot be described as an unpaid seller.

Second, the unpaid seller can exercise his right to retain the goods at any time before they have been delivered to the buyer. They may not have been dispatched to the buyer, or perhaps you can recall them in transit. As soon as the goods have been delivered into the buyer's possession, however, this right is lost, and you are restricted to claim for damages.

Once you have retained the goods as an unpaid seller you can do one of two things. You can simply hold on to the goods until payment is made, or you may sell the goods as if they were yours. If you do so, the ownership in the goods will revert to you. You can only do this if one or more of the following conditions are satisfied:

(1) the goods must be disposed of quickly because they are of a perishable nature;
(2) you as the unpaid seller have given notice to the buyer of your intention to resell and the buyer has not paid the price within a reasonable time thereafter;
(3) you as the unpaid seller have expressly reserved the right to resell the goods in these circumstances, by use of a *Romalpa* clause (see Chapter 4).

Damages for breach of contract

The most frequently made claim for damages in contract is for 'loss of bargain'. One party promised the other certain benefits if he made a contract with him. He fails to provide those benefits and may be made liable to the extent that he has damaged the other. The aim of this form of damages is to put the injured party in as good a financial position as if the contract had been properly performed.

This general rule applies provided two requirements are satisfied. First, the losses which you claim must have been foreseeable as the natural and probable consequences of the breach.

If you are both specialists in a particular field, you may well have knowledge which enables you to foresee loss over and above that which would normally have been foreseen. In this case the plaintiff may recover a higher sum. But the loss is not recoverable if it was not reasonably foreseen.

Second, the plaintiff must mitigate his loss so far as is reasonable. For example, goods are delivered to you which are defective or unsuitable (and which are not, or cannot be, returned); you cannot simply sit on them or throw them away. Provided the goods have some value you must act reasonably by obtaining a reasonable price for them. If you fail to do so, the price which ought to have been obtained will be deducted from the final award of damages. On the other hand, if a machine, for example, is operative but is less efficient than promised, you may recover the cost of putting it right or, if that is not possible, the loss that its inefficiency is likely to cause.

You have six years within which to bring your action. This period of limitation is measured from the date on which the breach took place or the time when you ought to have discovered the breach, if later.

PART II
LIABILITY IN NEGLIGENCE

Introduction

You may sue in 'negligence' those who cause you loss by their carelessness, whether or not you have any contractual connection with the person causing the loss.

The law of negligence developed out of the great variety of circumstances in which accidents are caused. Many involve injuries to individuals by defective products. Although the new law of product liability will affect many cases, most accidents remain governed by the law of negligence.

Negligence is now primarily concerned with accidents which cause loss to those who sue other than in their capacity as individuals. A common example of a business enterprise taking action in negligence, rather than contract, arises where the party from whom goods have been purchased is insolvent, or simply not worth suing. In this case it may be reasonable to trace back to a party in the chain of supply who has the means, or the insurance, to meet an award of damages.

7   The general duty of care

The manufacturer owes duties defined by the individual contract and by contract law towards those with whom he has a contractual relationship. But thanks to the decision of the House of Lords in the remarkable case of the dead, black snail, he must also take due care to protect 'the ultimate consumer' of those products. That 'consumer' is his 'neighbour'; and even though he is a total stranger, he may sue the manufacturer for damages. True, he must prove fault (or 'negligence'). But one day soon, even that ultimate liability to the eventual sufferer may be 'strict'.

Miss Donoghue was a shop assistant who was taken out by her friend for refreshment at a local café. The proprietor duly opened a bottle of ginger beer, ordered for her by her friend, and poured some of it into a glass. The bottle was opaque and the contents were invisible. Miss Donoghue drank.

The hospitable friend then poured the remainder of the beverage into the tumbler. And out swam the limp and slimy remains of the most famous snail in legal history. Not surprisingly, Miss Donoghue not only suffered gastric illness but also 'severe shock'.

Miss Donoghue could scarcely have sued the lady friend, who had bought the defective drink for her. If you serve up poison to a friend, the fact that she does not pay for it will not free you from potential liability. But clearly, Miss Donoghue's friend was not at fault.

Or Miss Donoghue might have sued the cafe, with which the friend had a contract in which there was an implied term that the food would be palatable and would poison neither her nor her friends. But the proprietor was not to blame. Neither did the sufferer have any contract with him.

Next up the line came the distributor. He was liable to Miss Donoghue neither in contract nor in tort. So she took a huge plunge backwards and sued the manufacturer, Mr Stevenson.

Sadly, Mr Stevenson himself died before the case was heard, no doubt himself suffering from deferred shock. But the case reached the House of Lords, where a majority led by Lord Atkin held that the plaintiff was entitled to succeed on the basis of a duty of care owed in the 'tort' or civil wrong of negligence. This duty exists independently of contract. Lord Atkin said:

> The rule that you are to love your neighbour becomes, in law: You must not injure your neighbour; and the lawyers' question: 'Who is my neighbour?' receives a restricted reply. You must take reasonable care to avoid acts or omissions which you can reasonably foresee would be likely to injure your neighbour.

So entirely independently of any contractual duty, you must avoid taking action which you 'can reasonably foresee' would be likely to injure 'your neighbour'.

Who is your 'neighbour', in law?

Lord Atkin: 'The answer seems to be persons who are so closely and directly affected by my act that I ought reasonably to have them in contemplation as being so affected when I am directing my mind to the acts or omissions which are called in question.'

As another judge once put it:

> One man may owe a duty to another, even though there is no contract between them. If one man is near to another, or is near the property of another, a duty lies upon him not to do that which may cause a personal injury to that other, or may injure his property.

This rule includes cases of the supply of goods

to be used immediately by a particular person or persons, or one of a class of persons, where it would be obvious to the person supplying, if he thought that the goods would in all probability be used at once by such persons before a reasonable opportunity for discovering any defect which might exist – and where the thing supplied would be of such a nature that a neglect of ordinary care or skill as to its condition or manner of supplying it would probably cause danger to the person or property of the person for whose use it was supplied, and who was about to use it.

Before *Donoghue*'s case, the duty seems to have been confined to goods 'used immediately' and 'at once, before a reasonable opportunity of inspection'. Now, 'reasonable foreseeability' was stretched much wider.

Lord Atkin, again:

A manufacturer puts up an article of food in a container which he knows will be opened by the actual consumer. There can be no inspection by any purchaser and no reasonable preliminary inspection by the consumer. Negligently, in the course of preparation, he allows the contents to be mixed with poison . . .

If the rules of law did not permit the sufferer to obtain damages from the manufacturer, then its principles would be 'remote from the ordinary needs of civilized society'. 'Where there is so obvious a social wrong', the remedy must be available.

By Scots and English law alike:

the manufacturer of products which he sells in such a form as to show that he intends them to reach the ultimate consumer in the form in which they left him, with no reasonable possibility of intermediate examination, and with the knowledge that the absence of reasonable care in the preparation or putting up of the products might result in injury to the consumer's life or property, owes a duty to the consumer to take that reasonable care.

The doctrine of the 'ultimate consumer' then spread out across the field of law.

A Dr Grant contracted dermatitis after wearing underwear manufactured by Australian Knitting Mills Ltd. The garments contained 'an excess of bisulphate soda.' The determined efforts of the defendant's lawyers to make a distinction between internal consumption and external wear were dismissed by the court. The doctor was the 'ultimate consumer' of the garments.

A solicitor's managing clerk, named Haseldine, went to visit a client who lived on the fifth floor of a block of flats. A porter showed him to the lift. When it reached the second floor, it stopped, reversed direction, and sped downwards, stopping with a violent jerk at the bottom, in the basement. Mr Haseldine suffered severe spinal injury.

The lift had been in use for some thirty-five years and a firm of engineers (A & P Steven Ltd) were under contract to maintain it. Mr Haseldine sued the owners of the building and the engineers.

The Court of Appeal held that the owners were not to blame as they had employed competent contractors and had reasonably acted on their advice. But the lift had been left in a dangerous condition through the negligence of the engineers; there was no reasonable opportunity for intermediate examination; so the engineers were liable to the visitor, who (in effect) was the 'ultimate consumer' of the engineers' services.

So the *Donoghue* v. *Stevenson* principle extended from the manufacturer of the goods to the supplier of services. Engineers, consultants, erectors, installers, repairers, maintenance men – all owe a duty to take care not merely for the safety of those with whom they contract, but also with anyone whom they ought reasonably to contemplate would be affected by their negligent act or omission.

In the case of *Green* v. *Fibreglass Ltd* the court again emphasized that the obligation of the repairer or engineer in this sort of case 'has nothing to do with the law of contract'. It depends upon negligence – which is quite separate.

Vacwell Engineering Company Ltd manufactured equipment designed to produce transistor devices. A Mr Neale was in charge of their applied physics department and worked side by side with a Russian, one Strouzhinski, in Vacwell's laboratory. While washing the labels off samples in two adjacent sinks, prior to using them in the manufacturing apparatus, there was a sudden white flash; Mr Strouzhinski was killed; Mr Neale was injured; and

Vacwell's premises were seriously damaged. Vacwell sued BDH, the suppliers of the chemicals, alleging that they were delivered without any adequate warning notice of the industrial hazard which might arise in their use.

There was no suggestion of any absolute duty on BDH to give warning of industrial hazards of dangerous chemicals 'whether they could have discovered them by the exercise of reasonable care or not'. But (said Mr Justice Rees), they did owe a duty 'to take reasonable care to ascertain major industrial hazards of chemicals marketed by them and to give warnings of such hazards to their customers'.

If that duty had been complied with, the explosion hazard 'would have come to light and a suitable warning would have been given'. This would have prevented Vacwell dealing with the ampoules as they did. The damage was foreseeable; there was no fault on Vacwell's part; the manufacturers were liable.

The same reasoning was applied by a court in *Boots* v. *Devilez*, a case brought against the manufacturers of corn solvent (and explained in detail in Chapter 1). The plaintiff was using the substance while dressed in his birthday suit. His hands were wet. The bottle slipped. The solvent allegedly spilled over his private parts – which duly dissolved.

'There had never been such an accident in the past', said the manufacturers. 'How lucky', replied the court.

'The user ought to have realized that corn solvent would dissolve other, more valued parts of the body than corns' they argued. 'Not so', said the court. 'That which will dissolve one substance will not necessarily dissolve another.' They owed a duty of care to the ultimate consumer. They should have labelled the product, 'Danger!'.

There, the health hazard was all too obvious. In the sad case of *Wright* v. *Dunlop Rubber Company Ltd* the court applied the same rules to carcinogenic substances. If, for instance, employers operate a system under which employees are allowed to put oily rags into their pockets and the oil eventually causes cancer of the scrotum, the employers will be liable because they have been negligent.

So 'ultimate consumers' include not only private but also business buyers; not only employers but also employees – all those whom you should expect to suffer as a result of your negligent act or omission, if you apply your mind to the problem.

The meaning of 'reasonable care'

In many cases, the care which ought to have been taken can be assessed by any reasonable man. Whether or not the driver of a motor car has driven carelessly is within the experience of reasonable people. So are many of the safety precautions taken at work to prevent injury to employees or consumers. Once the existence of a danger has or should have been reasonably foreseen, reasonable precuations should be taken to minimize or avoid it. The ordinary man on the street, 'the man on the Clapham omnibus' as he is sometimes called, can assess what ought to have been done.

However, as the state of commercial and technical life becomes more sophisticated, occasions arise when the ordinary reasonable man cannot be expected to be knowledgeable. The design of a complex piece of machinery or apparatus, or the standard of behaviour expected of an expert in a particular field, are not matters for laymen to decide. In cases of this sort the court must be assisted by the advice of specialists. They are asked to testify as to what they would have done if they had been faced with the facts of the case. Would they have acted the same way, or would they have considered the danger or the risk of loss to be too great and, therefore, have taken different decisions or action?

In cases which come to court, the issue may be finely balanced, with experts on both sides. The question the judge must decide is: Given the state of knowledge possessed by a particular profession and the standards of care normally required of its members, did the conduct of the defendant in the case in question fall below the standard which ought to have been adopted by other members of the same profession?

In the past this test has been applied to doctors, architects and the professions in general. It has also been used to regulate those whose business is to develop items of equipment for general industrial, commercial and consumer use.

Although the answer to the question may be clear in some cases, in others the particular problem may be so novel that no generally agreed standard is available. In that case, if there is room for legitimate differences of opinion there will be no liability in negligence for following one sensible and reasonable path rather than another.

Reasonably foreseeable injury

The obligation to take reasonable care has been imposed to try to prevent reasonably foreseeable injuries from occurring. What does the law consider to be reasonably foreseeable? The question is crucial because if the damage is not foreseeable, no liability will attach to the person responsible for it, even if it is acknowledged that he failed to take reasonable care for his neighbour.

Generally, the foreseeability of a particular course of action is a matter of ordinary human experience. The consequences of a failure to manufacture, or design, goods to the required standard, or of failing to describe their characteristics adequately are not difficult to imagine. The same may be the case for careless deliveries or supplies, provided the deliverer or supplier ought to have known why care should have been taken in performing his service.

In cases where the layman could not be expected to know what consequences ought reasonably to have been foreseen, the reasonable specialist in the field may again be called upon for advice. There the question becomes: What knowledge of the consequences of his action ought the defendant to have had, given the specialized field in which he was working? There may be circumstances in which he could be excused for being ignorant of a particular event. The test is that of the reasonable man knowledgeable of the standards adopted by the trade or profession in question. On the other hand, the court will be very reluctant to relieve you of responsibility for full knowledge of the consequences of your action if safety is at stake, or large sums of money at risk. As the potential loss increases, so you will be expected to know about the dangers presented by your product.

It sometimes happens that damage from a person's carelessness is perfectly foreseeable, but the extent of the loss suffered on a particular occasion was vastly more serious than expected. The nature of the loss was foreseen, but not its extent. For example a chemical may be known to react with another substance, but not to the extent that actually happened when it reacted so violently as to kill someone. In this case the defendant is made liable for the full extent of the loss.

Equally, there are occasions when damage of a particular nature is known to arise in a certain way. In some cases, however, a breach of the duty to take care gives rise to precisely that nature of damage, but in a different way. The nature of the damage was foreseen but not the manner of its infliction. Again, the defendant will be made liable.

Intermediate examination

Liability in the 'tort' of 'negligence' rests on the supplier of the product, where there is no reasonable prospect of 'intermediate examination'. But when can blame be laid against the distributor, the wholesaler, the retailer or anyone else who physically comes into possession of the property before it reaches 'the ultimate consumer'? When is 'intermediate examination' reasonably practicable?

Suppose that you are a supplier of components. If you mass-produce the goods, you will probably recognize that a percentage (however small) will be defective. If one of these is incorporated into the eventual product, that product will itself be defective – possibly dangerously so. How far, then, can you expect your customer (or, perhaps, what we might call 'the ultimate manufacturer') himself to test the items?

If you yourself are to inspect each tiny item, your quality control department will multiply and so will the (probably originally modest) cost of the individual product. Therefore you rely on the customer.

In criminal law, if your customer gives you a *written* undertaking that he will carry out all necessary research and testing, you are in the clear. Otherwise, you may have to rely on his good sense or his industrial knowledge or commercial intelligence.

The manufacturer or other supplier who wishes his customer to examine goods should say so. Include a term, if you wish, in your own written, standard terms. A judge may (under The Supply of Goods (Implied Terms) Act 1973, see Chapter 2) hold that this clause is 'unfair' or 'unreasonable' and therefore void (under the Unfair Contract Terms Act 1977) but he may not. Your customer may not even challenge the exclusion, probably because he does not know his law or because he sees the exclusion as reasonable and fair in the circumstances. Alternatively–and better still–why not draw your customer's attention to the need for intermediate

testing or examination by him? Do so orally by all means. But if
you wish to prove your case, take the trouble to write.

These rules are important, of course, even today when 'fault'
must be proved by the plaintiff. They will become more vital in
future, when the law will impose liability without fault – and when
fault will therefore become relevant when enabling the parties
sued to impose or to apportion blame as between their erring or
innocent selves.

Now let us look at some of the decided cases on 'intermediate
examination'.

In *Griffiths* v. *Arch Engineering Company (Newport) Ltd* the
plaintiff was injured by a portable pneumatic grinding machine
hired by subcontractors from a plant-hire company. He was given
permission by the subcontractors to use the machine; the grinding
wheel shattered because the speed of the machine was too fast for
the diameter of the wheel; and the question was: Should the
subcontractors or the plant-hire company or both be held liable?

The plant-hire people maintained that 'intermediate examination' should have been carried out by the subcontractors. However,
the judge emphasized that 'the mere existence of a reasonable
opportunity for intermediate examination will not exonerate a
manufacturer or hirer out of a chattel'. The proper question is:
'Whether he should reasonably have expected that the person to
whom he has passed the article would use the opportunity for
inspection in such a way as to give him an indication of the risk and
the means of warning any subsequent user of the article.'

The possibility or probability of intermediate examination

> is merely one facet of the wider principle ... Was there a
> reasonably foreseeable risk that the plaintiff who was in fact
> injured would sustain such injury if no precautions were taken
> to guard against the risk? There is a lot to be said for the view
> ... that the customer would rely on his supplier and assume that
> what his supplier handed out to him was sound and in proper
> order – particularly if he was paying for it.

So the possibility of intermediate examination is not enough to
free the supplier from liability. Was it reasonably to be expected
that the intermediate party would inspect?

In *Clay* v. *A. J. Crump & Sons Ltd* builders employed demolition contractors to demolish an old building and building con-

tractors to erect a new one on the same site. They employed an architect to prepare plans and supervise. A wall collapsed and injured Mr Clay, a labourer employed by the building contractors. He sued the architect, the demolition contractors and the building contractors. The trial judge held that all three were partially liable and this view was upheld by the Court of Appeal.

The architect had argued that the building contractors should have examined the wall. But the court held that the architect knew or ought to have known that the building contractors' examination would be likely to be cursory, in reliance on his having left the site safe; that he had failed to take steps to satisfy himself that the wall was safe to be left, although he had had the opportunity of doing so; and that the fact that the building contractors had the last opportunity to examine the wall did not, in the circumstances, break the chain of causation. The architect's negligence was one of the causes of the plaintiff's injuries. Blame was shared and so, therefore, were the damages.

This decision was followed in the case of *Driver* v. *William Willett (Contractors) Ltd*. Here, a firm of counsulting safety and inspecting engineers had agreed to advise the employers on safety requirements in compliance with the relevant regulations. They had not advised the employers to discontinue the unsafe use of a hoist. They were 60 per cent responsible for the accident, even though the employers themselves were negligent and could have avoided the accident, had they followed the rules.

Even a local authority building inspector may be responsible on the same basis. In *Dutton* v. *Bognor Regis Urban District Council* the Court of Appeal held that the inspector owed a duty of care to the purchaser of the house. His failure to make a proper inspection before he gave his approval imposed liability on his employers, even though the building contractors had been negligent.

These rules are, of course, of great importance to all consultants and others who are not necessarily as expert as their title suggests. They are bound to carry out their jobs in a proper and workman-like manner and to use that degree of skill reasonably to be expected of a person of their standing, experience and repute. If they fail so to do and as a result someone is hurt, they cannot avoid responsibility merely because of the possibility of intermediate examination. The 'chain of causation' may have begun with their faulty advice. Alternatively, they may have had the opportunity to

break the chain and to avoid the accident, by the giving of the correct advice or information. Either way, they may be liable in law.

Again, whether the courts are dealing with a defective product,
in the sense of something manufactured, or a dangerous structure,
the rules are essentially the same. If, but only if, there was not only
a probability of intermediate examination but also that this
examination could, should and would have rectified the defect,
will someone higher up the chain be likely to throw off the entire
responsibility on to those lower down it.

Of course, if the intermediate examiner discovered the defect
and failed to do anything about it, the situation would be very
different – as was illustrated in the case of *Taylor* v. *Rover
Company Ltd & Others*. Mr Taylor was injured when a splinter of
steel flew from the top of a chisel which he was hammering. He
lost his eye. The hardness in the chisel was caused by negligence in
the original heat treatment. However, the employers kept the
chisel in circulation after they had discovered the defect. There
was actual knowledge of the defect. 'This was a dangerous chisel
... It ought to have been taken out of circulation ... It was the
keeping of the chisel in circulation with the knowledge that it was
dangerous that caused the accident.'

So if intermediate examination of the defective product does
take place and reveals that defect, the manufacturer may avoid
liability even though he was originally at fault. The chain of
causation was broken and the link between him and the sufferer
has been cut. The sole, effective cause of the damage was the
supervening intervention.

When negligence may be presumed

As a general rule, the burden of proof is always on the plaintiff
to prove his case against the defendant, on the balance of
probabilities. When the defendant's behaviour has been clearly
negligent, the placing of the burden of proof makes very little
difference to the outcome of the case because the court can infer
from the events which have taken place that he must have been at
fault.

Where the fault of one party is more doubtful, the burden of
proof may be sufficient to win or lose the case. The plaintiff must

show that it was more likely than not that the defendant was negligent. If the likelihood is even on both sides the plaintiff loses.

So if the burden of proof is reversed, and put on to the defendant, the results of the case may change. Such a procedure is available in one class of case known under its Latin tag of *res ipsa loquitur* – where 'the thing speaks for itself'.

Suppose that an accident occurs from goods that are, or have been, under the control of the defendant. The accident ought not normally to have happened if due care had been taken but no one is able to explain how it came about. There is a total absence of evidence, apart from the fact of the accident itself. On the face of it, therefore, the plaintiff cannot prove negligence and the defendant cannot disprove it. Their cases are equally balanced. On facts like this the courts have been prepared to reverse the burden of proof where 'the thing speaks for itself'. Here the defendant will be held liable unless he is able to show that the accident occurred without negligence on his part.

This rule has been applied where, for example, there has been a departure from the standard to which goods should have been constructed or assembled. If the defect is one which ought not to have occurred, there will tend to be a presumption that it must have arisen by fault unless contrary evidence is adduced (see Chapter 8).

Of course, if a satisfactory explanation is available from the defendant, the presumption cannot apply. The rule has been applied to help people injured by burst tyres, goods which have fallen from warehouses and passing vehicles, foreign bodies in foodstuffs, swabs sewn up into patients or cars mounting the pavement.

The presumption only applies to one person, however, and if there is more than one possible defendant, and no indication as to which is responsible, the principle cannot apply. For the purposes of the law of negligence, however, a number of employees are all regarded as under the control of their employer. As a result, the presumption can be applied to the general system of work adopted by the employer (see Chapter 10).

8 Physical loss

The chain of production and supply of goods has a variety of commercial links. Each one is subject to the general duty of care, the 'neighbour principle', imposed by the law of negligence. So what is the standard of care applicable to these various links in the chain of production and supply?

The manufacturer

Your duty as a manufacturer is to take reasonable care in the design and construction of your goods. If an error occurs in the process of construction the courts may attribute negligence to you, unless you can show why such an error could not, or should not have been anticipated.

You have the same duty to take reasonable care in the design of your product. Of course, design is often a complex matter. It may be impossible to foresee every eventuality. Subject to the new rules on strict liability for defective products, you will not be made liable for the dangers that no reasonable designer could have foreseen. But courts require you to take special care if you deal with a product that is potentially dangerous.

If things have gone wrong, therefore, the law is inclined to say that it ought not to have happened, that it was under the manufacturer's control and that, until he can show otherwise, he should be responsible for things going wrong.

You may also be criticized for failing to recall a product once its dangers have become known. The more dangerous the product, the more likely it is that prudence demands recall. But if the defect gives rise to the prospect of breakdown alone, and not to injury, it may be reasonable to leave the purchaser to take up the complaint with his supplier. In cases of doubt you should obtain specialist advice. If you deal with products that could be dangerous, formulate a recall policy that can be put into operation at short notice. So far as possible, keep a record of your distributors (and, if possible, their purchasers).

The requirement will depend on what is reasonable. A notice in a trade newspaper may be sufficient if it is reasonable to expect that the message would be communicated to the people it is aimed at. Notices in the national press may be required if the product presents a danger to large numbers of the public.

In many cases, a product cannot both serve the purpose for which it has been designed and be totally safe. Chain saws have to be used with care. So do cooking oil and bleach. Adequate instructions for the use of your product plus warnings of danger and damage are vital. Warnings must be sufficient to cover the various uses, and misuses, to which the product might foreseeably be put. The dangers that must be plain and obvious to all do not generally require notification, although the foreseeable carelessness of the user should be considered, together with the inquisitiveness and lack of care of children, especially in respect of many household goods and 'allurements' (see the Occupiers Liability Act).

Intermediate distributors

Distributors must in general rely on their suppliers. Intermediate suppliers have not usually been required to carry out extensive checks of the goods for which they have become responsible. Often such an examination will be impossible because the goods will have been pre-packed by the manufacturer and are out of sight.

Naturally, distributors must take reasonable care in handling and shipping the goods. They may be obliged to maintain the goods in suitable conditions of warmth, or cold, wet or dry and to keep them generally safe. In normal circumstances, it will be the duty of the distributor's suppliers to inform him of the relevant requirements. Those who sensibly follow instructions will rarely be liable in negligence.

If you have any reason to suspect that the goods you are dealing with are not safe, you must minimize the danger – for example, if the manufacturer is known to supply goods of poor quality. The same would apply if the defects of the goods in question were obvious. Your duty is to take reasonable care not to harm the people who you can foresee are likely to come into contact with them.

What is not yet clear is the legal position of the distributor who receives goods from a person with whom he has had no previous dealing and who has no commercial reputation. It may be, however, that if the goods were of a type which could present danger, a limited duty to inspect might be imposed provided that inspection could be conducted reasonably quickly and efficiently.

The position of importers is also unclear. Of course, if you import goods which you ought to have known would expose the public to an unreasonable degree of danger, you may be negligent. On the other hand, what if the goods have been negligently assembled abroad, but you had no reason to suspect that negligence? If it is effectively impossible to sue the manufacturer abroad, could you as the importer be made liable for the negligence of the foreign manufacturer? Under the law of negligence, the answer is probably no. But under the new rules of product liability the importer of goods from outside the EEC may be strictly liable if the product is unsafe and causes injury or damage.

Retailers

The duty owed by the retailer to the consumer is similar to that of the distributor. You are entitled to believe that the goods you have been supplied with are reasonably safe unless you have reason to think otherwise. For example, your customers might take the trouble to inform you of the dangerous characteristics of a product, in which case the duty of care might require you either to warn subsequent purchasers of the danger in question or, in more serious cases, to withdraw the product from sale altogether, and return it to your supplier.

You should also try to ensure that your goods are not sold to those incapable of understanding the dangers they present – again, take special care for children.

A difficult problem faces sellers of secondhand goods – such as motor cars – which are known to be less than perfect. There is an elementary obligation to check, for instance, the steering and the brakes. Equally, the purchaser should understand the need for a thorough check, especially as the age of the car increases and its condition deteriorates.

Suppliers of service and repair facilities

As a service contractor you must take reasonable care that machinery you are dealing with is maintained in a safe and efficient condition. What standard of service has been promised? Is it a general service designed to check, recondition or replace all parts of the machine whenever required, or a more limited form of service, restricted to certain parts only? You cannot be made responsible for failing to notify a danger which you were not and should not have been expected to discover.

Within the scope of the duty imposed by your contract, you must perform your work with reasonable care and skill. As in the case of the manufacturer whose goods fail to meet his own standards of construction, if a machine breaks down owing to the fault of a part which should have been replaced or refitted, or which has been wrongly fitted, you may be made responsible.

This duty is owed not only to the party with whom you have a contract. It also applies to all those whom you ought to have foreseen being affected by your carelessness. The duty has been applied, for example, to those responsible for servicing motor cars, lifts, heating systems and fire extinguishers.

Failure of service provided by a public body

Both central and local government, and other public bodies, undertake responsibility for providing services to the public. In a number of circumstances these services may affect the condition of goods. For example, much responsibility is given to public bodies to inspect goods and establish standards (for example the Department of Trade and Industry, the Health and Safety Executive and the Department of Health and Social Security). Sometimes they require a certificate of safety to be obtained, a safety standard fixed, a product to be withdrawn from circulation, or a municipal service maintained. What if damage arises following a failure in this respect?

The law is slightly different from that which applies to private interests, because public bodies may have to exercise discretion as to the way in which they spend their time, money and resources. It may be, for example, that they are well aware of the need for close inspection of a trade or service, but their financial constraints enable only the most serious cases to be regulated.

In this case liability in negligence may arise in two circumstances. First, if the public body carries out its function but does so carelessly, so that others suffer damage as a result, the ordinary 'neighbour principle' applies. In performing the task, they must take that degree of reasonable care for the safety of their 'neighbours' expected of a body entrusted with the functions in question.

Second, if the public body does not carry out its function, liability may only be imposed if its failure to do so was caused by negligence. For example, did the authority simply forget to perform its task, or did it make a conscious decision not to do it? If it decided not to act, was the basis of the decision a reasonable one? Did it make a reasonable effort to balance its resources against the apparent danger? Did it make a responsible decision? You should note that, given the numerous demands made of central and local government finances, it will not be easy to establish liability on this ground.

9 Economic loss

Who can recover for *economic* loss – as opposed to actual *physical* damage?

In cases of physical loss the damage is tangible; it is clear for all to see. It is also quantifiable because, by its nature, its effects are limited. Even if the extent of the physical damage is colossal, it is possible to prove where it starts and finishes.

Economic loss is often less provable. If, for example, a commercial institution is unable to trade because of a power cut, they may suffer loss of business. So may their customers, who themselves may have to let down their own clients, all of whom may lose business. If the power cut was caused by negligence, for how much should the defendant be held responsible?

In cases like this, the law does not allow all the foreseeable loss from the careless act to be recovered. Financial loss can be recovered if it arises from damage to a particular product.

Spartan Steel Ltd v. *Martin & Co. (Contractors) Ltd*

The plaintiffs were the owners of a factory which manufactured stainless steel. The factory obtained its power by a direct cable from the Midlands Electricity Board. The defendants were contractors

71

working on the road a mile or so from the factory. They had been
given a map indicating where cables, pipes and mains were laid but
they failed to examine it with sufficient care. They damaged the
cable which supplied power to the plaintiffs' factory. The factory
was working around the clock and lost power for 14 hours.
The plaintiffs suffered the following loss.

(1) Molten metal being processed in the furnace at the time of the
    power cut had to be released from the process before comple-
    tion. It was, therefore, of less value than was intended. The
    actual physical damage to the melt was valued at £368.
(2) In addition, once the melt was made ready for sale it was of a
    lower quality than intended and had to be sold at a price which
    represented a £400 loss of profit.
(3) During the time the power was off, the factory was unable to
    process four additional batches of melts into the furnace. They
    did not suffer physical loss, but their lost production amounted
    to a lost profit of £1767.

The Court of Appeal decided that the actual physical damage to
the melt was recoverable. So was the loss of profit which arose out
of that damage. Thus the sum of £768 represented the loss which
was the direct consequence of the negligence. But the loss of profit
from lost production could not be recovered. It was 'pure' loss of
profit. If that was allowed, there would be no knowing where
liability might stop.

In the ordinary case where lost profit cannot be traced back
directly to damage to a particular product, it may not be claimed in
damages. This very strict rule has recently been modified. There
are some circumstances where the economic loss which may be
inflicted may not be open-ended, but restricted to a precise
amount. Similarly, the class of people who may be affected may
not be vast. It may only be one person. Pure economic loss may
now be claimed when these factors exist and there exists between
the parties 'a special relationship'. The meaning of this phrase is
illustrated by the leading case of *Junior Books* v. *Veitchi*.

Junior Books Ltd v. *Veitchi Co Ltd*

The plaintiffs arranged for a firm of building contractors to build a
warehouse. A certain amount of specialist work was required and

the plaintiffs specifically named the defendants as the company by which the work should be done. So the plaintiffs entered into a contract with the building contractors, and the building contractors with the subcontractors. There was no contract, however, between the plaintiffs and the subcontractors, but they were in reality far from strangers. For example, the subcontractors were specially appointed by the plaintiffs because of their expertise. They knew that it was their skill, rather than that of the main contractors, on which the plaintiff was relying, and could foresee the nature of the damage which would be suffered if they performed the work carelessly. They alone were responsible for the composition and construction of the work.

The House of Lords held that the degree of trust and reliance invested by the plaintiffs in the subcontractors was such as to create a 'special relationship' between the parties. When the subcontracted work failed the plaintiffs were therefore entitled to recover the loss of profits suffered while the warehouse was out of use.

So, there is a category of case in which pure economic loss may be recovered. But later cases have given a very narrow application to the rules in the *Veitchi* case. It seems most unlikely that it would be applied to mass-produced goods. The ultimate consumer in such case may be entitled to proceed against the seller in contract, but probably not against the manufacturer for his pure economic loss. Neither will the producer of goods to a particular order be liable unless he assumed responsibility for the goods directly to the consumer.

Economic loss caused by negligent advice

The possibility of recovering for the consequences of negligent advice has already been considered (see Chapter 1).

It is another example of the type of 'special relationship' which can give rise to liability for pure economic loss. In many cases, of course, the advice of a consultant, on whom it is proper to place trust and reliance, is sought under a contract. An action for breach of contract may lie if the advice is given without reasonable care or skill.

Where advice is given by a party outside a contract – for

example as a means of persuading one party to enter a contract at some future time, or simply gratuitously as a form of professional advice – liability may arise in negligence.

Liability depends on there being a 'special relationship' between the parties arising from the trust and reliance placed on one party by the other, such that a duty is placed on the adviser to take reasonable care in giving the advice.

10 Responsibility of employer for negligence of employee

The employer is responsible in law for the negligent acts of his employee, provided those acts were committed within the scope of his employment.

If you are an employer, you are not entitled to say that you selected your employees responsibly and with reasonable care and that you as an individual were not at fault. You are said to be 'vicariously liable', that is, liable on behalf of your employee.

When does this liability end? Clearly you are not liable for your employee when he happens to have an accident in one of the works' vehicles which he happened to be borrowing over the weekend. This is so because the employee had not behaved negligently within the scope of his employment. At the time of the accident he was not at work. He was on an 'independent frolic'.

The scope of employment

The meaning of the phrase 'within the scope of employment' is broader than might be imagined. It goes beyond those activities which you, the employer, have specifically authorized. You are responsible not only for such acts, but for the unauthorized acts which have been done for the good of the business. So, if the employee has been careless in doing the job he has been employed to do, you will be liable. Employers have been liable for a petrol tanker driver who threw a match near an underground petrol storage tank and caused an explosion; for a bus driver who injured pedestrians and passengers by careless driving; and for a driver of a fork-lift truck whose way was blocked by a lorry, and which he drove into a wall. In each case, the employee was attempting to further the interests of his employer.

This is so even when the employer has specifically forbidden a particular form of conduct. If the employee ignores the instruction, but does so in an attempt to benefit his employer, you remain liable.

Once the employee's acts move outside the scope of his employment, vicarious liability ends. An employer is not generally liable for the time spent by the employee driving to work (although a different result might be reached for time taken off for a tea-break, or even for lunch), or for the chauffeur who takes his employer's car for a joy-ride, or the delivery man who deviated from his responsibilities by driving in the opposite direction for the benefit of a friend who wanted a lift. In these cases, the employee was not seeking to further his employer's interests or doing something reasonably incidental to his employment.

The essence of the distinction, therefore, depends on the reason why the employee had undertaken the activity which caused the harm. As so often happens in law, however, while the principle behind the previous cases is easily stated, the application of that principle to specific cases is difficult.

Liability for agents and independent contractors

So the employer may be made liable for the negligent acts of his employee. But what is the position when the person responsible for the negligence is not an employee, but an *agent* of the employer; or an *independent contractor* in business on his own account? Can a business which has contracted work out to a separate firm of (say) designers, assemblers or deliverers, be made responsible for their negligence?

Normally, you are not liable for your agent's negligence. He is not your employee: he is responsible for himself. So, provided you have chosen him with reasonable care to perform the work, you will not be liable for his carelessness.

You may be made liable if the goods or services you supply are inadequate, even though the fault lies with your agent. You may be responsible – not in negligence, but for breach of contract. If you wish, you may ask an agent to carry out your obligations on your behalf. But if he fails, it is still your promise that has been broken.

If your agent cannot make you liable for his negligence, can he make contractual promises on your behalf?

Naturally, you give certain power to those who operate for you or on your behalf. They have your 'actual' authority, normally within limits which you specify. You are bound by any deal made by your servant or agent within the limits of the authority you gave him.

What, though, if your agent exceeds your authority? Suppose, for instance, that he is offered a deal which he regards as both important and beneficial to his employers. Unfortunately, to tie up the arrangement he would have to go beyond the authority you gave him. If he is selling, perhaps the customer is offering a fraction less than he is authorized to accept; or if he is buying, the price may be a little more than he was told to pay.

Usually, your agent tries to contact you, his principal. To no avail. You are out, away, unavailable. So he is in a well-known spot. If he exceeds his authority, he is likely to be in trouble. After all, what is the point of putting a limit on his powers and informing him of that limit if he is going to go beyond it on his own initiative? On the other hand, if he allows the deal to escape him, you may say, perhaps with total justification: 'Why didn't you use your initiative? What's the use of employing a person like you at your level, if you are not prepared to take a decision off your own bat?'

Precisely the same rules would apply to an agent who gave a warranty about a product which he is not authorized to give – or who recommends a product for an unsuitable purpose. If he is acting within the scope of his apparent or implied or ostensible authority, his employers will have to accept legal responsibility for the results of his incorrect statement.

In countries, companies and firms where an employee who makes a mistake is likely to suffer while one who does well rarely benefits, the employee will play safe and stick to his authority.

Elsewhere, he is likely to shrug, to take the plunge and to hope for the commercial best.

If all goes well, the deal is approved – no problem. But if the contract goes sour for the employers or principals, they will not only protest to the employee, they will probably also contact the other party and say: 'We are very sorry, but Mr So-and-so had no authority to make the deal on our behalf.'

At this stage, the law will intervene on behalf of the innocent other party, deceived into entering the arrangement by his reasonable belief that your servant or agent was entitled to do the deal on your behalf. If you gave him your 'apparent' or 'ostensible' authority, the other party is entitled to rely upon it and to insist upon the carrying out of the contract in precisely the same way as if the individual concerned had your 'actual' authority.

You must take care, then, not to 'clothe' your servants or agents with authority which they do not possess. If you 'hold out' a servant or agent as entitled to make a contract on your behalf, you are bound. This concept is technically known as 'the doctrine of holding out' – which is not (as a solicitors' examination candidate recently suggested) a branch of the law on indecent exposure!

In each case, then, the law looks to see whether the employee or agent was 'held out' as having the authority which in actuality he did not possess. Would a person of his status or standing, with the credentials which you provided for him, reasonably be expected to be entitled to make the deal in question?

You might, of course, put the other party 'on notice' of the limits on the authority of the servant or agent. 'We enclose herewith details of the research and testing which we are willing and able to carry out, if required, on our products. No employee is authorized by us to extend those limits without my personal, written authority . . .' Or: 'I am pleased to introduce our Mr Black. He has authority to place orders on our behalf up to a maximum of £ . . .'

Alternatively, the other party may impliedly have notice of limits on authority. You would hardly expect an office boy to be able to place an order for intricate machinery, or the junior clerk for a major computer. But directors, company secretaries, senior managers and other executives are likely to have implied authority to take major decisions.

11 Statutory and other standards

In a number of industries, compliance with standards is a relevant factor in deciding whether or not conduct has been negligent. Standards may be laid down by the government in the form of a statute, or by a statutory instrument in which a specific code of practice is provided for. Alternatively, standards may be required or recommended by either non-governmental bodies or official ones. Finally, standards may exist wholly informally as matters of practice generally adhered to within a particular industry.

Statutory standards

Many statutes require manufacturers to maintain certain standards. Some standards are imposed in relation to the organization of the workplace, for the benefit of employees (for example, by the Health and Safety at Work Act 1974 and regulations made under it). Others govern the process of production itself, for the benefit of the consumer (for example, the Consumer Protection Act 1987). Some statutes impose standards for other purposes entirely, for example to promote good business practice (the Trade Descriptions Act 1968) or general standards of public health (the Food and Drugs Act 1984).

What if you fail to adopt a statutory standard? Evidence of the breach of a standard imposed by a statute does not automatically lead to a finding of negligence. Before this is possible the intention behind the statute must be discovered. Was it intended to confer a right of action on an individual in negligence? In some cases, this intention is expressly stated in the statute. The Consumer Protection Act 1987, for example, specifically provides that those who suffer injury owing to a breach of a standard required by the statute shall have a right of civil action in negligence (see Chapter 20).

Where the statute makes no reference to a right of action on behalf of an individual, the intention has to be gleaned from the implication of the Act as a whole. Courts have developed a number of general rules of guidance but judges are reluctant to confer additional rights on the consumer, in cases of this sort. Their reasoning is that when there is a variety of suitable remedies available to the consumer in contract and negligence, the courts should not presume that an Act of Parliament intends to add to them.

Finally, note that even if you have complied entirely with a statutory standard, this does not automatically preclude an action in negligence. The ordinary remedy in negligence will still be available unless the statute forbids it. Again, the intention of the statute has to be interpreted. Your compliance with the standard is not conclusive, but it is strong evidence in your favour. Equally, it is uncommon for the courts to find that the standard required by a statute falls foul of the law of negligence.

Informal standards

Informal standards are those not enforced by statute or statutory instrument. They may be recommended by governmental agencies (like the Health and Safety Executive), non-governmental bodies (like the British Standards Institution) or simply by a particular industry's own code of practice or trading standards.

The courts have always said that, in deciding whether the practice of an industry is negligent, the test turns on the standard of care which ought to have been adopted by a reasonably prudent industrialist in the area in question. Would he have regarded the practice adopted by a business to have fallen below an acceptable standard?

The courts insist that it is their job to consider all the evidence, to listen to all the experts and to form a conclusion on the matter. They will not be bound by the standards of conduct which may have been adopted by others. But they are not blind to such standards. The more trouble and care which has been taken in their formulation, the more likely it is that the courts will adopt the same standards. At the other end of the scale, there are a number of cases where judges have said that the standards generally adopted by an industry were inadequate – in effect, that an entire industry ought to have taken greater care.

12 Defences to an action in negligence

In deciding whether to defend an action or not it is necessary to balance delicately the strengths of the cases of each side. Clearly, if an employee has performed his job carelessly, for example, and not achieved the standard of work required of him, you will be inclined to settle the dispute out of court. There is no point in wasting time and money attempting to defend the indefensible.

There are a number of circumstances in which there may be genuine disagreement about who should bear responsibility for an accident and, in such cases, you must consider the grounds law provides as defences to allegations of negligence. Before any decision is taken whether or not to defend, it is essential to have an accurate and detailed account of the accident and its surrounding circumstances. Then the question of a defence can be considered.

Contributory negligence

It may be that as a producer of goods you are prepared to admit that your product presented an unreasonable danger to its users but that, for a number of reasons, the user ought himself to have been more careful in using it. In other words, that the user contributed to his own injuries by his own negligence.

The Law Reform (Contributory Negligence) Act 1945 permits an award of damages to the injured plaintiff to be reduced by a percentage which represents a fair and equitable estimation of the extent to which the plaintiff caused or contributed to his own loss. The reduction could be 1 per cent, 100 per cent or any figure in between.

The defence is available when you can show that the plaintiff has failed to take reasonable care of his own safety, that is, that he himself behaved negligently. The elements of the defence involve a plaintiff who has, or ought to have, reasonable knowledge of the dangers to which he is exposing himself; a willingness to expose himself to those dangers; and who suffers damage of the type foreseen as a result.

It is not sufficient if the danger was not appreciated by the plaintiff, or if he could not reasonably have been expected to avoid it, or if damage arises of a nature which was not foreseen. Dangers which are not obvious to the user, therefore, will not attract the defence. So attention must be paid to the knowledge he possessed. Was he (for instance) a child, or known to be inexperienced in dealing with the goods in question?

To a certain extent, warning people of the dangers can increase your chances of being able to use the defence. The more knowledge others have of a danger, the more they may be considered to be responsible for avoiding it. On the other hand, if the very fact of exposing people to the danger is itself unreasonable, it would be difficult to argue that it was the user's fault when he suffered injury.

Voluntary assumption of risk

This defence is difficult to establish and is unlikely to succeed – but it is a complete defence to an action in negligence. Unlike the defence of contributory negligence, the defendant who success-fully pleads this defence (known to lawyers as '*volenti non fit injuria*') is relieved of liability altogether. A volunteer cannot complain of injuries suffered through risks knowingly undertaken.

This defence may apply where an individual has knowingly exposed himself to danger. The entire responsibility for the accident may then rest with the individual.

The reason the defence is uncommon is because of the difficulty in proving it. The defendant must show both that the plaintiff voluntarily undertook the conduct in question and that he had full knowledge of all its likely consequences.

It is highly improbable that an employee who was acting under the instructions of his employer could be met by such a defence. His action was not entirely voluntary. If there is any good reason why a person might expose himself to danger it is unlikely that his conduct would be regarded as wholly voluntary. Similarly, the defence must fail if the person did not possess full knowledge of the extent and nature of the risk he was running. It would be difficult to apply to a child, or to a person who had little experience in the workings of a particular product.

PART III
THE CONSUMER PROTECTION ACT 1987: CIVIL LIABILITY

13   When are goods defective?

The Consumer Protection Act 1987 introduces new law – the law of product liability. Under the law of negligence, the plaintiff can succeed only if he can establish fault against the producer. The new rules impose liability irrespective of fault. All it requires is that the product has caused injury when it was in a defective condition.

It is essential, therefore, to know when a product is 'defective'. The Consumer Protection Act lays down that 'there is a defect in a product if the safety of the product is not such as persons generally are entitled to expect'. And 'safety' shall include safety in the context of risks of damage to property, as well as in the context of risks of death or personal injury.

The safety a person is entitled to expect

When will your products not give a person the safety he is entitled to expect? Safety means freedom from danger. When, then, will your product expose people to unreasonable danger? Your products will not fall foul of the Act just because they do not work. If they simply do nothing, they do not expose people to danger. In this case, there will be the normal remedies in contract and in negligence but not under the 1987 Act.

It is the same if the product is put into operation and causes damage *to* itself. Say, for example, that all the lubricant leaks out of a machine – no question of safety arises. The 1987 Act does not apply, although you may well be made liable in contract or in tort.

But what if your product causes damage to other property? Is it 'unsafe' if it goes out of control, for example, even though it causes no personal injuries? It may well be unsafe for this reason. The 1987 Act provides: 'Safety shall include safety in the case of risks of damage to property.' It is not 'safe' to have it among other property. If it causes damage in this way, you may be liable provided the danger is caused to 'consumer goods' (see below).

Of course, if your product happens to injure someone, this *is* a question of safety. If injury arose from the product when it was being used in its intended way, subject to your defences it will be 'defective'.

What, then, are the different types of defect?

Manufacturing defects

A common type of defect arises because something goes wrong with your manufacturing process. You know the form your product should take, but it did not leave you in the form intended. Perhaps a part of it has not been attached or has fallen off, or a valve has stuck, a pump has broken or a connection sheered. This is a defect of manufacture. If it is unsafe, you may be made liable for it. The difference between this law and the law of negligence is that you will now be liable regardless of whether or not you were at fault. The relevant question under the 1987 Act is: Was it defective?

What is the position of goods assembled on a production line? You allow for a proportion to contain faults. Absolute quality control is unrealistic and you are prepared for some goods to be defective, but you do not know in advance which ones they are. No one has criticized you for making this judgement and other manufacturers do the same. Will you still be liable?

It is impossible to know exactly how the court will react to the problem; you would probably be liable. You should therefore estimate as accurately as you can the quantity of defective goods to be expected and arrange insurance cover accordingly.

A different question arises in connection with defects that no one could have foreseen because the state of scientific and technical knowledge at the time the product was developed did not recognize the danger. In this case you may have a defence (see Chapter 15).

Design defects

Defects of design will generally occur in two sorts of situation: when the product has been assembled according to your specifications but it simply is not up to the job (an *unintended* defect), and when you make a deliberate choice in the design of the product which gives rise to danger (an *intended* compromise).

Unintended design defect

Unintended design defects are governed by the same rule as manufacturing defects. You may not have foreseen them and you certainly do not intend them, but you will be liable if they cause danger. Unlike manufacturing defects, however, design defects may arise in the production line itself. An entire run of products may possess the defect. Of course, if you discover the danger and do nothing about it, a large claim could be made against you. What should you do?

First, insurance cover may be available (see Part VII). Also, you may be able to minimize the potential loss by a campaign of providing information to the users or, where possible, by recalling the product. The Society of Motor Manufacturers has developed an effective recall procedure for its members when things have gone wrong at the design stage and been incorporated on the production line. For those manufacturers who are able to keep reasonably accurate records of the whereabouts of their products, a similar response must be considered.

If your goods are of the type generally made available to the public from the shop counter, the most effective measure may be a publicity campaign to warn of dangers. This may adversely affect the reputation of your company. But apart from the moral responsibility to your customers, it may be the most effective way of reducing the potential claim against you for damages.

Intended design compromise

Intended design compromise raises a different problem and a difficult one. You have to pitch your products to the right area of the market. You must get the price right. The style must be appealing. It might have to be fast, or efficient, or durable ... All these factors may have a bearing on the safety of your product. Of course, you could always make it more safe, but that would affect something else. In the end you arrive at a compromise. You make your goods available, knowing that they are the best you can do for the price, but that they could be made safer.

For example, do you sell a car with a safety cage that reduces the danger to its occupants in a crash? Or an economical car, made as light as possible, to cut the cost of motoring? Or a car capable of high speeds? Or anti-skid brakes? If injury results, can you be made responsible?

You are entitled to offer the public a choice in the variety of goods for sale. The consuming public demand different things. But in making that choice available, you must not expose the user, or others that could be affected, to unreasonable danger. You cannot, for example, offer a sports car at a bargain price because substandard brakes have been fitted. Neither must you supply a dangerous grinding machine without fitting an adequate safety guard or cut-off mechanism.

You must take reasonable care in the design of your product to ensure it is safe for the uses, and misuses, to which it will foreseeably be put. You will not be able to say: I offered it so cheaply that the buyer was not entitled to expect reasonable safety from it.

So what is 'reasonable safety'? The product must be capable of being used without exposing people to unreasonable danger. As standards change, so must the safety of your product. But if your product is as safe as those others you compete with and, in all the circumstances, was capable of being used safely by the general public, it is likely to be considered safe under the Act.

So far, there have been very few cases in the law of negligence on this sort of design compromise. Expect the 1987 Act to give rise to significant developments here.

Warnings

The 1987 Act specifically mentions the importance of instructions and warnings attached to a product. The product itself is as you intended it to be and works satisfactorily. But if it could pose a danger, what would otherwise be unsafe and therefore defective may be rendered safe by a warning or instruction. When should you attach them to your product?

You should take the steps necessary to make reasonably safe those you can reasonably foresee coming into contact with your product. Note that it is not necessarily enough for you to have in mind what the reasonable user would do with the product. If you can reasonably foresee your product being misused, take precautions to warn.

For example, children like to put things in their mouths. So remind the consumer to keep household cleaning agents and gardening chemicals well out of children's reach. So, too, with electrical goods. They can easily injure people. Make your instructions as plain and clear as possible.

On the other hand, of course, if you were to try to warn against every foreseeable accident that your product could cause, you would end up with a pamphlet or even a book. If you specialize in sophisticated machinery, instructions to that level of detail may be necessary. But, so far as warnings are concerned, you must strike a balance. Some dangers are so obvious that the user should be expected to be aware of them. Carving knives are sharp – no warning of that fact is needed; that is why they are bought.

Take reasonable care. If a warning can be easily incorporated, warn. In all these cases where this rather imprecise requirement of 'reasonable care' is used, you might like to take advice. As a general rule, if in doubt do not leave it out.

If you are in the business of supplying component parts to other manufacturers, your position is different. If your product has hidden dangers that the other manufacturers might not know about, warn them, for the sake both of their employees and their customers. It will probably be their job to attach the relevant notice. This is particularly so if your component part will be absorbed into their products, out of sight. But if your component could cause danger and is simply attached to an outer part of the main product, ready to be seen, so that you could easily attach your own warning, then be safe – warn.

Goods not covered by the Act

Certain types of goods are not covered by the 1987 Act. They are still subject to the law of contract and of negligence. So you may be liable to your buyer for breach of contract if the goods are unmerchantable or they fail to comply with their description. In negligence, you may be liable if the product causes damage as a result of your carelessness.

Agricultural produce

Agricultural produce means any produce of the soil, of stock farming or of fisheries. You will not be liable for the defects in your agricultural products, or for game, if you supplied them when they had not undergone an industrial process.

What is an 'industrial process'? Clearly, if you are a farmer who has taken produce from the land and sold it directly on the market, no industrial processing has occurred. The problem arises as soon as something is done to the produce. Potatoes and carrots are washed, peas are shelled. Even though these processes are relatively minor, they may still be 'industrial'. We will have to wait for the judges to decide – but do not take chances, take out insurance.

The significance of this new law is not that you will be liable if a foreign body is mistakenly included in your bag of chipped potatoes. In this type of case you will probably be liable in negligence in any case. Under the 1987 Act, if your produce has undergone an industrial process, you will be responsible irrespective of your mistakes. If the produce is defective – if (say) it contains harmful fertilizer – you will be liable.

The defective product itself

You will not be liable under the 1987 Act for the damage caused *to* the product itself. If you install a defective oil gauge which fails to indicate loss of pressure, you will not be liable for the consequent damage to the machine. The same rule applies if you are the supplier of a component part which fails and causes damage to the product to which it has been attached.

But note: you may be liable for the other damage which the

defect causes. If the defective oil gauge causes the machine to damage other goods, you may be liable for them.

If the defect has arisen through your negligence, you may be made liable for the damage caused to the product itself. Therefore, if negligence is alleged against you, you may be made liable for the machine to which the oil gauge was attached (see Chapter 8).

Goods not intended for private use, occupation or consumption

When a claim is made against you for damage to goods, the 1987 Act applies only for the benefit of consumers in relation to consumer goods. The claim can only be made under the Act in respect of goods ordinarily intended for private use, occupation or consumption and which were intended to be used in that way by the person who suffered loss.

If the goods concerned are either normally used in a commercial setting, or if they were consumer goods being used in a commercial context, the Act does not apply. Of course, the law of contract and negligence will still apply in these cases.

Many goods are equally suitable for both business and private use and may be used both at home and at work.

Property damage not exceeding £275

If you have caused damage to property, an award will not be made against you under the 1987 Act for damage not exceeding £275. A claim may, of course, be made for a lesser sum in contract or negligence.

14   Who may be made liable?

Once a product has been found to contain a defect, and to have caused injury or damage to a consumer's personal property, who may be made liable?

The producer

The producer may be made liable. Who is a 'producer'? If you have manufactured the goods, you are their producer. This is usually straightforward enough. But if you are engaged in mining operations and you win or abstract material, you are regarded as the producer of that material. If it is defective, you may be liable regardless of your fault.

You are also regarded as the producer of produce that you have subjected to an industrial process. The farmer will not be liable under the 1987 Act for his defective farm produce. It is excluded from the Act. But if you are responsible for cleaning, dicing, cooking or mixing, you become the producer of that produce. You may be held strictly liable under the 1987 Act.

The Act defines the word 'product' in a broad way. It means any goods or electricity, but not gas. If a user is injured by electricity, or his domestic property is damaged by it, you may be responsible for the damage caused by your product. 'Product' includes the packaging in which it is contained. Make sure that it is up to the job, that it will not corrode or explode. Be aware (for instance) of the need for child-proof lids and caps where danger may reasonably be foreseen.

Own-brand products

If you buy your products from someone else and then attach your own brand or trade mark to that product, so as to say the product is yours, you will be regarded as its producer. Chains of supermarkets and departmental stores commonly do this.

The defect may have arisen through no fault of yours. The product may have been pre-packed, or canned, and totally immune from inspection. Nevertheless, you will be its 'producer' under the 1987 Act. You may be made responsible for its defects.

There is nothing to stop you coming to an arrangement with your supplier about who should be responsible for the payment of damages, if the need arises, or in what proportion you should both pay. So far as the injured person is concerned, that is your problem, not his. He is entitled to damages from you.

Importers

You may be liable as an importer if you have imported a defective product into the EEC. As an importer, you will not be caught if you imported from one EEC country into another, even if the goods were originally imported into the EEC from elsewhere.

Are you likely to be sued if you import defective goods into Germany, to a supplier there, who then sells them on? Will the German consumer's first line of attack be against the German supplier, or you?

If you have acquired your goods from a German importer (who himself brought them into the EEC), will the injured consumer turn first to you, to the supplier, or to the German importer? Guidance on this complicated question is provided in Part VI.

Suppliers

You may be liable for the defects in a product if you are a retailer, a wholesaler or otherwise no more than one of the links in the chain of supply, and even if you have nothing to do with the production process. A number of conditions must be satisfied before that can happen. These are:

(1) The person who suffered the damage must have been in touch with you with a request that you tell him the names of either the producer, the own-brander or importer of the product.
(2) That request must have been made within a reasonable time after the damage has occurred, and when it is reasonable to expect him (the damaged party) to find out who these people are.
(3) You, the supplier, must have failed to comply with his request within a reasonable time. If you do not know the identity of the producer, own-brander or importer, you may escape liability by telling him the name of your supplier. Then the process can start again, against him.

So it is essential to keep thorough and up-to-date records. Know who supplied you with what, in what quantity and when. If possible, know too who you sold it to. And as a retailer or other non-producer, importer or own-brander, the Act should not worry you.

Sharing liability with other 'producers'

If you are sued by someone for a defect in your product and there is another producer of that product who could also be liable, you can insist on joining that other producer as a co-defendant. This procedure is made possible by the Contribution Act 1978. It means that he will be made to contribute to any damage you have to pay.

When can you join others as a co-defendant?

If an employee is injured through defective equipment you supplied, you are strictly liable in law and he may sue you for damages. But you may pass the blame back to your suppliers, if they were really at fault.

If you supply defective goods to your customers, they may successfully sue you for damages for breach of contract. But if you can show that someone else was the real culprit, you can make him liable.

You may be manufacturers incorporating a sealed part into a final product without the possibility of intermediate examination – so if that part is defective, why blame you? Or you may be distributors or retailers, landed in contractual trouble through your suppliers' default.

How, in practice, though, do you bring the true blame home to rest on the party who was really at fault? What are the legal procedures?

If you are sued, you may issue 'third-party proceedings' against those whom you say are really responsible for the default. You may bring that company, firm or individual into the action as 'third party', seeking an appropriate contribution towards any damages which you may have to pay, or (better still) a total indemnity. If the other party was partly to blame, he will have to make a contribution; if the fault was totally his, you should get an indemnity.

The third party may try to pass the blame further up the line. You sell to the public and are sued by your customer because you sold him defective goods? Then you may bring the wholesaler into the action as third party and he may join the manufacturer who sold the goods to him as a 'fourth party'.

Precisely the same procedure applies in safety cases. A boiler or vessel exploded killing a workman. His widow sued his employers, alleging that they had supplied him with faulty equipment or alternatively had failed to train or supervise him adequately or at all. The employers claimed contribution or indemnity from the erectors or installers who (they said) put up the machine without unsealing the safety valves, properly or at all or (alternatively) without adequately informing their (the defendants') employees as to how the job could and should be done safely.

The erectors and installers then joined the manufacturers, claiming that the machine was faulty in the first place. Ultimately, the three lots of insurers split the agreed damages.

These, of course, are the rules in civil law. Similar principles apply to crime. If you are prosecuted under Section 6 of the Health and Safety at Work Act for failing to take such steps as were reasonably practicable not to make it a dangerous product, then you may blame the consultants who advised you ... those who supplied you with your parts or accessories ... or anyone else whom you say was really responsible. The inspector may then prosecute them – together with you or in your place.

Strict liability law is a largely civil concept, designed to give the sufferer the right to direct legal access to the bank account of (usually) the manufacturer. It in no way prevents that unhappy defendant from seeking contribution or indemnity from someone else, if he was not at fault. Unfortunately, that 'someone else' may be insolvent or in some far off land ... which is a matter for regret, but one which the manufacturer should have foreseen and (through insurance) guarded against.

A businessman once owed £100000, payable the following day. Knowing that he could not find the money, he tossed and turned, sleepless in his bed. Finally, he arose, dressed and drove to his creditors' house.

'Joe', he called out, as he knocked at the window. 'I want to speak to you'.

'What is it?'

'You know I owe you £100000 which I am due to pay tomorrow morning?'

'That's right.'

'Well, I am sorry to tell you that I won't be able to pay. Until now, I've not been able to sleep. Now you can stay awake and worry. ...'

To some extent at least, product liability law concerns he who should stay awake at night and worry. That person should not, at any rate, be the innocent individual who suffers because someone has – for his profit – put a defective product into circulation.

Who may sue, and for what?

Who gains rights from the Act? And what type of damages must they suffer to be able to recover?

Victims of breach of consumer safety regulations

This subject is discussed in Chapter 20.

The purchaser

Your purchaser who suffers damage as a result of the defective product you have sold him has rights under the 1987 Act against you. He may also have rights in the law of contract – rights far more extensive than those under the 1987 Act.

Third parties

The real significance of the 1987 Act is for those who are not purchasers – the third parties, the public in general, who happen to be injured by your product. These people have always been able to sue you in negligence, but they had to prove fault against you. Now that requirement has gone, if the person sues under the 1987 Act.

For some types of defect, the Act will not make much difference. Manufacturing defects, where your goods have been incorrectly assembled and caused injury as a result, have tended to attract liability in any case. But design defects have not been considered much in the courts. If you use asbestos in your products, if you add preservatives and other chemicals to food, if you know your product causes danger in some circumstances but have not given adequate warning to the public about it – in these types of situation you may find more people pursuing you.

Physical injury

Physical injury is the most obvious case in which a product defect will make you liable. Some injuries are one-off, due to one incidental trauma. But what of those that arise insidiously, over years? Some drugs, for example, can reduce vision or damage digestion.

There have been very few cases of this sort in UK law. But if the American experience is a guide, more are on the way.

Damage to property

'Property' means personal belongings, or land. In both cases, a claim may be made only for property ordinarily used for private use, and the claim may be made by a person who put it to that use. Commercial bodies, therefore, cannot claim for loss suffered by their property.

15 Defences under the Act

Liability under the 1987 Act is 'strict', but not 'absolute'. The fact that your product contains a defect which has caused damage or injury will not necessarily make you liable. The Act provides for a number of defences.

State of the art

The 1987 Act provides that the producer of a defective product will have a defence if he can show:

> that the state of scientific and technical knowledge at the relevant time was not such that a producer of products of the same description as the product in question might be expected to have discovered the defect if it had existed in his products while they were under his control.

The 'relevant time' for the producer and the supplier of the product is the time when he supplied the product to another person.

What is 'scientific and technical knowledge'?

The main purpose of the defence is to protect the producer or supplier when the defect was undiscoverable. He simply could not have been expected to have foreseen it and to have taken precautions against it. But note that it is not all unforeseeable or undiscoverable defects that are covered – only those hidden from view and the current state of 'scientific and technical knowledge'. Therefore, the pharmaceutical, chemical and aerospace industries may be expected to turn to the defence because they work at the forefront of scientific knowledge. To a certain (hopefully small) extent their products are bound to contain hidden dangers.

Not all industries are in this position. Take the following example (reported in the national press in 1986). A bunk bed is designed for use by infants. The designers are aware of the need to stop infants in the upper tier from rolling out. They put a wooden bar along the length of that bed. What they do not consider is that some toddlers may wriggle between the safety bar and the mattress. In the case in question, a little girl was tragically killed after she had managed to fit her body through the gap but not her head. She was left hanging from the upper bunk.

Would the producer now be entitled to say: 'I admit the design was defective but I could not have been expected to have discovered this defect because nobody would have foreseen such an awful thing happening'?

It may well be that he will not be allowed to shield himself with the defence. It was not 'scientific and technical' knowledge that prevented him from foreseeing the accident. It was simply that he failed to piece together a sequence of events that anyone could understand – after the event. In other words, it may have been unforeseeable, but not by reason of a lack of 'scientific and technical' knowledge.

Which defects ought to be discovered?

How much ignorance is excusable? According to the Act, you must know as much about your product as other producers of the same kind of product. If they could not have been expected to have discovered the defect in question, neither will you.

This means that your ignorance of a defect will be excusable if you have taken reasonable care in the research and development of your product. It will be a strong indication that you have taken reasonable care that your standards are as high as other producers in your particular field. Conversely, if they are not so high, you will find it difficult to prove that you could not have been expected to discover the defect.

It will be no excuse for you to say that you are new to an industry and therefore cannot be expected to be as careful as other well-established manufacturers. If you are in this position you will require to get independent advice to help you.

Consider the following situation. Assume there is a university in New Zealand, with a department dedicated to research in plastics, and it discovers a circumstance when spontaneous combustion might occur. Could you be made liable the week after they made their discovery? Or the week after their research paper was published? Or the week after their findings were published in America? Should your own company have discovered the possibility first?

It is impossible to know exactly what sort of approach the judges will take. Expect that you will be required to know as much about the dangers in your product as a reasonable manufacturer in your position ought to know. This will depend on the nature of your product. Drugs, for example, are recognized as being capable of causing injuries in a large variety of ways. Very extensive research must, therefore, be conducted to discover them. Pocket handkerchiefs, on the other hand, present fewer opportunities for danger, and less effort has to be spent in research for safety defects.

The more your product has a potential for danger, the more you will be expected to know about it. You will probably not be expected to have read everything that has been published in the relevant area. But you ought to be acquainted with the leading findings. If you have reason to believe that knowledge concerning your product is available elsewhere, make use of it. If in doubt, take specialist advice.

The fact that you have behaved in accordance with industry standards is some evidence of the reasonableness of your behaviour. But in several cases judges have criticized an entire industry for being slack, and held a manufacturer responsible for injury.

Reversal of the burden of proof

You will have noticed that the question, 'which defects ought you to be aware of?', is very difficult to answer in precise terms. The answer turns on broad generalizations: you must take reasonable care, and so on. It all depends on the particular facts of the issue in dispute.

This has another consequence under the 1987 Act. The state of the art defence is only available if the *producer* is able to show that he could not have been expected to discover the defect. The burden of proof (which is normally on the plaintiff) is now put on the defendant. It is up to the producer to show, on the balance of probabilities, that he is protected by the defence. It will be presumed that he ought to have known about it until he can prove the contrary.

This is an important concession to the consumer. There will be cases in which it is difficult to know one way or the other whether the producer ought to have known of the defect. There are experts on both sides, all of whom have plausible arguments. In cases like this, the consumer will be given the benefit of the doubt. You will be held responsible unless you can convince the court that you were excusably ignorant.

Note, however, that the state of the art defence only becomes relevant once the consumer has proved that the product was defective and that it caused his injuries. In those issues, the burden of proof is on the consumer.

Mandatory government regulations

Government involves itself in the standards of safety that have to be adopted in a number of industries. Electrical appliances for use by the public have to be colour coded. Heating appliances must have guards. Cosmetics must comply with standards of safety. Novelty goods must be safe for use by children. There are a large number of such regulations. If your business is covered, you must know about the relevant regulations.

The question is: If you do everything which the appropriate regulations require of you, and your product still causes damage, will you be able to say: 'Don't blame me. I was only doing what the regulations said.' Will your goods not be regarded as defective if they comply with these regulations?

The defence is available provided you have complied with *mandatory* government regulations. But not all of them are mandatory. What is the difference?

Mandatory regulations are those which insist that you adopt a specific standard. In the Upholstered Furniture Regulations, for example, a specific warning tag must be attached to the furniture warning of the danger of fire from cigarettes and matches. The regulations lay down what is to be said and how it is to be presented to the consumer. It is a mandatory requirement. Nothing else will do.

Most regulations are not mandatory. All they do is set minimum standards which you are free to exceed if you wish. They are not mandatory in the sense that you are free to improve on them if you think fit. Compliance with this form of regulation will not provide you with a defence under the 1987 Act.

Whether a regulation is mandatory or provides for a minimum standard only is not always easy to tell. It will depend on the wording of the regulation. If in doubt, take specialist advice.

Component parts

What happens if you have supplied a component part to a manufacturer, he has included your component in his machine, and because of a defect in that machine your part has caused damage?

In this case you may have a defence. The person who has suffered damage is advised to look to the manufacturer of the machine for his damages.

And what if you have supplied a component part to a manufacturer according to the manufacturer's own design specifications? You build the component in the way required by the specifications, but the design is defective. It causes injury. Who is liable?

If you have complied with the manufacturer's specifications, and it is the design itself that is defective, you have a defence. The manufacturer should be responsible for damages. But if the fault in your component lies with you, the defence is not available. Neither is it open if the responsibility for it is partly yours and partly the manufacturer's.

Non-business distribution

The 1987 Act applies to products distributed for commercial purposes. All personal injuries are covered, inside the workplace or out. But if the complaint relates only to goods that have been damaged, consumers have a claim but businesses do not (see Chapter 13).

16   When action must be taken

Once your product has caused damage or injury because it is
defective, what period of time is allowed for the victim to bring his
action? The law imposes what is called a 'limitation period'.

Damage to property

The consumer whose property is damaged has three years to
commence proceedings. The period begins to run at one of two
points in time. Either when the damage occurred – when the type
of damage caused is plain and obvious for all to see – or when the
damage ought to have been known.

This second point, where the product has caused damage which
has been hidden from view, is less straightforward. If it is not plain
and obvious, when does the three-year period begin? When ought
the damage to have been known?

The 1987 Act provides that the key time is when the damage
ought to have been *observable* by the owner (which could be years
later), or when it should have been known to a specialist adviser
and a reasonable person ought to have asked for his opinion –
when a reasonable owner should have been alerted by something
that things were not what they should have been. Although he

could not have known exactly what was wrong, he should have been sufficiently concerned to seek independent advice.

Personal injury

The same rule applies to the personal injuries caused by your defective products. The injured person has three years either from the time the injury was caused or the time that he ought reasonably to have made the connection between defect and injury.

In most cases, there will be an obvious link and no room to doubt that the product caused the damage. But for pharmaceutical products, for example, the link might be much more difficult to prove. There could be injury in the form of a symptom which the patient thought was natural. Time will not run against him unless something ought to have alerted him to the connection. This will often be the advice given to him by a doctor. Once 'on notice', time runs.

Death

What if your defective product causes someone to die? Alternatively, what if your defective product injures someone who dies later, from natural causes or some action which has nothing to do with you?

Action on behalf of the deceased person

Once a person died, all his rights of action used to die with him. In a sense, it was cheaper to kill than to injure. Since 1934, all the rights of legal action that a person had while alive may be proceeded with by his personal representatives after his death. They are able to step into his shoes and sue on his behalf. If they do so, the damages are awarded to the deceased's estate.

If the personal representatives decide to sue, what time limits apply? When may they bring the action on the deceased's behalf?

Once a person has a cause of action, he has three years to take it to the courts. If he dies within the three years (either as a result of the defect in a product or for any unrelated reason), the personal representatives have a further three years to bring their action. Their three years is measured either from the date of the death, or the date they ought to have had knowledge that the deceased had a cause of action, if that is later.

Action on behalf of the deceased's dependants

It is not only the deceased person who may have a cause of action against you. If a defect in your product has been responsible for causing the death of a person, his dependants may also recover for their own loss due to the death of the breadwinner.

To be a 'dependant', a person must have had a reasonable expectation of financial support from the deceased during his lifetime. It will usually be a wife, husband, parent or child. But the category could cover grandparents and grandchildren, brothers, sisters, uncles and aunts. The test is, were they dependent on the deceased? Damages are assessed in terms of cash. They do not include the dependants' emotional suffering.

What is the time during which the dependants may make their claim? The dependant takes the action that would have been available to the deceased. Therefore, the deceased must have died within the three-year period in which he must take his action. Thereafter, the dependants have a further three years from the time of his death, or from the time they ought to have known of the cause of the injury and the identity of the producer of the defective goods. (In addition, if the dependant is a child, the period runs from his or her eighteenth birthday.)

All the dependants' actions must be brought at the same time. They are not permitted to take successive actions.

When no action may be taken

No action may be taken under the 1987 Act against the producer or other person responsible for the product after a period of ten years from when the product in question was put into circulation. It does not matter that the product caused damage that no one could have been expected to discover until after then. No action may be taken.

Note, however, that an action is still available in negligence.

Suppose that a product causes damage four years after being put into circulation. The damage arose through the producer's negligence. But it was not discovered for a further four years. The plaintiff has three years from then to bring his action in negligence. But his action under the 1987 Act is extinguished after a total of ten years.

17 The American experience of product liability

The American experience of product liability has given rise to anxiety. In a number of cases very large sums of damages have been awarded to plaintiffs, sometimes when the product has scarcely been shown to have been defective, at other times when the defendant may not have been responsible for the damage, because it could have arisen from natural causes (for instance in the case of drugs).

It is not expected that the same thing will happen in the UK for a number of reasons. First, American civil cases are still heard by juries who decide all the questions of fact in the case. Naturally, juries are sympathetic to plaintiffs who appear in wheelchairs or who have been blinded by a product. They tend to award them very high sums of damages.

In the UK juries do not generally sit in civil cases. All matters of fact are left for the judge to decide. Judges are less prone to be excessive in awards of damages. Every pound claimed must be accounted for. In addition, the availability of the National Health Service means that our medical expenses are a fraction of the amounts that have to be claimed in America.

Second, American lawyers work on what is called a contingency fee basis. They take a prearranged percentage of the final sum of damages awarded. This means that they have a direct interest in obtaining the largest sum they can for the client. This system has the advantage that no poor client will ever find that he is unable to afford a lawyer. But it also helps to increase awards and damages and, therefore, the insurance premiums payable by producers. No such arrangement is allowed between lawyer and client in the UK, where a fixed fee applies.

Third, if one looks at what judges say in America, rather than what juries do, the principles of law they have laid down in product liability cases are largely similar to the ones that have been developed here in the law of negligence. As has been explained (see Chapter 13) manufacturing defects will now be subjected to a more strict regime of liability, but design defect cases will not attract significant change. This position is now well established in most of the American states.

The biggest change that we must expect is a change of attitude. Lawyers and potential litigants are likely to take a fresh look at many of the claims that in the past they would not have thought worth fighting. The pendulum has certainly swung in favour of the consumer, but we are looking at a process of evolution, not revolution.

PART IV
CRIMINAL LIABILITY

18 The civil law and the criminal law

Almost any wrongful act may lead to two consequences, one civil, one criminal. The civil law gives a remedy against the wrongdoer to any individual or company who suffers loss. The criminal law imposes sanctions on the wrongdoer in breach of minimum standards designed to protect the community.

You drive carelessly and cause a crash? Then you may be *sued* by anyone hurt in the crash – under civil law and in the civil courts. You may also be *prosecuted* for careless or dangerous driving – under criminal law and in the criminal courts.

A thief steals your property? *You* may sue for its return and *he* may be prosecuted for theft.

An employee is injured at work? He may claim damages and those responsible for the unsafe practice may be prosecuted under the Health and Safety at Work Act 1974.

You produce or market a defective product? You may be liable under the civil law to anyone who suffers loss in consequence, either in contract if that person has a contractual relationship with you, or otherwise in tort because of your negligence or for breach of the Consumer Protection Act 1987, if the product is for consumer use.

Differences between civil and criminal law

If you lose a civil action brought against you for the supply of a defective product, you will probably have to pay damages to the person harmed. If you are convicted in a criminal case brought against you for a similar wrongdoing, you will probably have to pay a fine. This will go not to the victim but to the state.

The civil action is brought primarily to compensate the victim; the criminal prosecution imposes sanctions and is designed to punish and deter the wrongdoer.

If you are found civilly liable, your insurers may pay the damages awarded against you. This may lead to a subsequent increase in your insurance premiums, but the immediate effects of your liability are not grave. If you are found guilty of a criminal offence, you are responsible. Your insurers cannot pay your fine, or replace you in dock or gaol. Similarly, your employer might offer to pay your fine for you, but there is no obligation on him to do so. The basic rule is that criminal liability rests on the individual wrongdoer.

These fundamental distinctions between civil and criminal cases are reflected in the fact that the actions are pursued in different courts. Civil claims for damages up to £5000 are brought in a county court; claims for higher sums go to the High Court (or their Scottish equivalents). Criminal prosecutions start in magistrates' courts; the more serious are usually 'committed for trial' by jury 'on indictment' before Crown Courts (or their Scottish equivalents).

Interaction between civil and criminal law

Despite the clear differences in content and purpose between civil law and criminal law, the two areas interact.

If you are found guilty in criminal law of supplying a defective product, that has no immediate consequences in civil law. If an employer contravenes the Health and Safety at Work Act and as a result an employee is hurt, the employer might be fined by the magistrates, but the employee would have to bring a separate civil action to recover compensation.

However, the fact that you have criminal conviction would be of great value to the civil litigant. It is strong evidence that you should be held liable under civil law. So in practice, if you are intending to bring a civil action against someone likely to be prosecuted for the same wrongful act, the best advice is – wait! Your prospects will be improved by a finding of guilt in the criminal proceedings.

The criminal court may even exercise its discretion to order the criminal to compensate you for loss suffered in addition to or instead of any criminal penalty imposed on the wrongdoer. This procedure under the Powers of Criminal Courts Act 1973 enables you to secure compensation without the trouble of pursuing your action in the civil courts. Useful though this is, it is a matter for the court's discretion and you have no *right* to demand compensation from the wrongdoer at the end of criminal proceedings.

Increasingly the criminal law is playing a more important role in the field of product safety. Standards of sound practice are laid down by statutory regulation, breach of which may lead to criminal penalties. Products are controlled pre-sale. The criminal law attempts to prevent injury; the civil law compensates for injury suffered.

19 Criminal liability for unsafe products for use at work

Section 6, Health and Safety at Work Act 1974

Section 6 of the Health and Safety at Work Act 1974, recently amended by the Consumer Protection Act 1987, is of outstanding importance.

'It shall be the duty of any person who designs, manufactures, imports or supplies . . .' So it covers those who design the product, produce it or supply it. 'Supply' is defined by section 53 as meaning supply 'by way of sale, lease, hire or hire purchase, whether as principal or as agent for another'. Any sort of 'supply' is covered.

'Designers' of potentially lethal 'products' have long been wary of this section. The word 'design' is not defined by the Act but rather by ordinary usage, and is broad in its application.

Importers are covered because they come within the jurisdiction of the UK courts, whereas the manufacturers of the articles they bring into the UK are not.

The word 'article' is not defined. It means a thing or product. An 'article for use at work' means 'any plant designed for use or operation (whether exclusively or not) by persons at work', and 'any article designed for use as a component in any such plant'. Articles of fairground equipment are also covered.

It is not the use actually made of the article that matters but

118

whether it was in practice 'designed' for use 'at work'. The statute is for health and safety *at work*. Consumers (who do not use articles 'at work') have other protection (see Chapter 20).

So what are the duties of designers, manufacturers, importers or suppliers? Each is bound:

(a) to ensure, so far as is reasonably practicable, that the article is so designed and constructed that it will be safe and without risk to health at all times when it is being set, used, cleaned or maintained by a person at work.

This is an important and wide-ranging duty. Note how it goes beyond 'use' in the narrow sense. It is linked to the next duty:

(b) to carry out or to arrange for the carrying out of such *testing and examination* as may be necessary for the performance of the duty imposed on him by the preceding paragraph.

Either he must carry out the research and testing himself, or make sure that someone else has done so.

Note: while the person or company must do what is 'reasonably practicable' to see that the design and construction are safe, there is no such proviso in connection with research or examination. He must take such steps as are 'reasonably practicable' to see that the article is 'designed and constructed so as to be safe and without risk to health when properly used'; and he must (without any provision as to reasonableness) ensure adequate testing and examination.

Finally, he must:

(c) take such steps as are necessary to secure that persons supplied by that person with the article are provided with adequate information about the use for which the article is designed or has been tested and about any conditions necessary to ensure that it will be safe and without risks to health at all such times as are mentioned in paragraph (a) above and when it is being dismantled or disposed of; and

(d) take such steps as are necessary to secure, so far as is reasonably practicable, that persons so supplied are provided

with all such revisions of information provided to them by virtue
of the preceding paragraph as are necessary by reason of its
becoming known that anything gives rise to a serious risk to
health or safety.

So the person subject to this duty, be he designer, manufacturer,
importer or supplier, cannot simply dispose of the product and
forget about it. Information relating to its safe use must be
supplied in the first place and thereafter relevant new information
which comes to light must, so far as is reasonably practicable, be
communicated to the person supplied with the product.

Section 6(2) provides:

It shall be the duty of any person who undertakes the design or
manufacture of any article for use at work or of any article of
fairground equipment to carry out or to arrange the carrying out
of any necessary research with a view to the discovery and, in so
far as is reasonably practicable, elimination or minimization of
any risks to health or safety to which the design or article may
give rise.

Again: research. And an absolute duty.

Section 6(3) provides:

It shall be the duty of any person who erects or installs any
article for use at work or any premises where that article is to be
used by persons at work or who erects or installs any article of
fairground equipment, to ensure – in so far as is reasonably
practicable – that nothing about the way in which the article is
erected or installed makes it unsafe or a risk to health

when used at work.

So 'erectors and installers' join 'designers, manufacturers,
importers and suppliers'. They must erect and install plant or
equipment so as to minimize danger to life or limb in so far as is
reasonably practicable.

Sections 6(4) and 6(5) apply almost identical rules to those who
'manufacture, import or supply' any substance. Substances are not
'designed', so the wording is slightly different. The duty covers
substances 'used' in a broad sense. The manufacturer, importer or

supplier must make sure, so far as is reasonably practicable, that the substance will be safe when 'handled, processed, stored or transported' as well as when 'used'. He must also provide information about safe disposal.

The word 'substance' is defined by section 53 as meaning 'any natural or artificial substance, whether in solid or liquid form or in the form of a gas or vapour'. This leaves unanswered the question: What about electricity? It would not appear to be a 'substance'.

Section 6(6) provides:

> Nothing in the preceding provisions of this section shall be taken to require a person to repeat any testing, examination or research which has been carried out otherwise than by him or at his instance, in so far as it is reasonable for him to rely on the results thereof for the purposes of these provisions.

If someone else has done the 'testing, examination or research', you have to repeat it only if it would not be reasonable for you to rely upon the testing already done.

This helpful exception can apply, though, only if you knew of previous work done on the product. So you should enquire, satisfy yourself that the testing, research and examination is adequate for safety purposes and then, if it turns out that the product is dangerous and that the hazards would have been discovered through adequate research, testing or examination, you must be prepared to prove that you reasonably relied on work done by others, ahead of you in the line of production or circulation.

'Impossible', you say. 'A politician's counsel of perfection, offered without regard to the realities of business life. How can we conceivably do as you suggest?' Fine. Then do not do it. But recognize that you will have removed your only likely defence if you are prosecuted. You may not like the statute, but – unless and until it is amended or repealed – it contains the law.

You may, of course, simply ignore these suggestions and hope for the best. All being well, there will be no complaint, no accident, no disaster, no prosecution and no civil claim. Indeed, so far section 6 has largely been held in reserve as a weapon for future use. But at least you now know the risks.

Section 6(8) offers you one other potential defence:

Where a person designs, manufactures, imports or supplies an article for use at work or an article of fairground equipment and does so for or to another on the basis of a *written* undertaking by that other to take specified steps sufficient to ensure, in so far as is reasonably practicable, that the article will be safe and without risks to health [when used at work] the undertaking shall have the effect of relieving the first mentioned person from the duty imposed by [section 6(1)] to such extent as is reasonable having regard to the terms of the undertaking.

In other (and more ordinary) words – if you design, manufacture, import or supply an article (but *not* a substance) for a customer and he gives you his *written* undertaking that he will carry out any necessary research, examination or testing to see that the article will be safe and without risks to health, then you may rely on that undertaking. Note: the undertaking must be in writing – an oral promise is not good enough.

Suppose, for instance, that you quote for the production of certain equipment. Your customer demands a decrease in price. You say: 'We have to quote high because we must carry out any necessary research, testing and examination, to ensure safety and absence of risk to health.' Your customer replies: 'We will undertake to carry out the research, inspection and examination ... So on that basis, kindly reduce your price ...'

Make sure that you get the customer's undertaking in writing and you may then proceed, without worries under section 6. If it turns out that your customer does not comply with that undertaking, then he may be criminally liable, if he has either incorporated your product into one which he is marketing for use at work or even if he simply puts it on the market in an unsafe condition.

The civil consequences of the transaction are also clear. Your customer is extremely unlikely to have any claim against you because of any defect in your product which would have been revealed by inspection, research or examination which you would have carried out, were it *not* for his undertaking. If the 'ultimate consumer' is injured and sues you, you would deny negligence and in any event claim an indemnity from your customer. If in due course the rules of strict liability are applied, you would be liable to that ultimate consumer because your product was defective, but (once again) you would have a good claim over as against your customer.

Section 6(9) applies similar rules to the supply of articles or substances under hire-purchase, conditional sale or credit sale agreements.

Delegated legislation

Duties are imposed in this area not only by the Health and Safety at Work Act itself, but also by regulations made under the statute. This is an 'enabling Act' – it enables others to make regulations which derive their authority from the parent Act. If you breach these regulations, you are liable to precisely the same penalties as those applicable to offences under the Act itself.

Schedule 3 of the Act is of central importance. It enables the Health and Safety Commission to make regulations covering almost any health or safety aspect of the manufacturing or distribution processes.

Design, construction, examination, testing, inspection ... manufacture, supply, use ... testing, labelling, examination ... research in connection with any (appropriate) activity ... provisions for registration and licensing ... for monitoring atmospheric or other working conditions ... keeping and preservation of records ... or even 'restricting, prohibiting or requiring the doing of any specified thing where any accident or other occurrence of a specified kind has occurred'. By all means beware of the Act. But do not ignore the regulations.

Regulations which have been made have covered a wide variety of products, such as safety signs, lead at work and dangerous substances conveyed by road.

In addition, the Health and Safety Commission issues Approved codes of practice, which contain useful and practical guidance about how to meet the statutory requirements. You should be aware of the precise legal status of these codes. Failure to abide by a code is not of itself a criminal offence, unlike failure to meet the general duty or failure to comply with a regulation. But if you are prosecuted for breach of the general duty or breach of a regulation in an area in which there is an approved code in existence, then your failure to follow the code will throw a heavy burden on you to show that you have met your obligations in some other way. Conversely, if you have followed the code, you can be confident of acquittal. So although the codes issued by the Health and Safety Commission are not binding, you would be well advised to pay them close attention – they are there to help you.

Enforcement

Powers of enforcement

The body primarily responsible for the enforcement of this legislation is the Health and Safety Executive, which carries out its functions through inspectors. The inspectors have important powers, such as the right to enter premises and to seize dangerous articles or substances.

Inspectors can issue notices. An improvement notice requires you to put matters right, generally within a set time limit. A prohibition notice prevents you continuing a dangerous practice. These notices are a very important means of enforcing the legislation. They are in effect a 'half-way house' between an informal warning that you are breaking the law and a criminal prosecution in respect of that breach. You are required to remedy the situation, but as long as you do so in accordance with the notice you will not be prosecuted. Which will suit you – and the inspectors, whose aim is not to prosecute but to suppress the danger. So you are well advised to comply with the notice and avoid prosecution. If you ignore a notice, that in itself is a criminal offence.

Finally, importers should be aware that customs officers can hold goods for 48 hours to assist the enforcement of the legislation.

Penalties

There are a number of potential offences that may be committed under these provisions. Several have been mentioned – breach of the general duty, breach of regulations, acting in contravention of a prohibition or improvement notice. The penalties vary.

The more serious offences are triable on indictment (by jury) and the penalties may be a fine (no upper limit) or imprisonment for up to two years. Contravening a requirement or prohibition imposed by a prohibition notice (though not an improvement notice), for example, may result in a gaol sentence. And the fine is unlimited.

In less serious instances, the offence will be tried summarily. Maximum penalty is a fine of £2000.

Naturally, financial sanctions are the most usual penalties. In the Crown Court, where indictable offences are tried and the fine has no limit, substantial fines have been imposed, sometimes exceeding £10 000.

Self-regulation

Formal enforcement is carried out by health and safety inspectors and you may find yourself prosecuted for breach of the legislation. Most enforcement work is carried out informally, by the inspectors.

Our advice: try to establish good co-operative links with the inspectors. Seek their advice and act on their informal guidance. Refer to relevant codes of practice. In this way, you can expect to avoid the loss of time and money consequent on a conviction, not to mention the bad publicity of being labelled a dealer in unsafe goods and the bearer of a criminal conviction.

Who is the defendant?

The duties imposed by the Act have been explained; it is now necessary to consider exactly who may be held liable for breach of those duties.

There are no private prosecutions under the Health and Safety at Work Act. Theoretically, a private individual or company may obtain the consent of the Director of Public Prosecutions to proceed. In practice, his consent has rarely been sought and has never been given. The inspector decides whom to put into the dock. So how is that decision made? Who is criminally liable, where a defective product leads to potential prosecution?

A few years ago, an elderly man went into a Tesco supermarket in Northwich; selected a packet of detergent from a shelf marked with a cut-price offer; took it to the pay-out desk; and was required to pay the full price. 'Sorry, Sir', said the girl by the till, 'but we have run out of the cut-price packets.'

The customer reported Tesco to the local consumer protection authorities who prosecuted. The Trade Descriptions Act makes it an offence to offer goods for sale at a price lower than that at which you are in fact prepared to sell them.

Tesco proved to the magistrates that they had given firm and adequate instructions to their managers. Goods on shelves marked with a special offer were to be sold at the lower price until the advertising material was removed. Unfortunately, the manager had failed to pass on the instructions to the pay-out girl.

The magistrates convicted. An employer, after all, obtains the benefit of what his employee does correctly and must bear the blame if he makes a mistake or does wrong. The Court of Appeal upheld the conviction. Tesco took their case to the House of Lords, clearly eager to avoid the establishment of a principle contrary to their interests. It was in this sense a 'test case'.

Unanimously, the law lords decided that Tesco had complied with their obligations. In civil law, of course, they could be held 'vicariously liable' for the wrongful acts of their employees. Had the customer sued in a civil court for damages for misrepresentation the company could not have avoided its responsibilities by saying: 'Blame the manager, not us.'

However, in a criminal prosecution, the accused is only guilty if he has done something wrong. Tesco had come up to the standard required by law and by society. The prosecution should have been brought against the manager.

The same principle applies under the Health and Safety at Work Act. Every 'director, manager or secretary' is personally liable if the default has occurred with his consent or connivance or as a result of his 'neglect'.

Worse, if the accused maintains that he 'took all reasonably practicable steps' to avoid the commission of the offence, he must prove his innocence. Usually, the prosecution must prove guilt beyond all reasonable doubt. But in Health and Safety at Work Act cases, once a wrongful act has been committed, the accused must show that the fault was not his.

If, then, you are prosecuted because of a defect in a product marketed by your company, you may maintain that the fault was not yours. You may prove that you did all that was 'reasonably practicable' to avoid the offence. And you may also show that the fault was that of some other person. The law allows you to pass the legal buck, if you can.

To do this, you must be well prepared to prove your case. Be able to show that you gave full and clear instructions to your juniors. Perhaps you told your superiors that you thought extra testing was needed, but they turned you down. If so, be ready to provide actual written evidence to support your claims. To avoid criminal liability, try to think ahead.

The same applies along the full length of the chain of distribution. In fixing the blame, the courts could investigate the actions of the eventual user, the installer, the manufacturer, the importer and even the designer. All would be well advised to be ready to show they took adequate precautions to ensure, in so far as was reasonably practicable, that the product would be safe. If they are found to be at fault by, for example, failing to test the product properly, they will be guilty of a crime under section 6 as strengthened by the 1987 Act.

Civil liability

Section 47 expressly states that breach of section 6 does not of itself give rise to civil liability. But in practice, conduct which is criminal under section 6 is likely to constitute a breach of the more general civil law. It may, for instance, amount to the tort of negligence.

So you can expect to be sued as well as prosecuted if you do not meet your legal duties.

Approved codes of practice will be relevant in civil proceedings, as they are in criminal proceedings. If you have departed from an approved code, you may find it difficult to show you acted reasonably for the purposes of avoiding liability in the law of negligence.

Defences

If you are prosecuted under section 6 of the Health and Safety at Work Act because of an alleged failure as 'designers, manufacturers, importers or suppliers' of an article or substance intended or designed for use at work, what possible defences are open to you? Here is a checklist.

(1) That you did all that was 'reasonably practicable' to ensure that the design or construction of the article (or that the substance itself) was safe and without danger to health or safety. Problem: The burden of proving that you did what was 'reasonably practicable' will rest on you.

(2) That you in fact carried out or alternatively arranged for the carrying out of such testing and examination as was necessary to ensure safety as above.

(3) That you took all necessary steps to ensure that adequate information was supplied concerning the design, etc., so as to facilitate proper (and hence safe) use of the article or substance.

(4) That any failure on your part to test, examine or research was due to reliance upon testing, examination or research which you reasonably relied upon others to carry out.

(5) That you obtained, in the case of an article, a written undertaking from your customer that he would take steps specified to ensure safety.

(6) That the offence was due to the act or default of some other person who may be one of the following:
  (a) the person who should have carried out the testing, research or examination (see (4) above);
  (b) the customer, who gave the written undertaking ((5) above);
  (c) your superior, whom you had advised and recommended to set aside appropriate funds, facilities or equipment to carry out the necessary research, testing or examin-ation but who had lamentably failed to follow your recommendations;
  (d) your subordinate, to whom you had provided proper and adequate instructions, which he had failed to follow.

(7) Section 6(10) provides a defence if you can show that the risk could not reasonably have been foreseen. This could be a valuable defence, but establishing it to the court's satisfaction will not be easy.

20 Criminal liability for unsafe consumer products

The Health and Safety at Work Act, considered in the preceding chapter, concerns products for use at work. Products for consumer use are covered by Part 2 of the Consumer Protection Act 1987 which imposes both criminal and civil liability on a supplier of defective consumer goods.

Certain similarities between the Health and Safety at Work Act and the Consumer Protection Act will become clear. Both are enabling statutes and much of importance is found in supporting regulations. The defences to criminal charges under both Acts are comparable. But differences do exist and if you are a producer of consumer goods your potential criminal liability is not the same as that of a producer of goods for use at work.

The general safety requirement

The supplier of consumer goods is under a duty to make sure that his goods meet the 'general safety requirement'. If they do not, a criminal offence has been committed.

There is therefore a general duty, supported by criminal sanctions, to supply safe consumer goods. This was introduced in 1987 and clearly complements the general duty to supply safe goods for use at work contained in the Health and Safety at Work Act. Much of what has already been said about the nature of that duty therefore applies equally to the duty under the Consumer Protection Act, albeit in connection with a different category of product. But the duties are not identical.

'Suppliers' of consumer goods which contravene the general safety requirements may be criminally liable. A wide range of people can be considered 'suppliers'; sellers, of course, but also hirers, lenders, those providing goods for a price other than money, even prize-givers.

'Consumer goods' are defined in the Act as 'any goods which are ordinarily intended for private use or consumption', although there are certain exemptions such as tobacco, controlled drugs and food, which are covered by separate specific legislation. Some goods may be used both at work and for private use; it may not be obvious whether they are subject to the Health and Safety at Work Act or the Consumer Protection Act. But it is certain that they will be subject to at least one of the Acts: they cannot escape the legal requirements entirely.

Exactly how safe your goods must be to meet the general safety requirement very much depends on the particular circumstances. If your goods are not 'reasonably safe', you have committed a criminal offence. So what should you do to make your goods 'reasonably safe'?

First, pay attention to published standards of safety. You should always take account of views on safety issues prevailing in your area of production. So devote resources to research – and keep yourself up to date. The work of the British Standards Institution should be of particular assistance to you. British standards are in principle not mandatory although they may, if 'approved', show what you must do to meet the general duty. Or they may be given formal legal effect in delegated legislation. In any event, you should pay close attention to them. If you conform to the relevant British standard, in practice you are likely to be held to have met your legal duties under the general safety requirement. Depart from the relevant British standard and supply a product which causes damage and you will find it difficult to show your product is 'reasonably safe'.

Much of what has been said elsewhere in this book about your civil liability is relevant in deciding whether your product is 'reasonably safe' for the purposes of criminal liability. If a product is defective within the meaning of Part 1 of the Consumer Protection Act, it is very probably below the standard required by Part 2 of the Act.

Delegated legislation

The Consumer Protection Act, like the Health and Safety at Work Act, is enabling legislation. Apart from the broad duties set out in the Act itself, delegated legislation imposes a variety of more specific duties in particular problem product categories. If the Secretary of State for Trade and Industry considers that precise rules are needed to deal with dangers presented by a particular type of product, he will make either a safety regulation, a prohibition notice or a notice to warn. Of course, the general safety requirement still applies – but more detailed guidance as to the standards of lawful manufacture is provided.

The safety regulation

This is the most commonly employed instrument and you should be fully aware of any measures which govern products in which you have an interest. Supply of goods in contravention of a safety regulation is a criminal offence.

Safety regulations are in general a guide to sound and safe methods of manufacture and can contain a variety of provisions. They might, for example, set standards relating to product design or construction. They might lay down rules governing tests or inspection of products. Or they might require warnings or instructions to be attached to goods.

Many safety regulations refer to British standards and in a number of cases such standards are made mandatory under the legislation. So, for example, if you are a pushchair supplier, you are required to ensure your products conform to BS 4792. If you are involved in the supply of child-resistant packaging, it is BS 6652 you must adhere to. Pedal bicycles must conform to BS 6102.

This brief list indicates the variety of products covered by these rules. The common theme is that all are consumer goods.

Usually, safety regulations will be introduced after careful consideration and you, the supplier, will usually be consulted (see the next section, Enforcement). However, there is provision for regulations to be made without delay, if the risk is particularly grave. You must then immediately stop supplying the prohibited product or else risk criminal prosecution. Such urgent measures expire after twelve months. Products which have been banned under this procedure include toy water snakes (filled with Taiwanese sewage), balloon-making kits (containing benzene, which may cause leukaemia) and expanding novelties (designed to grow bigger when immersed in water, but equally and horrifyingly effective when swallowed by children).

Prohibition notices

These are also available to the minister if he feels that a specific measure is needed. Under this procedure, a particular trader can be banned from supplying a particular product considered unsafe. Such notices are rare and will only be used where there is information about a very specific item. For example, in 1983 a south London supplier was issued with a notice prohibiting supply of a particular brand of rice cooker. It is a crime to contravene the notice.

Notice to warn

This is the remaining measure available to the minister. Under this procedure, the trader may be required to publish a warning about his goods in the manner specified in the notice. Obviously, this can be used where the danger presented by the product is not so serious as to require a total ban but, nonetheless, there is a risk of which the consumer should be made aware. Again, failure to observe the notice is a crime.

Enforcement

Powers of enforcement

Local authority trading standards officers are responsible for enforcing the law relating to consumer safety. There is no body specifically responsible for enforcing this legislation comparable to the Health and Safety Executive. They have at their disposal an array of powers which you should know about.

First, if an enforcement authority reasonably suspects that you hold goods which fall below the general safety requirement or which infringe any other more specific measure, it may serve you with a *suspension notice*. This prevents you supplying these goods and is backed by criminal sanctions. You can appeal against the imposition of the suspension notice and, in addition, if your goods are in fact safe you may be entitled to compensation from the enforcement authority. This is discussed below.

As part of its investigation, the enforcement authority can make test purchases of your goods. Trading standards officers also have power to search your premises and in exercising this power they may seize and detain goods they reasonably suspect to be unsafe. This power of seizure extends to records which may be needed as evidence in a subsequent criminal prosecution. Importers should also be aware that customs officers may seize and detain suspect goods for 48 hours at the port, with a view to alerting trading standards officers. If you obstruct authorized officers pursuing their duties, you may be committing a criminal offence.

Eventually, if your goods are indeed unsafe and unlawful, they may be forfeited by order of the court.

But don't be too alarmed! If you are innocent, you are given important protection under the statute. You can claim compensation if you suffer loss as a result of the actions of trading standards officers as long as, first, your goods conform with the law and, second, you have not been at fault in any way. If you have, for example, misled the enforcement authority into suspecting you of holding unsafe goods, your claim for compensation will fail, but as long as you have behaved properly and your goods are safe, any loss you may incur can be reclaimed from the authority. So you should try as far as possible to co-operate with the trading standards officers.

If you are an importer whose goods are held for up to 48 hours by customs officers, you have no right to compensation. But if trading standards officers involve themselves in your case, you can then seek compensation if your goods are safe and if you have acted properly.

Penalties

If you are in breach of the general safety requirement, a safety
regulation, a prohibition notice, a notice to warn or a suspension
notice, you may be liable to up to six months' imprisonment or a
fine not exceeding £2000.

Under the old Consumer Safety Act, in the year ending 30
September 1985 there were 215 convictions in reported cases for
breach of regulations. The total amount of fines was £66 755
(roughly £300 per conviction). Regulations relating to electrical
equipment have given rise to the largest number of convictions;
regulations relating to the safety of toys are the next most
commonly breached.

Self-regulation

Much of the work of enforcement is carried out informally.
Prosecution of offenders is generally a last resort. Trading
standards officers will be keen to point out breaches in the
expectation that the supplier will choose to remedy his practices
without legal compulsion. This is particularly true in the case of
first offenders and those unaware that they are infringing the law.
After all, informal enforcement is quicker and cheaper and
preserves mutual goodwill.

You may also be able to influence the law at an earlier stage,
while regulations are actually being made. In making safety
regulations, the minister is under a duty to consult interested
parties and this will certainly include representatives of industry.
Before making rules regulating novelty toys, such as stink bombs
in 1980, the minister consulted sixty-six bodies. So you will
probably have a say in the drawing up of the rules to which you will
be subject. And even if your views are rejected, you will have
ample opportunity to modify your processes in accordance with
the new rules.

There are provisions in the Act for regulations to be made
without formal consultation. You may be afraid that new rules will
suddenly be introduced unannounced, disrupting your business –
but in practice, this is most unlikely. Usually, although there may
have been no formal consultation, informal negotiations between
suppliers and the regulators will have taken place. The measure
will have been introduced because informal efforts to curb the

danger have failed. So you will already be aware of the possibility of regulation.

An importer of scented erasers went to court in 1985 to challenge a measure prohibiting the supply of these products, claiming he had not been formally consulted and that he had suffered loss as a result of the ban. He failed. The measure had only been introduced after several months' effort to secure the voluntary removal of these items had proved fruitless. So the ban had not come out of the blue.

You should therefore always be receptive to informal contacts by enforcement authorities. Co-operate and communicate with them. In this way you may be able to forestall action contrary to your interests; if not, at least you will be forewarned of such action.

Civil liability

If you breach a safety regulation, your primary concern will be potential criminal liability. Your conduct may, however, also expose you to an action in tort for breach of statutory duty. So you may have to pay a fine to the state and damages to the injured consumer as a result of your wrongdoing.

This action in tort specifically granted by the Act has not proved to be of practical importance. But the possibility of civil proceedings as well as a criminal prosecution should never be discounted.

Defences

Although you may be able to make use of more specific defences, if prosecuted for breach of the general safety requirement your first thought should be to try to show that your goods are reasonably safe having regard to all the circumstances, and that therefore you have actually met the legal requirement placed upon you. You could, for example, show that you could not have taken any reasonable steps to make the goods any safer. Or that you have done all that is required by approved standards of safety.

More specifically, you have a defence if you can show that you reasonably believed the goods would not be used in the UK. The exporter is thus protected. If you are a retailer, you have a defence if you neither knew nor should have known that the goods were not of the required standard. So if the fault lies with the manufacturer, you may be able to avoid liability, but only if you have behaved properly. You will have no defence if you have 'turned a blind eye' to defects, the existence of which you suspected. The retailer also has a defence if he can show the goods he supplies are secondhand.

A defence of 'due diligence' is available to anyone prosecuted under these provisions. If you are charged, you can escape conviction if you can show that you 'took all reasonable steps and exercised all due diligence to avoid committing the offence'.

The most common situation in which you might wish to rely on this defence is where someone else, usually your supplier, has told you the goods are safe. Can you rely on such promises as a defence if you supply goods which turn out to be defective?

In 1977 a shop was prosecuted under the old Consumer Protection Act for selling a toy with too high a lead content. Their defence was that their suppliers, French manufacturers, had guaranteed the goods as sound and that therefore they, the English sellers, could not be held responsible. Their defence failed. The regulations had been changed between purchase and sale, yet the shop had made no attempt to check the old stock. They had failed to meet their legal responsibilities and were criminally liable. They should at least have had samples analysed.

A 1987 Divisional Court decision makes it clear that you must do something positive to be able to use this defence. A toy wholesaler from Anglesey was prosecuted for selling pencils with twenty-six times the level of lead permitted by regulations. The pencils had been made in Hong Kong and, in ordering the items, the defendants had specified that goods should conform to British legislative requirements. But they had done no more. It was held that they could not rely on the defence of due diligence. They should have sought specific assurances about the safety of these goods, guarantees of conformity with these particular regulations. A non-specific, blanket requirement of conformity was insufficient to allow them to rely on the defence.

It is quite clear that you cannot rely on confirmation provided by someone else if, for any reason, the information is suspect or if you could and should have checked the accuracy of what you have been told. Relying on someone else's word will only protect you if that reliance was reasonable.

One final point: if you are alleging that someone else was responsible for the offence, you must provide the prosecutor with details at least seven days before the hearing.

21 Other statutes

If you are responsible for the supply of an unsafe product, you can expect to be criminally liable under either the Health and Safety at Work Act or the Consumer Protection Act. These are the key statutes relating to product safety and you should now understand the way in which they operate.

There are, however, certain other statutes which may impose duties on you backed by criminal sanctions. These statutes fall conveniently into two categories for present purposes: first, those which have only incidental relevance to product safety and which are in this sense broader than the statutes already discussed; and, second, those which govern specific products and are therefore narrower than the legislation already discussed, which is of more general application.

Statutes of broader application

Statutes such as the Trade Descriptions Act 1968, the Weights and Measures Act 1979 and the Fair Trading Act 1973 may affect you as the supplier of goods, although none of these Acts is directly concerned with the safety of goods.

The Trade Descriptions Act outlaws misleading descriptions of goods. It is enforced by trading standards officers in a similar manner to the Consumer Protection Act. It is discussed in detail in Part V.

The Weights and Measures Act controls unlawful practices relating to the quantity of goods. It, too, falls within the responsibilities of the trading standards officers.

The Fair Trading Act is of broad application and all suppliers of goods should be aware of its operation. The Act provides the Director General of Fair Trading with broad powers across the whole spectrum of consumer interests. He can act, by regulation, to curb unacceptable trading practices as and when they arise. This is a flexible power and it resembles the making of regulations under the legislation previously considered when specific hazards emerge. The Fair Trading Act, however, goes beyond safety alone.

Under Part III of the Act, the Director General has useful powers to remedy unacceptable practices. The aim of this part of the legislation is the rapid and essentially informal removal of infringements, without the need for formal legal action. If the Director General considers a trader is acting unlawfully, he will seek a written assurance that the misconduct will cease. If the trader gives this assurance and adheres to it, no further action will follow. The problem is solved and neither side has had to undergo the expense and embarrassment of litigation. Ideal!

There are many examples every year. A Manchester fancy goods firm gave an assurance in 1984 that it would in future comply with various regulations made under the consumer protection legislation relating to the safety of electrical equipment. In 1985 a company based in Leyton, east London, gave an assurance that in future it would abide by the regulations relating to the safety of toys.

So, if you are asked to give such an assurance you are in effect being given a 'second chance'. Give the assurance and you will not be prosecuted for your previous misconduct.

Assurances may relate to any breach of civil or criminal law, not just the law relating to consumer safety. Commonly, traders give assurances that they will refrain from breaching the Trade Descriptions Act or various other criminal provisions such as the Food Act (see below). Or that they will in future abide by their duties under the civil law, such as those imposed by the Sale of

Goods Act or the Supply of Goods and Services Act, or simply contractual duties in general.

Usually, once the assurance is given, the matter is closed. If a trader refuses to give an assurance or if an assurance is broken, the Director General can apply to a court for a 'cease and desist' order against the trader. In 1985, for example, a Belfast retailer and repairer of electrical goods failed to observe a previous assurance and was ordered by the court to stop breaking consumer contracts by failing to do the work properly. A Sheffield trader was the subject of a similar order: he was also ordered to stop breaching the regulations relating to the safety of electrical equipment. These court orders have real teeth. Ignoring them is a contempt of court, for which the penalties are unlimited.

Statutes in particular product areas

Certain product areas are thought to need particularly detailed control, usually because the item is especially hazardous or of particular potential importance.

The Fireworks Act 1951 provides an obvious example. Specific rules are laid down, enforced by health and safety inspectors. The Farm and Garden Chemicals Act 1967 contains in particular provisions for weedkillers and insecticides.

The Food Act 1984 consolidates a large mass of previous legislation in this area. It regulates both the quality and labelling of food.

If you have any responsibility for the supply of an unsafe product, you should be concerned about more than the likelihood of having to pay compensation to anyone who suffers loss. In addition, you may find yourself on trial before a criminal court. The chapters (18–21) in this part of the book have indicated the extent of your potential criminal liability and the steps you need to take to avoid charge and conviction.

Remember also that the criminal law does not exist simply to burden you and to protect the consumer. It also aims to protect you, the honest, against the unscrupulous. The rogue seeking to undercut your prices by failing to spend money on safety design is to be deterred from behaving in such an unfair way by the provisions of the criminal law.

PART V
THE TRADE DESCRIPTIONS ACT 1968

Introduction

The criminal law also protects the consumer against those who misrepresent their goods. The wrongful description might relate to the quality of the 'goods' or services, their quantity or their price. This is the purpose of the Trade Descriptions Act 1968.

A consumer who enters into a contract because of a wrongful description will often have a remedy in contract. He may have an action in the law of contract for misrepresentation (see Chapter 1) or for breach (see Chapter 3). In reality, however, these remedies are not frequently pursued. More often than not, the goods in question are relatively inexpensive and it is not worth the time and expense of taking legal action.

The 1968 Act protects the individual in cases where he would not take action himself. Equally important, it protects other traders. If there were no way of maintaining standards, the trader who gained by fooling the public would have an unfair advantage. So the 1968 Act is available to maintain standards, both for private and commercial interests. It applies to 'trade descriptions', irrespective of whether a consumer has been taken in by them or not.

22 What is a trade description?

False descriptions of goods

The Act deals with false descriptions applied to both goods and services. In relation to the former, the Act lists ten different circumstances in which goods are said to contain a 'description'.

(1) Descriptions relating to *quantity, size* or *gauge*: you attach a trade description to your goods if, for example, you put sizes on shoes or clothing. Or if you sell goods by weight or number.

(2) Descriptions in relation to *method of manufacture, production, processing* or *reconditioning*: champagne must emanate from that area of France. Wilton carpet must be manufactured to that quality. Patent leather shoes have to be treated in the appropriate way.

(3) Description in relation to *composition*: clothes described as containing a certain percentage of mohair or silk must do so. An 'all wood surround' cannot contain plastic.

(4) Descriptions in relation to *fitness for purpose, strength, performance, behaviour* or *accuracy*: a motorbike said to be suitable for moto-cross has to be so. Similarly, a car described as capable of 115 mph and 35 mpg, or a 'waterproof' watch.

144

(5) Any *physical characteristics* not included in the preceding paragraphs: that a vacuum cleaner operates silently. And other descriptions which are not directly relevant to the nature and use of the goods themselves.

(6) Description relating to *testing* by any person and the *results* of that testing: that a hi-fi system is capable of 150 watts power without distortion or that a product has been issued with a British safety standard.

(7) Descriptions relating to the *approval* by any person or *conformity* with a type *approved* by any person: sports equipment is often said to be endorsed and used by sports personalities. Similarly, goods may be said to have received the approval of a respected body or professional association, for example 'as approved by the Consumers' Association'.

(8) Descriptions relating to the *place or date of manufacture, production, processing* or *reconditioning*: an antique may be said to be of Roman origin or a car manufactured in 1923; 'English' lamb.

(9) Description relating to *person by whom manufactured, produced, processed* or *reconditioned*: a painting by Constable or a car by Bugatti; china by Wedgwood.

(10) Other history, including previous ownership or use: 'one careful lady owner', '24 000 miles'.

These are all examples of the sorts of descriptions of goods covered by the Act. Clearly they are intended to cover the broadest range of cases in which goods carry descriptions.

Misleading indications as to price

All manner of inducements are made to the consumer to buy goods by means of a bargain offer of one sort or another. The Consumer Protection Act 1987 has increased the scope of the 1968 Act to control some of the more subtle means of misleading the consumer.

The broad categories of circumstances in which misleading pricing occurs are as follows.

Overcharging

It is an offence to indicate that the price of your goods is less than it in fact is. Advertisements which are false, in the press or in your shop window, fall foul of the Act. It is also an offence to describe your goods as being sold at a discount when they are not. The statement that 20p has been knocked off a packet of soap powder – when it has not – is false.

Previous prices

Traders often offer goods at prices which appear attractive because they are apparently lower than the previous price of the same goods. Goods may be marked '£5 off recommended retail price' or 'Closing Down Sale, 15 per cent off all marked prices'. Sale items may also be treated in this way. If these descriptions are false so that the consumer might reasonably be expected to be misled by them, an offence has been committed.

Hidden charges

If goods are apparently offered together with a number of accessories, those extras may be charged for or included in the price. What is not allowed is for the goods to be offered at a price which includes accessories, and for an additional price then to be charged for them. This sort of practice has occurred on a wide range of domestic equipment such as cookers and cars, as well as services like holidays.

Closing offers

This is a method of attracting customers, similar to referring to previous prices. The trader may say, not the price was higher in the past, but that it will be higher in the future. 'Prices held while old stock lasts', 'buy now before January price increase'. If the seller has no real expectation that his prices are in fact going to be increased, he has misled the consumer. The 1968 Act will apply.

Misleading comparisons

Consumers often judge the attractiveness of the price of a product by comparison with other, similar products. They shop around. It is misleading falsely to inflate the price of other goods and then to claim yours are less expensive. 'Normally £25, our price £15', 'elsewhere £40, introductory offer £30'. If these statements are untrue an offence has been committed.

Misleading methods of determining price

It may be that the trader does not specifically state a price for his goods. Instead he describes a method by which the consumer can work out the price for himself. It may be, for example, that he introduces an incentive scheme on the basis of the greater the purchase, the larger the discount. This form of price structuring is equally open to attack by the 1968 Act if it is misleading. Broadly speaking, it will be misleading if it is false in any of the respects described above.

Misleading descriptions of services and facilities

If you give a misleading description of a service or facility you provide, an offence may have been committed. The 1987 Act extends liability in this area. The following are examples of the areas to which the provisions apply.

A service contract is one where you promise to give the consumer some benefit other than in the form of goods. Consultants, in whatever area of expertise, give a service. Agencies provide a service when they put you in touch with the business with which you wish to work. Banks provide a service. A facility is a benefit you are promised as a result of entering into a contract. It might be a product or a service, for which money is paid or not. It is an inducement.

The holiday business provides a service. Tour operators have been held liable under the 1968 Act for statements in brochures describing hotels and holiday resorts. Hotels have not been completed, air-conditioning has not been provided, accommodation has failed to include a bathroom, or a sea view. Others in the business of providing services may be made liable in the same way. An airline has been held liable for over-booking its aircraft with passengers.

The professions also supply services and they may be made

liable if they falsely describe themselves or the services they are able to offer. Services include those provided by banks, by insurance companies and by those in the business of buying and selling currency.

If you offer to provide a form of guarantee, or a free product following the sale of another, this may be regarded as a facility; examples are a guarantee on a new house or the offer of a free radio with a new car. If your statement is false, you may be held liable for falsely describing a facility available to the consumer. The same may be the case if goods are offered with credit facilities, or subject to fourteen days' approval, and those conditions do not apply. Equally, if those facilities are promised to be available at a certain time but in fact are not, liability may arise.

23   When may liability arise?

So far we have considered the meaning to be given to the words 'trade description'. The next question concerns the circumstances that must exist to give rise to criminal liability for a false trade description.

'In the course of business'

The Trade Descriptions Act 1968 applies only if you falsely describe your goods, services or facilities 'in the course of business'. It does not, therefore, apply to private, domestic transactions. When do you trade in the course of business?

If you supply goods or services as your means of earning money, you are in business. This is clearly so when the goods you sell or supply form the main part of your business. But what if you run a business which very occasionally gets involved with trading in a small way on the side? For example, you are a textile company and you buy cars for your representatives. If you sell the cars after a period of time, can you be made liable for any false descriptions applied to your cars?

The answer is: Yes. Although selling cars is by no means your primary area of business, it is nevertheless a normal and accepted

part of it. The sale therefore takes place in the course of business.
This happened in a case which concerned a car hire business that
occasionally sold its vehicles.

But what if the sale of goods in question is not really a normal
and accepted part of your business. What if you are a self-
employed courier? You own a small number of vans which are
used for the purpose of transporting customers' goods from one
place to another. You reckon you sell on average one van per
year. Is that a sale made in the course of business?

In a case on similar facts, it was said that the phrase 'in the
course of business' meant that some degree of regularity was
needed. The very infrequent nature of the sale of the vans was not
enough to be caught by the Act. Of course, as the size of the
business expands, and these incidental sales increase, it becomes
more likely that they will become part of the normal activity of the
business.

Some companies are established for the purpose of doing one
thing only. After that, they are dissolved. Here, there is no
regularity of business. Is the business covered by the 1968 Act? It
is, because the whole nature of the business is to concentrate its
activities on one thing. So far as that thing is concerned, it is done
'in the course of business'.

Strict liability

Liability under the 1968 Act for falsely describing goods is strict. It
can arise without dishonesty. In fact, there are two separate
offences under the Act: one covers the person who fixes the false
description to the goods, the other concerns the person who sells
the goods with that description.

Applying a false description to goods

This offence applies to the person who attaches the false description to the goods themselves, or the container, or other thing with
which it is supplied. So the Act applies to labels and packaging. It
also covers markings on display units and vending machines which
are intended to refer to the goods. In addition, it includes any oral
statements made about goods.

A crime may be committed under this provision if a person misleads the consumer by actively falsifying the nature or quality of the goods. You may also be held liable for saying nothing. A customer writes to you and asks to be supplied with a particular product, of a particular size and quality. You supply a different product without informing the customer of the difference. You may be liable. This is because you have accepted the customer's order for goods. It is as if you have said: 'Yes, I can supply what you want.' If you then supply something different, which the customer believes is the thing he wanted, you may be liable.

The same could happen in a shop. If a customer asks for a suit made of wool, and is in fact given one made of wool and polyester without being told of the difference, the goods have been falsely described.

Supplying goods with a false description

This offence is of more interest to you if you are a retailer whose goods are supplied by manufacturers or other distributors. The Act applies to displays in shop windows and advertisements.

In this case, of course, you may not be responsible for the false description. Secondhand car dealers may be in difficulty with odometers on the cars they wish to sell. Can they be made liable if they do not know that the odometer has been falsified? They may be if they are aware of the description. This is so even though they are not actually aware that it is false.

The dealer, therefore, may be liable if he knows of the reading on the odometer. But if the car was damaged in the factory and was repaired so that the damage was invisible, he could not be liable for describing it as being in pristine condition (provided, of course, he did not actually know the situation).

Falsely describing services

The rule regarding services is different from that relating to goods. This is not a strict liability offence. You may be liable for falsely describing services only if you have done so 'knowingly' or 'recklessly'.

A 'reckless' statement is one made regardless of whether it is true or false. Therefore, if you know your statement is false, or simply do not care one way or the other, you may be held liable. But if you honestly and reasonably believed it was true, you will not.

What if you are a holiday company? Your statement about the accommodation to be provided is true when it is made and was honestly intended to be good for the short-term future. But subsequently circumstances change and it becomes false. You will not be liable, provided you did not know of the error. This is so even though someone may actually have been misled by your statement.

Neither will you be liable if your statement is false but you honestly believed it to be true. However, as soon as you discover the error, you are under a duty to correct it. It will not be sufficient merely to take reasonable steps to correct it. You may tell your agents to correct the statement in your brochure, but if they fail to do so, you may be liable for the false statement. In a way, this offence is strict because you could have done no more to try and correct it. But you knew of its falsity and someone has been misled by it.

Liability for advertisements, catalogues and price lists

Advertisements take a variety of forms. Those in shop windows do not usually cause problems because they normally refer to the stock specifically held inside. The difficulty arises with advertisements in the press or on hoardings. For liability to arise under the Act the false description must be taken to refer to goods. To which goods does an advertisement apply?

The answer: All the goods of the class mentioned in the advertisement. Therefore, if the advertisement talks about a particular brand of cat food, or lawnmower, it will be taken to refer to all the goods in that particular category. It does not matter that they have yet to be manufactured. The advertisement can apply to them when they are made, so long as it is still valid.

If there is any doubt about whether the advertisement does apply to those goods or not, the matter is to be resolved by asking what a reasonable person would think. This involves looking at where the advertisement was displayed, when and how it conveyed the message and for how long.

Note that this provision also covers your catalogues, circulars and price lists. If you do not intend them to contain accurate descriptions of your goods, say so clearly. If you are prepared to be bound by some things but not others (for instance specifications but not price) make that clear.

However, if you are in the business of publishing advertisements, brochures, catalogues and so on, you have a defence provided you did not know, and had no reason to suspect, that the material was false.

Can you disclaim liability?

A practice has developed of trying to avoid the Trade Descriptions Act by attaching disclaimers to goods. The disclaimer will say that the descriptions given to the goods cannot be guaranteed and that the customer should satisfy himself that the goods meet his requirements. Are such disclaimers effective to insulate you from the 1968 Act?

If you have been responsible for attaching a description to goods, you cannot disclaim your liability for that description. You cannot both describe goods in a certain way and then deny that the description is accurate. A manufacturer who attaches descriptions to his goods, therefore, may be made liable for them. So may a butcher who says his turkeys are English when they are not; or even a car dealer who describes a car as having scrap value only when it could easily be repaired. But so too may a motor dealer who winds back the odometer. By reducing the mileage shown on the clock he is responsible for attaching a new description to the goods, relating to its history, or use (see the section, False descriptions of goods (items 9 and 10), in the preceding chapter).

If you are responsible simply for supplying goods to which a false description has already been applied, you may be able to disclaim responsibility. A number of requirements must be satisfied for you to be able to do so.

You must disclaim responsibility before you supply goods. It is no use selling them to a customer and then telling him later that you disclaim responsibility for their description. Neither will it be good enough to bring it to the customer's attention immediately before the time of sale if, by that time, he has made up his mind to buy. He must be able to make his decision in the light of all the facts, including the disclaimer.

It will not be sufficient if it is not properly brought to the customer's attention. The more important the disclaimer, the more it qualifies the description of the goods being purchased, the more it should be brought home to the buyer. It should be enough to let him know what he is – and what he is not – about to buy.

You can bring your disclaimer to the buyer's attention by any reasonable means. But do not rely on oral statements – there may be a difference of recollection about what was said. Equally important, it will be extremely difficult to prove that your oral statement carried sufficient impact. The customer is likely to be believed if he says: 'I didn't think the statement meant that.'

You could put up a notice on the premises. But here again, it will be very difficult for you to prove that the notice had its intended effect. If the customer never saw it, or saw it but never read it, it will be simple for him to say: 'I was misled. The notice was not enough to explain what I was being promised.'

In some cases it is possible to place your disclaimer on the goods themselves. This may be sufficient provided the customer is not being misled. In one case, a car dealer wound back the odometer and then stuck a disclaimer notice on it. Was the disclaimer effective? It was not, because the very purpose of winding the clock back was to deceive the customer. A disclaimer cannot protect you from that.

If you honestly present goods to the customer, but do not know their date of origin, pedigree and so on, an adequate disclaimer may protect you.

Another way of attempting to disclaim is by including a term in the written contract of sale. Again, this may be effective, but only provided the term is sufficiently drawn to the buyer's attention. It will be no good if it is written in small print and tucked away in an obscure part of the contract. It must be made known to the buyer in a way that allows him to know exactly what it says. So it must be both conspicuous and clear.

In essence, you must do enough to prevent the customer being misled. This is most important for those businesses which deal with items which are known to be misleading to the consumer.

24 Defences to liability

The Trade Descriptions Act relies heavily on strict liability. Normally, liability will be imposed without fault. Nevertheless, the Act still recognizes some circumstances in which it could be grossly unfair to convict traders. The public and other traders generally deserve protection from false descriptions, but not at the cost of imposing injustice on those who do not deserve a conviction. For this reason a number of defences have been provided to those who make false statements about their goods or services.

Note that these defences are not easily established. The burden of proof is on you, the trader, to show they apply, and the courts require very persuasive evidence that you ought not to be convicted. This normally means that you had a suitable system of control in operation at the time, capable of preventing most things from going wrong.

Offence due to mistake or default of another

You will be able to plead this defence provided you make a mistake beyond your control, or you were reasonably relying on information supplied, or the offence was committed due to the fault of another person. But this can only be done provided you took all reasonable precautions and exercised due diligence to prevent it (see the following section).

When the Act talks about the 'default of another person' it includes employees. Be careful, however, because the courts will be very keen to hear from you how your business was supervised. You will not be able to pass the blame on to someone else if you failed to give adequate instructions and he did not know what action to take. In that case it is your act of default that is responsible for failing to organize your business properly.

Note also that the civil principle of vicarious liability (see Chapter 10) does not apply in criminal cases. You will not be made liable for your employee's act or omission provided you can establish the defence.

The defence is not available if the default occurs due to the act of a director, as opposed to an employee. This is because employees are 'others', but directors are the body of the company itself. The act of one director is the act of the company, not the act of 'another'.

The defence has been successfully pleaded by a supermarket against the actions of one of its employees who mislabelled the price of a household cleaner, and by a holiday company whose employee inserted a misleading photograph in their brochure.

Reasonable precautions and due diligence

To establish the defence of mistake or default of another, you must also show that the offence occurred despite reasonable precautions and due diligence on your part.

In essence this requires the business to have a system designed to ensure that offences under the Act do not occur. And it must be a reasonable system. It is not possible to say what will be considered reasonable without the facts of the individual case.

A secondhand car dealer advertised a car as being in good condition. He obtained an MOT certificate for the vehicle and sold it. He did not know of corrosion which had been hidden by undersealing. He had attached a false description to it. But had he taken reasonable precautions to prevent the offence from being committed? He had not. He had no system whatever for checking the condition of his cars. It was not sufficient simply to rely on an MOT certificate.

The same happened when jewellers sold a watch described as 'waterproof'. It let in water. They had placed complete faith in their suppliers. This was not enough. It would have been very simple for them to take a small sample of the goods and test them themselves.

Clearly, a heavy onus is put on traders to show that they behaved reasonably and diligently.

Accident or mistake beyond your control

This defence is similar to that discussed above, except that here the circumstances responsible for the offence are entirely beyond your control. Again, you have to show that the accident or mistake could not have been discovered by reasonable diligence on your part.

It was not beyond the control of the motor car dealer to check the accuracy of a car with a 'clocked' odometer in view of the fact that it had a suspiciously low reading. Again, however, reasonable diligence required some sensible enquiries to be made, but not the entire history of the vehicle to be traced.

In another case a normally accurate machine occasionally and unpredictably made bags of crisps at less than their described weight. The company tried to cope with the problem by increasing the average weight of all the bags. Nevertheless, the problem persisted and one bag was again found to be under-weight. It was held that they had reasonably and diligently attempted to deal with a problem that was out of their control.

Making somebody else liable

Where A commits an offence under the Act, but the person responsible for it is B, B may be prosecuted for the offence committed by A.

You are a car dealer. You buy a car from B and he has wound back the odometer. You sell the car with a false description. You may be made liable (subject to your defence) or B may be liable. If B is prosecuted, it may be for committing the offence himself when he sold the car to you, or for causing you to commit the offence.

You cannot take advantage of this defence, however, if you have taken advantage of B's action. If you do that you have committed a separate offence for which you may be prosecuted. The defence is available provided only one offence has in reality been committed, by B.

25 Enforcement and penalties

Criminal law

The responsibility for enforcing the Trade Descriptions Act belongs to trading standards (or consumer protection) officers, employed by local authorities. The Act gives them power to see that the Act is enforced by purchasing goods, services or accommodation to check that they comply with their descriptions. They may enter your premises to make spot checks and, if they have a reasonable suspicion that you have committed an offence, examine your business documents.

A prosecution must be brought within three years, normally by the local authority concerned.

The penalties that may be imposed are a fine or imprisonment. You may be convicted either in the magistrates' court or the Crown Court. The less serious matters are heard by the magistrates who can fine you up to £2000 for each offence. In cases of 'serious dishonesty' the case may go for trial in the Crown Court before a jury. Here there is no limit on the fine that may be imposed and you may be imprisoned for up to two years. Cases in which individuals have produced counterfeit goods have been dealt with by considerable fines and imprisonment.

A prosecution may be brought by each local authority in which the crime has been committed. In effect, therefore, if you have goods, or advertise services in a number of areas in the country, you may be prosecuted more than once for the same item.

Civil law of passing off and trade marks

The fact that you are held liable in criminal law does not necessarily affect your position in civil law. If you have made a contract it remains valid. Of course, the remedies of misrepresentation and breach of contract may still be open to the consumer.

More important to other traders may be the potential damage to their reputation if defective goods are being sold as theirs, or their trade name has been pirated.

The name of a well-known product is likely to be the seller's greatest asset. He may have spent a fortune on building up the goodwill which attaches to that name. If he has been able to register it, he will have the sole right to use it and will be able to take proceedings for infringement of his trade mark. But even if he has not registered the name, he may still take steps to prevent other people's goods from being 'passed off' as his. It is a civil matter (as opposed to a criminal offence) to 'pass off' goods as being those of someone else.

In one famous case, the manufacturers of Babycham champagne perry discovered that when customers went into a certain public house and asked for 'Babycham', champagne perry of a different brand was being poured into their glasses. So the manufacturers of the other drink were cashing in on the popularity of the Babycham label. Babycham brought a 'passing off' action and obtained an injunction – an order restraining the publican from passing off champagne perry not manufactured by them as being Babycham.

So, if a customer comes into a shop and asks for 'Brand W wool', it will not do to wrap up 'Brand V wool', leaving the customer to believe that she is getting the brand she asked for. If someone demands an 'A-line corset', she must not be sold a 'Z-line', in such a way that she may be deceived.

This is not to say, of course, that a seller must give the customer that which he asks for. There is nothing whatsoever to prevent a retailer, for instance, when asked for 'Brand W' wool from saying: 'We don't stock Brand W, I'm afraid. But I have some Brand V, and I think that you'll find it just as good. It's also rather less expensive . . .' Alternatively, when asked for 'A-line' corsets, their manufacturers have no valid complaint if the shopkeeper, honestly expressing his bona fide belief, tells the customer, 'We think that A-line are unshapely. Would you like to try the latest Z-line?'

The essence of 'passing off', then, lies in the probability that members of the public will be deceived. If a manufacturer can show that people have actually been deceived, he will probably win his case. But he is not bound to show actual deception. It is enough if he shows the likelihood that deception will arise.

Take the famous case of *Daks* v. *Kidax*. The manufacturers of the world-famous Daks slacks tried to prevent the use of the name Kidax, on the ground that members of the public would be likely to believe that these were kiddies' Daks. But they lost their case. They could prove no actual deception and as Kidax had been on the market for a long time, the court was unwilling to accept that deception was likely in the future.

Of course, deception may arise not only from the name but also from the make-up or presentation of the product. Suppose, for instance, that 'D-line' corsets had become famous for the D-shaped box in which they were sold. Another manufacturer produces a product with an entirely different name, but markets it in the same-shaped box. There may be just as active 'passing off' here as if the name had been identical. Once the particular box had become associated in the minds of the public at large with a particular company's goods, that company acquires a right to the sole use of that make-up for the class of goods in question, just as successfully as if the design had been registered.

'But suppose that we manufacture, say, woollen garments and either the name or the make-up happens to be similar to that of one already on the market – but we don't know of this. We have no intention of deceiving anyone. Could the other manufacturers do anything about it?'

Certainly. To succeed in a 'passing off' action, the plaintiffs do not have to show any actual intention to deceive anyone.

'So it's really up to us to make sure that we don't come too near to anyone else's name or to the way in which they market their products?'

Correct.

'What can an aggrieved manufacturer do about it?'

He can apply to the court for an injunction, restraining the competing manufacturer from putting out goods in the deceptive way or under the deceptive style in question. If the goods are already in the factories, he can seek an injunction, to prevent their sale in the way complained of. He may also recover damages, if he can show that as a result of the 'passing off', his trade was adversely affected.

Naturally, if the plaintiffs succeed in this sort of action, the defendants may suffer heavily. If you are at the wrong end of a 'passing off' action, you may lose all you have spent on wrapping, packing, naming the goods, printing or marketing them. If the design is deceptive, you may lose everything. If you are simply selling them, in so far as you have been actively doing the 'passing off', you may find that you have to pay the costs of a legal action and damages into the bargain. And while you may be entitled to an indemnity from your suppliers if they were responsible for the 'passing off', you may still yourself be held responsible in the first place.

So respect other people's goodwill.

Even if you give something away as part of a sales drive this does not mean that you can pretend that it was the creation of someone else who did not create it. Merely because you do not charge for an object does not mean that you can pass that object off as your own, if it was someone else's – and that other person had not given his permission. And if you sell premium goods, because the people who buy from you are going to give away the goods, rather than sell them, you are no more entitled to use other people's names on those goods than you would be if you were selling them directly to the public or if your customer was going to do so. All this was made abundantly clear in the High Court case of *Société Anonyme Unic* v. *Lindeau Products Ltd*.

Towards the end of 1961, Lindeau Products sold over a million pens to Lever Brothers, to be given away with packets of Omo. It was the defendants' business to sell promotion ideas 'to leading companies', and it was their suggestion that this give-away should be attached to the purchase of this famous detergent. After all, a gift will add brightness and lightness to the lives of the giver and the receiver – provided that the receiver buys more of the goods with which the gift is handed out.

Anyway, all would have been well were it not for the fact that the pens each had the word 'Everglide', written in very small letters around the button at the top of the pen.

Unfortunately for Lindeau Products, 'Everglide', was a registered trade mark. It had been registered 'in respect of pens and parts of pens' by Société Anonyme Unic, of rue Juliette Dodu, Paris. As soon as they discovered what had happened, they sued for an injunction and for damages. After all, anyone who goes to the trouble of registering a trade mark and succeeds in his application is entitled to protect the goodwill which lies in that trade mark. Anyone who infringes that goodwill by using the trade mark without permission is liable to be dragged into court and to be restrained by an order of that court from continuing his wrongful behaviour in the future – and damages will be assessed to compensate the proprietors of the mark.

When the case came to court, Lindeau Products argued that when pens were bought by Lever Brothers, the purchasers were 'completely unaware of the existence of the mark on the pens'. The pens were then 'distributed as gifts without reference to any brand'.

During the course of the evidence, witnesses were asked whether they could read the word written around the button at the top of the pen. Some managed to read it with the naked eye, but others needed a magnifying glass. The judge, Mr Justice Ungoed-Thomas, was satisfied that 'the word had been used on the pens as a trade mark', but he questioned whether the sale of the pens to the distributors of the detergent or the distribution of the pens to the public constituted an infringement of the mark.

Eventually the judge decided against the defendants. 'It seems a matter of inevitable inference', he said, 'that among the persons who bought the packets of detergents there would have been some conversant with trade marks used on ball-points, who would have recognized the mark and assumed the pens to have been connected with the plaintiffs. The plaintiffs will be granted an injunction to restrain further infringement of their mark, and an enquiry as to damages.'

Now, this was no joke for the defendants. The damages might well be heavy. The court costs would not be light. And the injunction might leave them with literally thousands of ball-points on their hands – the fact that these were not to be sold but merely to be given away would make them no less of a waste. What may be 'free' to the lucky members of the public to whom they are given, is far from free to the buyers of the premium product.

The moral, then? Be careful of the names which you apply to products, even those you give away. If you are infringing someone's trade mark, you will be in trouble.

Neither is that the end of the matter, as we have already seen. 'Passing off' actions can be as effective as actions for infringements of trade marks.

You will note that while you must take care not to deceive the people to whom you sell goods, you also have a responsibility which goes a stage further. You must not let those to whom you sell goods deliberately or unconsciously deceive those members of the public to whom they pass those goods on. You must not 'put into their hands that which may become an instrument of deception towards others'. That was, in effect, what Lindeau Products did when they handed over to Lever the pens with the 'Everglide' registration mark. Lever Brothers were not deceived. The brand name was no part of their bargain. But when they gave away the goods to the public, members of the public might well have been deceived into thinking that those pens were the product of the plaintiffs' work. The fact that the pens were given away rather than items to be sold, was completely irrelevant.

How you 'put into the hands of the public' the goods concerned is irrelevant. If those goods become 'instruments of deception' you are in trouble. In these days when so much advertising is lavished and so little expense is spared in the building up of a trade name, its infringement seldom goes unnoticed. If the mark has been registered as a trade mark, an action may lie for infringement of that mark. But even if it has not been registered, to be at the wrong end of a 'passing off' action brings joy to no one.

PART VI
INTERNATIONAL ASPECTS

26 Suing outside the EEC

If you buy or sell products overseas, you may need to enforce your rights against your foreign customer or supplier. Whether or not you can do so in the UK courts – and, if so, which law wil be applied by those courts – will depend upon some complicated rules – which you should know, at least in outline.

If you wish to bring a foreigner before our courts, you have to serve him with the appropriate writ or summons. A private individual who is physically in the UK is just as subject to our laws as he is entitled to their protection. Equally, if you deal with an overseas company which has a registered place of business in the UK, you will be able to serve your process on the company at its business address. Otherwise, you will have to serve your writ 'out of the jurisdiction'. To do so, you will need the leave of the court.

Actions in negligence

If the action is founded on negligence, the question is: Was the wrongful act or omission 'committed within the jurisdiction' of our courts? The 'jurisdiction' means England and Wales, but not Scotland, where the rules are different. It would appear to include territorial waters up to the three-mile limit.

Next question: If a product is negligently manufactured and causes damage, is the negligence committed within or outside the jurisdiction?

American Cyanamid & Chemical Corporation manufactured Cyanogas gas, used for destroying rats. George Monro Ltd imported Cyanogas gas and sold it to a local authority which supplied it to a farmer for 'de-ratting'. The farmer sued the local authority, claiming that he had suffered loss through a defect in the gas and the authority, in its turn, sought and obtained an indemnity from George Monro, who applied for leave to sue American Cyanamid in New York.

Clearly, the damage (if any) caused by the negligence was suffered in the UK. But the Court of Appeal unanimously agreed that any negligence occurred in the production process which was carried out in the USA; there was therefore no wrongful act committed within the jurisdiction; and while the manufacturers owed a duty to 'the ultimate consumer' in the UK, there was no breach of that duty in this country. So George Monro (or, hopefully, their insurers) had to bear the blame.

The place of the wrongdoing is technically called the *locus delicti*. Two other important decisions have shown how the courts fix it.

In one of the Thalidomide cases, a child in Australia attempted to apply an equivalent rule to serve the manufacturers in the UK. The Privy Council held that the court must ask the question: Where was the wrongful act committed? The plaintiff complained of a manufacturing defect. Then where did the breach of duty of care arise?

Second, in the case of *Cordoba Land Co* v *Black Diamond Steamship Corporation* the plaintiffs sued shippers, alleging that they fraudulently issued clean bills of lading. The trial judge held that if (as the plaintiff contended) a fraudulent misrepresentation had been made in Massachusetts, that was the *locus delicti*. The wrongful act did not occur in Britain, where the plaintiff had relied on the defendant's statements or (again in Britain) where he suffered his loss.

This approach might create difficulty for people in the UK seeking product liability damages based on the negligence of a manufacturer in some far-off land. In the Thalidomide case, the plaintiff attacked the distributors, alleging that they should have issued due warnings. And in criminal law (section 6 of the Health and Safety at Work Act), a specific responsibility is placed on importers (as well as on designers, manufacturers and suppliers – see Chapter 19).

So negligence must be established within the UK. What, then, of product liability cases founded on breaches of contract?

Actions in contract

The Rules of the Supreme Court state that:

> If the action begun by the Writ is brought against a defendant not domiciled or ordinarily resident in Scotland to enforce, rescind, dissolve, annul or otherwise affect a contract, or to recover damages or obtain other relief in respect of the breach of a contract, being (in either case) a contract which:
>
> (1) was made within the jurisdiction, or
> (2) was made by or through an agent trading or residing within the jurisdiction on behalf of a principal trading or residing out of the jurisdiction, or
> (3) is by its terms, or by implication, governed by English law,

then the court may give leave to serve out of the jurisdiction.

So we first exclude defendants 'domiciled or ordinarily resident in Scotland'. To sue them, you go to the Scottish courts – unless (as explained in the preceding section) they have a presence within the jurisdiction.

Much of the law which applies in England and Wales is also effective in Scotland. But some is not; and the administration of justice in these parts of the UK frequently differs. Anyway, you cannot get leave to serve English or Welsh process against a defendant 'domiciled or ordinarily resident' in Scotland.

In broad terms, a person (which includes a company) is 'domiciled' where he has his permanent residence; he may at one time have more than one residence; but an individual may be permanently domiciled (either as a result of origin or choice) somewhere other than in the country in which he 'ordinarily resides'. If you run into difficulties over these definitions, consult your lawyer.

Now assume that the proposed defendant is not domiciled or

ordinarily resident in Scotland. You wish to sue for damages for breach of contract. Maybe your supplier has failed to deliver the correct quality or quantity of goods, or your customer has refused to pay . . .

First question: Was the contract 'made within the jurisdiction' of the UK courts?

If your customer comes to your factory and makes a deal on the spot, the contract is made within the jurisdiction. But if you go abroad and place your order in someone else's country, it is made outside the jurisdiction. The main complications come where the deal is made by telephone or correspondence – whether by letter, cable or telex. The normal rule is that if a deal is done by cable or letter, the contract is 'made' where the offer is *accepted* by the posting of a letter or the dispatching of a cable of acceptance. But a telexed contract is 'made' where the offeror *receives* the notification of the offeree's acceptance.

In the case of *BP Exploration (Libya) Ltd* v. *Hunt* 1982 it was held that if you make a contract within the jurisdiction and then amend it outside, unless the amendment has the effect of substituting a new agreement for the old, the amended contract is still taken to have been made within the jurisdiction. Whether or not a new contract has been substituted for the old is a matter of immense complication – as, indeed, is much of the law in this and the following chapter.

Now suppose that the contract was made outside the jurisdiction. Question two: Was it made 'by or through an agent trading or residing within the jurisdiction, on behalf of a principal trading or residing out of the jurisdiction'? The person (or the company or firm) acting for the defendant must have 'made' the contract – or have negotiated it (so that it was made 'through' him) – even if the principal abroad actually concluded the deal.

Finally, question three: Was the contract, wherever made, 'by its terms, or by implication, governed by English law'?

Parties to a contract may decide which law applies. They may (and, if wise, they probably will) say: 'This contract is governed by English law.' In that case, English courts will assume jurisdiction and will normally give leave for the process to be served outside that jurisdiction.

Conversely, recognizing that foreigners sometimes have a preference for their own laws or customs, the contract may expressly provide that it be governed by the law of (say) the USA or France or anywhere else 'outside the jurisdiction'.

Difficulties arise in deciding whether a contract is 'by implication' governed by English law. Unless the parties expressly agree as to 'the proper law' governing the contract, there may be real difficulties. It seems from the cases of *Compagnie Tunisienne de Navigation SA* v. *Compagnie D'Armement Maritime SA* and of *Coastlines Ltd* v. *Hudig Chartering* that the ultimate test should be: 'What is the system of law with which the transaction has the closest and the most real connection?'

Finally, 'Where was the contract broken?' Once again, the law is exceedingly complicated. The chances are that in a contract for the sale of a product the breach occurs when the goods are sold and not when the defect comes to light. In the case of *Crowther* v. *Shannon Motors*, for instance, it was held that the contract was broken at the time of the sale and not when the vehicle broke down.

Where does a breach occur? Probably at the place of shipment – especially if that is the time when ownership of the goods was transferred. But when we talk of transfer of ownership, that is also a legal quagmire. So this area is yet another in which you should take all relevant documents and a statement of the facts to your solicitor, to sort out the rule most likely to apply in your particular case.

Permission to serve the writ abroad

The fact that a judge has power to give leave to serve process out of the jurisdiction does not mean that he will necessarily do so. He must exercise his discretion in accordance with the rules, or risk having his decision overturned by an appeal court. However, this discretion is wide. So if you are involved in a product liability case involving an overseas defendant, you must consider on what basis a court is likely to give you permission to serve your writ or summons outside its jurisdiction.

The application must come not only within 'the letter of the rule' but also within its spirit. Would it be right for the court to order before it the foreigner who owes no allegiance to it? Is there a good arguable case, made out on the facts and on the law? Has

there been an 'inordinate delay' in seeking leave to serve the writ?
Do the interests of justice demand that leave be granted?

One important factor: Which is the most convenient forum for
the consideration of the dispute? In legal terms, what is the *forum
conveniens* for the trial of the matter? What would be the
'comparative cost and convenience' of hearing the matter in
England or Wales, as opposed to the trial taking place elsewhere?

As in the case of the assessment of 'reasonableness', so here in
the exercise of a court's discretion – in each case, all will depend
upon the view taken by the particular judge who hears the
application.

Still, if you can bring yourself within the rules set out in the
previous chapters; if you have a *prima facie* case, a good, arguable
case on the facts made apparent to the judge; and if it is apparently
convenient that the hearing be held in the UK – leave is likely to
be given.

Enforcing foreign judgments

A barren judgment is one which cannot be enforced. To sue a
'man of straw' is to throw good money after bad. Equally, to
obtain a judgment against a foreign defendant is useless if it goes
unsatisfied. Conversely, if a foreign customer obtains judgment
against you because of a defect in a product which you have sold
abroad, you can laugh all the way to the factory if that judgment
cannot be enforced against your assets. So consider: When is a
foreign judgment enforceable in the UK – or your judgment in
some foreign land?

The first place to look for the defendant's money is within the
jurisdiction of the UK courts. Even if the defendant is overseas, if
he has assets in the UK you may use the resources of the UK
courts to enforce your rights. You may, for instance, 'levy
equitable execution' on his property, that is, obtain an order for
the sale of all buildings belonging to him, so that the judgment
debt may be satisfied. Indeed, you may even send in the sheriffs,
to take hold of his movables.

Equally, if you have assets in (say) the United States and an
American court gives judgment against you, the resources and
methods of the US enforcement processes may be used to snatch

up your property, real or personal, to obtain satisfaction of the judgment debt.

If, as is more likely, the judgment must be enforced against you in the UK or against the other party in his own country, you must look to see whether there are arrangements with that country for the reciprocal enforcement of judgments. It is unthinkable, for instance, that the judgment of a court of that country would be enforceable in the UK against you, while you remained unable to enforce your rights through the courts of that country.

So in each case you must look to see whether one of the various Acts of Parliament which provide for the reciprocal enforcement of judgments applies as between the UK and the country with which you are concerned. If so, then you would be able to register your judgment in the court of that country, which would then enforce your judgment as if it were its own. Conversely, if the successful foreign plaintiff is able to register his judgment with the UK courts, you had better prepare for payment.

The Administration of Justice Act 1970 provides for the reciprocal enforcement of judgments by superior courts in many parts of the Commonwealth. The Foreign Judgments (Reciprocal Enforcement) Act 1933 has been applied to Austria, Belgium, France, West Germany, Guernsey, the Isle of Man, Israel, Italy, Jersey, the Netherlands and Norway – and also to certain Commonwealth and former Commonwealth countries not covered by the 1970 Act (including India and Pakistan). Judgments obtained in Scotland or Northern Ireland are, of course, mutually enforceable – in this case, through the Judgments Extension Act 1868. Finally, it is possible on occasion to sue on the foreign judgment in the UK courts, recommencing the proceedings on the basis of the foreign judgment.

If any question of the enforcement of a foreign judgment against you should arise, you should at once consult your solicitors. The rules are complicated and there are even some useful wrinkles in the enforcement procedures.

For instance, if a foreign judgment is registered against you in the High Court, there are grounds upon which you may be able to set it aside. Examples are:

(1) Would the enforcement of a judgment be contrary to public policy in the UK?

(2) Was the judgment obtained by fraud?
(3) Is the wrong person applying to enforce the judgment? Are the rights in the judgment vested in someone else?
(4) Did the courts of the country of the original court have jurisdiction, in the circumstances of the particular case?
(5) Was the judgment registered in contravention of the provisions of the Act concerned?

Note that you cannot get the registration set aside merely because the claim would not have succeeded had it been brought in the UK courts. If, for instance, the overseas plaintiff obtains judgment against you on the basis of strict liability for your product, when you would not have been held liable in Britain, you will still have to meet the judgment in the UK, if the appropriate reciprocal arrangements for the enforcements of judgments exist with the country in question.

Unfortunately for the British judgment debtor in a foreign court, though, it may be possible for the judgment creditor to bring a new action in the UK, based on the foreign judgment. He may sue in the UK courts, claiming the amount judged due abroad. He would not then have to show the original 'cause of action' but he may win his money by a roundabout but well-tried route. If you face this problem, your first step should be a swift one in the direction of your solicitors.

27 Suing within the EEC

If you have business dealings outside the UK but within the EEC, a different code of law applies. The idea behind the European Community is to open up the markets of all the member states to free competition from other countries within the Community. Therefore there are laws which guarantee the freedom of people to work where they wish, and for goods to be sold anywhere in the Community.

This aim can only be fully recognized when there is a common system of enforcing laws between the member states as well. Such a common system was introduced amongst the founder members in 1968. Now the UK has followed suit, under the Civil Jurisdiction and Judgments Act 1982.

Judgments in one state, enforceable in another

The central purpose of the 1982 Act is to bring Britain into a common system of law in Europe. Now, whether a breach of contract, or the damage caused by a product, arises in Dieppe, Düsseldorf or Dover, it should not make any difference. If you have a right of action in one country, it can be enforced in another. Likewise, if an EEC company, or individual from abroad, has a right of action against you, it is the same. Judgments in civil and commercial matters in one member state will be recognized and enforced in another.

Say, for example, the judgment from a French court has been given against you. The other party can bring proof of the judgment to the UK High Court, and it will enforce the judgment against you. And if you have been successful against a German manufacturer in the UK, you can take the judgment to the German courts for enforcement there.

However, if you want to appeal against a judgment, you have to do so in the courts of the country in which the action was started. If a Dutch company has won against you in Holland and now seeks to enforce its judgment in England, you will not be allowed to appeal against the Dutch judge here, you must do so in Holland.

In which state should the action be started?

Before any question of enforcing a judgment arises, you have to decide in which country you should begin proceedings.

Defendant's country of domicile

The basic rule of the 1982 Act provides that a defendant should be sued in the country in which he is domiciled. The laws of domicile are not the same in every member state of the EEC. So if you wish to sue elsewhere in the European Community, you will have to find out about the law of domicile of that country. In the UK, however, domicile means that you are a resident of England or Wales and have a substantial connection with them. It will be presumed that you have a substantial connection if you have lived there for more than three months.

Even if you do not reside in England or Wales, your business connections may be sufficient to make your business domiciled here. It will be domiciled in England either if it was formed or incorporated here and has its registered address here, or if its central management and control is exercised here.

It may be possible for a person, or business, to be domiciled in more than one country.

Having said you should sue the defendant in his country of

domicile, there are some significant exceptions to the rule. In fact, the requirement of domicile is no more than an additional factor which may entitle you to choose where you wish to proceed.

Contractual rights

You have made an agreement with another party in (say) Belgium. Everything is going well until a dispute arises. In what country should the dispute be settled?

In most contracts of this sort your agreement will specify the country in which settlement should occur. You are perfectly entitled to do this and your wishes will be respected. Therefore, if you indicate that English courts will supervise the contract, the Belgian courts will refer the case to England.

If, however, your contract has not specified in which country disputes shall be settled some other solution has to be found. The general rule is that the dispute should be settled in the country where the contract was to be performed. This normally means the country where the seller performed his services, or provided his goods. However, this is such a complicated area of law (like much international law) that you should immediately seek advice in the event of a dispute.

Damage caused by party with whom you are not in contract

The carelessness of a person has caused damage. A German mining company has polluted a river which flows into France. A French market gardener uses water from the river to irrigate his crops. The polluted water damages them. In which country must he proceed? Is it the place where the carelessness took place, or where the damage was suffered? It is established that the plaintiff can choose either one of these places. It is up to him.

Presence of branch, agency or other establishment

If a dispute arises out of the operations of a branch office of a company that is based in another country, then you can proceed in the country of the branch. However, for this to apply, the defendant must be domiciled somewhere in a member state. The branch office or agency must be established in the country in question and be equipped to do business in that country.

Disputes will arise out of the activities of a branch office in matters relating to its management or staff, and in issues concerning the obligations that it has been responsible for creating.

Co-defendants

You may be made a co-defendant, for example as a supplier of a component of a machine, or as its distributor or carrier. In this case, if a main action has been brought against the seller of the machine in one country, you may be brought in as a co-defendant to that action in that country.

In product liability cases this rule is clearly very important. Take, for example, motor cars. One foreign manufacturer had a slogan that said 70 per cent of the vehicle was British because most of the component parts were made in Britain. So, if one of the British component parts was defective, the British manufacturer could be made a co-defendant with the car maker.

This provision is likely to lead to some very complicated litigation, and if you happen to get caught up in it, seek specialist advice quickly.

PART VII
PRODUCT LIABILITY INSURANCE

by Peter Madge

28 Introduction

The aim of product liability insurance

A typical product liability policy protects the insured against his legal liability to pay compensation or damages to third parties who have sustained bodily injury or loss or damage to their property arising out of any product sold, supplied, repaired, serviced or tested by the insured. The policy is a legal liability policy not a moral liability policy.

Growth of product liability insurance

Product liability insurance has made enormous advances in the last twenty-five years as consumerism and increasing claims-consciousness on the part of the general public have created a demand for protection. Although separate product liability policies are issued by insurers, it is usual market practice to include the product liability risk as part of the general public liability policy. A public liability policy protects the insured against his legal liability for injuries to third parties, or for loss of or damage to their property, by general business risks, for example the ownership of property or acts of employees, but specifically excludes liability arising out of any goods sold or supplied by the insured. An amendment to this exclusion is normally the way in which insurers provide the product liability cover. However, for the purposes of this chapter it will be more convenient to assume that a separate product liability policy has been issued, and examine that policy in detail to ascertain the scope of the cover provided.

Some types of insurance have been governed by a tariff which determines not only the premiums to be charged but the scope of the policy cover. Where such a tariff existed, there was a marked degree of conformity between competing insurers in the policy document. Product liability insurance has never been subject to a tariff and there is therefore no standardization on rating or cover. Indeed, between various insurers there is much competition for business not only on price but on the breadth and width of the policy cover. It is for this reason that many firms use insurance brokers to advise them. It is necessary, therefore, to make it clear that there is no such thing as a standard policy wording available from the insurance market. The specimen policy reproduced in Appendix A and examined in this chapter, however, is typical of the cover generally available. It is used simply as a guide.

Completion of a proposal form

Before any insurer issues a product liability policy, he has to obtain certain underwriting information from the insured. This may be collected by means of a written proposal form or by other means. This aspect will be considered in more detail later. At this point it is sufficient to realize that since the underwriter bases his acceptance of the risk and his premium on the information given, it must be accurate. Inaccurate information which misleads the underwriter into his acceptance of the risk or calculation of the premium may give the underwriter an opportunity to avoid the policy if he so wishes.

Moreover, the insurer must be kept up to date. As the risk or the products change he must be told.

Underwriting and premium assessment

To assess the risk and calculate the premium the underwriter needs certain information. He will normally obtain this from a proposal form, which is completed by the proposer. A specimen is shown in Appendix B. Questions are mainly self-explanatory. The main features the underwriter will take into account are the following.

(1) The type of product and the dangers attaching to it, for example pharmaceuticals are a heavier risk than paint manufacture.

(2) The past record of claims, since the past is often a guide to the future. How many were there? What did it cost to settle them?

(3) The turnover. Premium is related to turnover by applying a rate for each £1000 of turnover. An initial premium is charged on estimated turnover, subject to adjustment at the year-end, when the correct turnover is known. Where there are exports to the USA, a higher rate may be charged because of the increased risk in that country and restrictions may be imposed on the cover.

(4) The experience of the proposer in the business and the time he has been established in that business.

(5) The limit of indemnity. The higher the limit, the higher the premium.

(6) How much of the risk the insured is prepared to carry himself, in other words an excess.

The premium to be applied is based mainly on the underwriter's personal assessment of the risk plus whatever statistics on that particular type of risk he may have. Statistics, however, are treated with caution in this class of insurance, since no one insurer has a sufficiently wide spread of business over all product ranges to make his statistics accurate. Moreover, whatever statistics the underwriter may hold are based on past events, whereas he is insuring the risk of claims in the future. Premiums for the same risk may also vary widely from one underwriter to another.

Some elementary insurance principles

A policy of insurance is a legal contract whereby one person, the insurer, in consideration of a premium paid by the insured undertakes to indemnify the insured against certain losses or liabilities. The contract of insurance is completed when there has been offer and acceptance and both parties are in agreement. Normally in a contract of insurance the proposer knows more about his business than the insurer. Insurance is transacted on the understanding that the proposer will disclose to the insurer all material facts to enable the insurer to assess the risk and the premium. Insurance practice is built on this basic principle of utmost good faith. (Until the risk is accepted by the insurer, the insured is known as the proposer.)

If the proposer is under a duty to disclose to the insurer all material facts, what is a material fact? A material fact is anything which would influence the judgment of a prudent insurer in fixing the premium or determining whether he will take the risk or not. Thus, the test is what a prudent insurer would require to know and not what a prudent proposer considers he ought to disclose. Proposers who withhold information from the underwriter in the hope that it will keep the premium down run a serious risk of invalidating their policy.

The proposer does not have to disclose everything which is material. Particularly he does not have to disclose the following:

(1) facts that lessen the risk;
(2) matters of common knowledge or matters which an insurer ought to know in the course of his business;
(3) matters on which the insurer waives information;
(4) facts that it is not necessary to disclose by reason of an express or implied condition in the policy document itself.

The duty to disclose all material facts is a duty to disclose not only facts that the proposer knows but those that he ought to know, for example facts which are available to him if he chooses to make enquiry among employees and others.

The duty of disclosure continues throughout the negotiations for the policy up to the point in time when the contract of insurance is completed. Thereafter it ceases and does not attach again until renewal of the policy, since insurance policies are annual contracts and at each renewal date the proposer and the insurer are entering into a new contract. The duty to disclose material facts therefore arises again at renewal date. However, a specific condition in the policy may require the insured to notify material changes in the risks that occur during the currency of the policy.

Failure by the insured to disclose a material fact gives the insurer the option to avoid the policy if he wishes.

29 The insurance policy

The recital clause

The policy opens with a clause which recites the parties to the contract and deals with certain preliminary matters. The clause reads:

> Whereas the Insured carrying on the business described in the Schedule and no other for the purposes of this insurance by a proposal and declaration which shall be the basis of this contract and is deemed to be incorporated herein has applied to the company (hereinafter called 'the Company') for the insurance hereinafter contained and has paid or agreed to pay the Premium as consideration for such insurance.

The following points are important.

'... carrying on the business described in the Schedule and no other for the purposes of this insurance'

The business the insurer is covering is that proposed to him and that for which he has obtained certain underwriting information for premium assessment. As will appear later, the premium varies from business to business, some being more hazardous than

185

others. The business the insurer is covering is described in the
schedule to the policy. It is this business and only this business the
insurer is covering, so that it is important the business description
is a full and accurate one.

Moreover, as the business expands or changes, the business
description should be kept under review. For example, the insured's occupation may be described as retailer of electrical
appliances, but in the course of time the insured may decide to
manufacture. Unless the policy is amended to cover the manufacturing activities, these remain uninsured.

'... by a proposal and declaration which shall be the basis of the contract and is deemed to be incorporated herein'

The underwriting information required by the underwriter to
assess the risk and the premium is often collected by means of a
written proposal form, the details of which are discussed later.
This proposal form contains a declaration signed by the proposer
to the effect that the answers and information he has given are true
and correct, and he agrees that they shall form the basis of the
contract of insurance. The proposal form and the declaration are
incorporated into the contract of insurance to form the basis of it;
the legal effect of this is that any wrong information on the
proposal form gives the insurer the right, if he so requires, to treat
the policy as void. Insurers would not normally take this course of
action for minor inaccuracies in the proposal form, but they would
naturally do so where the inaccuracy related to a material aspect of
the risk, as, for example, a failure to disclose that the product in
question was known to be defective or had previously caused
accidents resulting in injury or damage.

'... has paid or agreed to pay the Premium'

The premium is the legal consideration for which the insurers have
agreed to accept the risk of injury or damage arising out of the
defective products. It is fundamental that the insured has paid or
agreed to pay the premium before the policy is operative. The
insured may not have paid the premium at the time a claim is
lodged against him. This does not mean he is not entitled to the

benefit of the policy: the policy will still protect the insured provided he intended to pay.

The insuring clause

This is the important part of the policy which sets out what the cover is. It reads:

> The Company will subject to the terms exceptions and conditions of this Policy indemnify the Insured against all sums which the Insured shall become legally liable to pay as damages in respect of
>
> (1) accidental bodily injury (including death or disease) to any person
> (2) accidental loss of or damage to property
>
> happening anywhere in the world elsewhere than at premises owned or occupied by the Insured during the Period of Insurance and caused by any Goods sold supplied repaired altered treated or serviced by or on behalf of the Insured from or in Great Britain, Northern Ireland, the Channel Islands and the Isle of Man in connection with the Business.

The points discussed in the following section are important.

Meaning of important expressions

'... subject to the terms exceptions and conditions of this Policy'

The words of the insuring clause which express the indemnity to the insured must be read in conjunction with the policy as a whole. In other words, in addition to looking at the insuring clause, one must also look at the exceptions and policy conditions to see whether the claim is within the scope of the policy and the conditions of the policy have been complied with.

'. . . indemnify the Insured'

To indemnify a person is to put him in the same position after the loss as he was before the loss, subject to the terms and conditions of the policy. In motor car insurance, for example, if a motor car is damaged and insured under a comprehensive policy, insurers pay the cost of repairs. Thus, after the repairs have been completed, the insured is in the same position as he was before the accident, that is, he has an undamaged vehicle.

The indemnity which the insurers are promising under a product liability policy is to pay any damages the insured may become legally liable to pay because of claims arising out of his products. The purist may argue that a person is not legally liable to pay unless a court so finds him, because, until such a decision has been reached, there is no judgment against which the insured can be indemnified. It is a theoretical argument. In practice, where the insured is faced with a product liability claim, insurers deal with the claim on his behalf. Where there is no legal liability, they will defend the claim on behalf of the insured. Where there is a legal liability, they will pay the damages on behalf of the insured, including the legal costs and expenses. In other words, they indemnify the insured. The worry of dealing with the claim is removed from him.

'. . . against all sums which the Insured shall become legally liable to pay'

There are many ways in which a person may become legally liable to pay damages to a third party. Liability, for example, may attach in negligence, breach of contract or breach of statute. The policy does not attempt to spell out the specific ways in which liability must attach. It does not promise to indemnify the insured against claims arising out of negligence, for example. The words 'legally liable' are extremely wide and cover all forms of liability. Thus legal decisions representing changes in existing law or Acts of Parliament creating new liabilities, such as the Consumer Protection Act are automatically included in the expression 'legally liable'.

Also, legal liability does not have to arise out of acts or omissions of the insured himself. Liability may attach to the insured because of the activities of others, for example agents, contractors or suppliers. Provided the insured is 'legally liable', the policy applies.

Sometimes the expression 'liability at law' is used rather than 'legally liable'. The intention under such a wording is the same.

'... as damages'

The person who has been injured or sustained damage to his property is entitled to sue for compensation. This compensation is referred to legally as damages, which are simply an amount of money given to the claimant to compensate him for the injury, loss or damage he has sustained. The object of civil liability is to compensate the plaintiff, not to punish the defendant. Punishment of the manufacturer of a defective product is the function of the criminal law and usually enforced by fines. These are not the subject of a product liability policy – it would be unlawful for them to be.

Damages may broadly be classified under two headings. Special damages are those damages which have to be specifically pleaded and proved before they are paid. In the case of a person injured by a defective product it may be damage to his clothing and doctors' bills and other medical expenses. General damages, on the other hand, are those damages which cannot be assessed precisely and therefore have to be negotiated or agreed by the court, as, for example, an amount of money to cover pain and suffering and the loss of future earnings of a person injured and unable to carry on his normal employment.

Although the policy form being considered refers to the word 'damages', the alternative word 'compensation' is often used. In most instances there is no difference between the choice of the two. It does become a matter of major importance for products which are exported to the USA. American juries may award sums of punitive damages where they think that the action of the defendant is reprehensible and they want to punish him. Such damages are not normally awarded in the UK (except for matters which do not concern us), which is why until the 1970s the choice of the word 'damages' or 'compensation' presented no problems. Technically, punitive damages are caught by the general expression 'damages' but are not thought to be caught by the word 'compensation'. The reason for this is that punitive damages are not truly compensatory. Insurers using a 'compensation' wording do not intend to cover punitive damages – leaving an area of risk uninsured.

There is much uncertainty in the insurance market whether or not punitive damages come within the scope of a policy, and it is in each case a question of interpretation by the insurers and agreement with them. Many policies specifically exclude punitive damages.

'... in respect of'

The policy protects the insured against his liability at law to pay damages to persons who have been injured or have sustained loss or damage to their property. The plaintiff's loss, however, may not stop solely at his injury or damage. He may incur other consequential losses. For example, a chemical manufacturer may supply a defective chemical to a factory. It may cause a fire, leading to extensive damage to the factory, with a consequent loss of production and loss of profits on the part of the factory owner. The policy protects the insured against his legal liability for damage to the factory and also for the consequential losses flowing therefrom. The object is not to protect only against the direct injury or loss. To take such a narrow view would be to leave the insured unprotected in what is very often the major area of the risk – the consequential losses.

'... accidental bodily injury (including death or disease) to any person'

The policy protects the insured against his liability for bodily injury to third parties arising out of the products. Some time ago it was argued that the words 'bodily injury' meant such things as cuts or bruises and did not cover death or disease, for example cancer or skin diseases. The words in brackets are added to make it clear that the object of the policy is to cover all forms of bodily injury, death, disease or sickness which may arise out of the use of the product. Most insurers prefer the words 'bodily injury', although lawyers and judges often refer to 'personal injury'. Personal injury may have a much wider meaning than bodily injury in the sense that it may include injury to a person's reputation, as, for example, libel or slander. Generally it is not the insurers' intention to cover risks of this sort, although as with many aspects of liability policies the meaning is negotiable.

'... accidental loss of or damage to property'

To the lawyer the word 'property' has a much wider meaning than that normally attributed to it by the layman. In a legal sense property is anything a person may own or possess. In the case of physical property, quite clearly a person may own a house or a motor car or valuable contents. There are, however, intangible forms of property which a person may own, such as the copyright in a book, patent and design rights, trade marks and trade names. Such intangible forms of property, often referred to as 'intellectual property', are covered by the all-embracing word 'property'. So what does the word mean?

The meaning is one of considerable importance to insurers, because when they assess their premium and issue their policies, they do not normally intend to cover interference with intangible property interests. Generally it is the intention of insurers to protect the insured against his liability for loss of or physical damage to *tangible* or *material* property. Thus, claims for damage to motor cars, houses, contents, machinery, and so on, are within their contemplation, but not non-material damage claims. Some insurers make their position clear by specifically referring to accidental loss of or damage to *material* property.

Some insurers do intend the word 'property' to have a wider meaning than material property. These tend to be in a minority. They are prepared to give the word 'property' its wide meaning in law but cut out those risks they do not wish to insure by means of a specific policy exclusion. Thus, the policy may exclude liability arising from libel or slander, or infringement of plans, copyright, patents, trade names, trade marks or designs. Other types of non-material damage claims other than the ones specifically excluded are thus covered.

In addition to protecting the insured against his legal liability for damage to property, the policy also protects the insured against his liability for *loss* of property. For example, the manufacturer of a burglar-alarm system may be liable for damage to the building due to a fire caused by a defect in the wiring of the burglar alarm. That would be a case of damage to property.

The burglar alarm, however, may not work. Thieves enter the premises and property is stolen. The manufacturer of the burglar alarm may be sued by the owner of the property for the loss of the property owned by him. This is an example where there is a liability for loss of property. The underwriting of those risks where the product presents an exposure to loss claims in addition to damage claims is carefully considered by insurers. Usually they are considered to be unattractive in that insurers feel that they are getting near to guaranteeing the product – something they do not regard as their role – and in many cases the policy may be amended to delete reference to loss of property in situations where the insurer does not wish to give this type of cover.

It is important to appreciate that the policy does not cover everything. It is limited in the sense that it only provides protection against legal liability for bodily injury to third parties or loss of or damage to property. The insured may be faced with a claim for a purely economic or financial loss on its own. Such a claim would not be covered. For example, a manufacturer may supply machinery to a factory, intended to provide power to enable the factory to produce its goods. If the machinery is defective and explodes, causing damage to the factory, and as a result the factory has to close down, sustaining several days' loss of production, the insured would be protected under his policy against the claim for the damage to the factory and the loss of production. If, however, the machine simply failed to operate, as a result of which the factory was deprived of its power (but without there being any damage to it) the claim against the manufacturer would be for a purely economic or financial loss not flowing from damage to property. That claim would not be covered.

The policy protects the insured against his legal liability for *accidental* bodily injury or *accidental* loss of or damage to property. The word 'accidental' is important. Insurers intend to cover claims arising out of products which are fortuitous but not claims which are inevitable. For example, in the process of manufacturing chocolate a piece of wire may accidentally find its way into the chocolate. A consumer may sustain a cut in his mouth or broken teeth through biting on the chocolate, and his subsequent claim against the chocolate manufacturers would be regarded as being covered by the policy, since it was accidental. If, however, the chocolate manufacturers knew of the existence of the wire in the chocolate but nevertheless deliberately put it on to the market knowing it was going to cause injury to the consumer, insurers would not regard the subsequent claim as being covered, since they would argue that the injury was not accidental. Much discussion has taken place in the insurance market regarding the interpretation to be placed on the word 'accidental'. It can be argued that from the customer's point of view his injuries were accidental, and therefore the insured ought to be entitled to indemnity under his policy. Insurers intend the word 'accidental' to be interpreted from the insured's point of view. In other words, standing in the place of the insured, can it be said that from his point of view the injury was accidental.

Some policies omit reference to the word 'accidental' and deal with the matter by means of a specific policy exclusion. Thus the policy may exclude bodily injury or loss of or damage to property which results from a deliberate act or omission of the insured and which could reasonably have been expected by the insured, having regard to the nature and circumstances of such act or omission. Several different wordings are in use.

Without going too closely into the meaning of the words, the insurers' intention is reasonably clear. If the insured deliberately puts on the market a product which he knows is going to cause injury, loss or damage, insurers do not intend to indemnify him against his legal liability for any resulting claim.

'. . . happening anywhere in the world'

Although products may be sold for consumption only in the UK, there is no certainty that they may not cause injury or damage abroad. Some products, particularly components, may be incorporated into other products which are exported. Often, too, the manufacturer will sell directly to overseas markets. The policy provides indemnity in respect of injury, loss or damage happening in any part of the world. That being the case, there is the risk that the insured may be sued in courts outside the UK: for example, a person injured in the USA through a defective product manufactured in the UK is not likely to come to the UK to make his claim. Apart from the cost and the physical inconvenience of so doing, there are advantages to him in bringing his claim in the US, not least of which is the higher scale of damages.

The attitude of insurers in giving cover for litigation in overseas countries varies. Some insurers may limit their worldwide cover by saying that they will only deal with claims arising from any injury, loss or damage abroad, provided the claim is brought in the courts of the UK (by no means as common now as it used to be). Others may issue a policy which provides that they will deal with claims in overseas courts if the insured does not have a branch office or any assets in the country in question. Both clauses represent serious limitations in the cover. Some insurers have no such limitations in their policies. The trend is to give worldwide cover without limitation – except where there is an American risk.

'... elsewhere than at premises owned or occupied by the Insured'

The object of product liability insurance is to protect the insured for injury, loss or damage caused by his products once they have left his premises or left his custody or control. If the injury, loss or damage arises while the products are on the insured's premises, the insured will be entitled to an indemnity under his public liability policy. For example, if a third party is visiting the premises of firework manufacturers, and a firework explodes and injures him, that is a public liability claim. If the fireworks are sold, leave the insured's premises and while being stored by a retailer explode and injure people, the injured persons' claim against the manufacturer would be a product liability claim.

'... during the Period of Insurance'

Policies are usually issued for one year. When they are renewed, they are normally renewed for a further year. The test of whether the policy cover is operative is: 'When did the injury or damage take place?' If it took place during the period of insurance, the insured is entitled to indemnity under his policy even though the claim may not arise till some time later, even perhaps after the policy has lapsed (provided he complies with the condition requiring notification of injury or damage to the insurer). The insurer is thus on risk for goods which may have been sold or supplied before he issued his policy, provided the injury or damage takes place during the currency of his policy. Conversely the underwriter is not on risk for injury or damage caused by goods which take place after his policy has lapsed, even though the policy may have been in force at the time the goods were manufactured or put into circulation.

Because of bad underwriting results in the USA, some insurers have converted their policies on to a 'claims made' basis. In other words they apply to *claims* made during the period of the policy regardless of when the injury or damage took place. The object of such policies is to protect the insurer against the long time lag associated with disease claims. In such cases the actual claim by the injured person may often be made many years after his disease occurred. Insurers have had to pay for claims made in the late 1970s for diseases which occurred under policies issued some twenty years previously. Generally there has been a marked resistance on the part of the policyholders to accept 'claims made' policies. They bristle with difficulties and the policyholder should be aware of the problems involved if he is insured under such a policy.

'... caused by any Goods sold supplied repaired altered treated or serviced'

Product liability policies are drafted so that they can apply to a variety of trades or businesses. In addition to liability attaching to the manufacturer or retailer of goods, liability may also attach because goods have been repaired badly or incorrectly treated. The housewife may take her electric iron to an electrician to be repaired, the repair may be carried out negligently, and the housewife may be electrocuted. The liability arises not so much out of the goods which have been sold or supplied but out of the bad repair. The words 'repaired altered treated or serviced' are therefore used to provide full protection.

The liability to be covered by the policy must be caused by any goods sold or supplied by or on behalf of the insured but only in connection with the business covered by the policy. In other words, the goods must bear some relation to the business as described in the policy, for example if the business is described in the policy as electrical goods manufacture, liability arising out of the sale of paint to the public is not covered.

The definition of goods will usually be defined, for example 'goods means any commodity, article or thing sold or supplied by the insured'. The policy is sometimes drafted to make it clear that liability arising out of the containers holding the goods is also covered. Most insurers intend to interpret their policy this way anyhow, since it is an important risk, and not to provide cover for defective containers may leave the insured unprotected. For example, the goods themselves may be in perfect condition and it may be the container which is defective, for example paint leaking from a tin or acid leaking from a container.

The policy may sometimes be restricted in the sense that it covers liability caused by any 'defective' goods sold or supplied, etc. At first sight it may appear that the word 'defective' is superfluous, since injury or damage will not arise unless the goods are defective. However, that is not always the case. The supply of an incorrect but perfect product may still create liability. For example, a person may go to a garage to buy paraffin to light a bonfire and by mistake be given petrol. He may be injured in the resultant fire. While there would clearly be liability on the garage, would it be entitled to indemnity under its product liability policy which limited the cover to the supply of a defective product? The petrol was not defective. As in many insurance cases, it is a question of clearing with insurers what they intend.

'... from or in Great Britain, Northern Ireland, the Channel Islands and the Isle of Man'

The particular policy under consideration only intends to provide cover for those insured persons who are carrying on business in the territories mentioned. Although the policy gives worldwide cover, it does so only provided the products have been sold or supplied from the insured's premises in the territorial limits specified. Where the insured has manufacturing premises or other premises abroad, the product risks arising from such premises are intended to be covered by policies issued locally in the overseas territories.

Facilities do exist in the insurance market to provide cover on a worldwide basis, no matter where the insured's premises are. The point is of great importance to large corporations and multinational companies, which require a common approach to their product liability insurance requirements. It is often possible to arrange one 'master' policy in the UK covering all the insured's activities on a worldwide basis. In most local territories, however, a policy will be issued to the locally domiciled subsidiary to provide local day-to-day service or to comply with local legislation. Where possible these local policies should be issued by the same insurer or panel of insurers issuing the 'master' policy. That way it is the same insurer or panel of insurers who are dealing with any claim no matter where it may be throughout the world. There is less danger of gaps appearing in the cover or arguments developing between different insurers as is often the case where the UK parent insures with one insurer and leaves the subsidiaries to insure with any insurer of their choice.

'... in connection with the Business'

Reference has already been made to this but it is worth repeating. The business is described in the policy and it is only in connection with goods sold or supplied, etc., in connection with that business which are intended to be covered by the policy.

The matter is of considerable importance. The business activities of the insured must be kept under review. Where the nature or type of the product changes, insurers must be advised.

Litigation costs and expenses

An analysis of the policy cover so far shows that the insurers will indemnify the insured against his legal liability for injury, loss or damage to third parties. However, an expensive part of any product liability claim is the legal costs and expenses incurred in resisting the claim or negotiating settlement. Merely to pay the damages but not the legal costs and expenses would leave the insured unprotected. Thus, the legal costs and expenses clause of the policy provides that:

> The Company will also pay legal costs and expenses recoverable by any claimant and all costs and expenses incurred with the written consent of the Company plus solicitor's fees incurred with the written consent of the Company for representation of

the Insured at any coroner's inquest or fatal enquiry arising from
any death proceedings in any court of summary jurisdiction
arising out of any alleged breach of a statutory duty resulting in
bodily injury or loss of or damage to property which may be the
subject of a claim under this insurance.

Litigation is expensive. Payments under this clause cost insurers a
lot of money. Although the costs and expenses payable by insurers
are in addition to any damages payable to the claimant, some
insurers include them within the limit of indemnity – effectively
reducing the cover.

Limit of indemnity

The liability of the Company for all damages in respect of
all bodily injury loss or damage happening in any one Period
of Insurance shall not in the aggregate exceed the Limit of
Indemnity.

If a person is injured or sustains damage to his property, there is
no limit in law on the amount of the claim he may bring. Provided
he can quantify his loss to the satisfaction of the defendant and the
court, his proved damages will be payable. Thus, for example, a
drug company may put on to the market a drug which is defective
and dangerous; the drug may be consumed by thousands of
people, all of whom sustain serious injury and all of whom lodge a
claim against the drug manufacturer. The claims may run into
millions of pounds. No insurer could run the risk of issuing a policy
for an unlimited amount – they lack the resources. Hence all
insurers limit their liability to a set figure. The figure is of course
negotiable, and the higher the figure the higher the premium. As a
broad generalization, no one insurer would be keen to expose his
account to a limit of more than £1 million per policy. Where high
limits of indemnity are required, the risk is shared by a number of
insurers. Thus, if a limit of indemnity of £10 million is required,
the risk may be shared amongst ten or so insurers or, alternatively,
the first insurer may accept the first £1 million of risk and other
insurers share among themselves a policy for £9 million after the
first £1 million. The first method is usually referred to as co-
insurance and the second method as excess of loss insurance.

The important point about the limit of indemnity is that it is an aggregate limit for any one period of insurance. It is not a limit of indemnity for any one accident. In this respect it differs from public liability insurance, where normally the limit of indemnity is a limit on any one accident or any one occurrence or any one event. Insurers use an aggregate limit of indemnity to protect themselves and their reinsurers. As has been pointed out previously, the policy protects the insured against his liability for *accidental* injury or damage to third parties. There is no certainty in law how a court would interpret the word accidental. It has been stated previously that the intention is to construe the word 'accidental' from the point of view of the insured, but the courts could take a contrary view. If they did, the repercussions for insurers could be serious. To take the case of the drug manufacturer. If the insurer issues a policy with a limit of indemnity of £1 million, his premium and his acceptance of the risk are based on the fact that in the event of a claim he does not intend to pay out more than £1 million in any one year. A batch of drugs, however, may be defective and may injure 1000 people. One could say that each individual claimant had been accidentally injured. If the courts took the view that the £1 million limit was a limit applying to each individual claimant, the exposure facing the insurer could be enormous. It is for this reason that the limit of indemnity is expressed as an aggregate limit in any one period of insurance. If the total claims against the insured exceed the aggregate limit, claims in excess of the aggregate limit must be met by the insured himself.

30 Exceptions to the policy

Why exceptions appear

Exceptions normally appear in most insurance policies. They are there to clarify the cover the insurer intends to give, and are used frequently by insurers as a method of controlling the premium and their underwriting.

Basically there are three main reasons why exceptions appear in insurance policies.

(1) Because the risks excluded are covered or can be covered under other policies. The product liability policy excludes injuries to employees because the insured's legal liability for injury to employees is covered under an employer's liability policy.

(2) Because the risk is a hazardous one or one which the insurer is not prepared to cover without making further underwriting enquiries. Thus the product liability policy may exclude liability arising out of the design or formula of the product because the insurer wants to be satisfied about the qualifications and experience of the designers before providing cover.

(3) Because the risks are uninsurable. This type of exclusion is not of any great relevance to product liability insurance but is in other forms of insurance, for example material damage policies exclude the consequences of war.

Exclusion and exception clauses in commercial contracts have long been regarded with disfavour by British courts and are normally construed against the drafter – known as the *'contra proferentem'* rule. Further limitations on the use of exclusion clauses arise by reason of the Unfair Contract Terms Act 1977. This makes exclusion clauses relating to bodily injury claims void and other exclusion clauses subject to a test of reasonableness. It is important to remember that insurance contracts are not caught by the Unfair Contract Terms Act.

Courts construe insurance policies strictly. Any doubts regarding the application of an exclusion are construed in favour of the insured and against the insurers on the basis that the insurers drew up the policy and should make their intentions clear.

There are well-established rules regarding the interpretation of insurance exceptions. The onus of proving that an exception to a policy applies rests upon the insurers. Conversely, the onus of proving that his claim falls within the insuring clause of the policy rests upon the insured. In other words, if the insured cannot prove that his claim is within the insuring clause of the policy, the question of proving whether or not an exception applies does not arise.

Although modern policies are drafted in such a way that any exceptions to the policy are clearly set out under a section of the policy headed 'exceptions', this is not universally so. The practice still exists with some insurers of including exceptions in the insuring clause of their policy. An example of such a clause from one policy reads:

> The insurers will indemnify the insured in respect of his liability at law for damage to property (not belonging to the insured or in his custody or control) and bodily injury to any person (other than persons under a contract of service or apprenticeship with the insured).

Where such exceptions are included in the insuring clause of the policy, the legal rules change and the onus of proof is reversed. Before the insured is entitled to claim indemnity under his policy, he must prove that the property damaged, for example, was not in his custody or control or that the injured claimant was not a person who at the time of the injury was under a contract of service or apprenticeship with the insured.

Exceptions to the product liability policy

The risks excluded by a product liability policy vary from one insurer to the other. In practice much negotiation goes on about them, and they are often changed. The risks excluded by the specimen policy under consideration are considered in greater detail below.

'... bodily injury sustained by any employee and arising out of and in the course of his employment by the Insured'

This risk is excluded because a more specific type of insurance exists to cover it. Claims by employees are the subject of employer's liability insurance. By virtue of the Employer's Liability (Compulsory Insurance) Act 1967, with certain exceptions, this form of insurance is compulsory.

'... loss of or damage to property belonging to or in the custody or control of the Insured'

This is an exclusion common to most forms of liability insurance. Insurers normally take the view that where the insured has property in his custody or control, it should be insured specifically under material damage policies, for example fire or theft, not under legal liability policies. As far as property belonging to the insured is concerned, this is an excluded risk, since the insurer only intends to cover liability for damage to other people's property.

'... liability assumed by the Insured under agreement unless such liability would have attached in the absence of such agreement'

Insurers assess premiums and underwrite product liability risks on the basis of common law legal liabilities and statutory liabilities known to them at the time. Thus, they keep abreast of legal developments both in the courts and through Parliament. The insured, however, may enter into contractual terms or agreements which substantially alter the common law or statutory provisions known to the insurers, often with a substantial increase in the risk. For example, the insured may supply a product which is perfect in

every respect, but in a buyer's market he may have to indemnify
his customer against any injury, loss or damage sustained by the
customer arising out of the use of the product, however that
injury, loss or damage is sustained. The customer may misuse the
product and injure himself. The manufacturer may be liable to
compensate the customer under the terms of the indemnity clause.

The use of indemnity and exclusion clauses in commercial
contracts is a common feature of business life and obviously has a
bearing on the underwriting of the risk. It is for this reason that
such risks are excluded by the policy. That is not to say that
insurers will not provide cover under such indemnity clauses but
they normally require sight of the clause first so that they can
assess the risk and decide the right level of premium.

A variation of the risk is where a manufacturer may buy
component parts from a sub-manufacturer. The component parts
are incorporated in the manufacturer's product and sold to the
public. A member of the public may sustain injury, loss or damage
because the product is defective, and the defective part may be
the component part. In these circumstances, although the manufacturer may be liable to the claimant, the manufacturer will have
rights of recovery against the component producer. However, the
component producer may have supplied his component to the
manufacturer on terms that he, the component producer, is not
liable for any injury, loss or damage. In effect, therefore, by
accepting such a clause the manufacturer has destroyed his (and
thus his insurers') rights of recovery against the component
producer. Some insurers attempt to cover this situation by a
specific policy exclusion which provides that:

The insurer will not indemnify the insured against liability
arising from bodily injury loss of or damage arising from goods
obtained by the insured on terms which prevent the insured
exercising his rights of recovery under the ordinary process of
law against the supplier or any other party.

Product liability often arises only because of a contractual agreement. For example, the shopkeeper who sells a product to his
customer will be liable to the customer if the goods are defective
and cause him injury. This is because the normal process of
contract law will imply terms of fitness and merchantable quality

into the sale. Insurers do not intend to exclude that particular type
of contractual liability. Sometimes, therefore, the exclusion of
liability assumed by the insured under agreement is reworded to
make this clear. The following is an example:

> The insurer shall not be liable in respect of liability attaching to
> the insured by contract other than any liability attaching solely
> by reason of a contractual condition or warranty implied by
> statute or ordinance of Great Britain, Northern Ireland, the
> Channel Isles or the Isle of Man.

Thus liability attaching under the implied terms of the Sale of
Goods Act or the Supply of Goods (Implied Terms) Act 1973 would
not be excluded.

*'... any action for damages brought in the courts of law of
any territory outside Great Britain, Northern Ireland, the
Channel Islands and the Isle of Man in which the Insured has
a branch or is represented by an employee domiciled in such
territory or by a party holding the Insured's power of
attorney'*

Reference to this particular exclusion has already been made. The
policy gives cover for injury or damage occurring anywhere in the
world, provided the defective goods are sold or supplied from
premises in the UK. This exposes insurers to claims in foreign
countries, where they may be subject to foreign law and judicial
processes they do not understand. Where the insured has no
branch or no representation in the country in which he is being
sued, and no assets, the insured and his insurers may feel safe in
refusing to deal with the claim unless the action is brought in the
UK courts. Conversely, they may feel satisfied that they can
respond to any action in the overseas courts on the basis that they
can withdraw from the action at any time or not pay the damages if
they think the decision is wrong, on the basis that, as the insured
has no branch, representation or assets in the country, these
cannot be seized to satisfy the judgment.

If, however, the insured has a branch, representation or assets
in the country in question, there is always a risk that they may be
seized, thus putting pressure upon the insured and/or his insurers

to deal with any claim. The particular exclusion under consideration is an example of a clause used by insurers who are prepared to deal with claims in overseas territories provided the insured has no branch, representation or assets there, but not if he does.

Sometimes a clause may appear limiting claims to those brought in the UK courts only. The subject is a difficult one and deals with complicated matters of international law. It has become increasingly difficult because of the growing problem of forum shopping. In other words, the injured plaintiff or his lawyers will seek out the best country in which to bring the claim (which may be different from the country in which the injury or damage took place). For obvious reasons the USA is the main risk.

Some insurers with no overseas representation or claims-handling facilities are reluctant to enter into litigation abroad. Other insurers with worldwide representation and worldwide claims-handling facilities are more flexible. Suffice it to say that there is no uniformity in the product liability insurance market. Jurisdiction clauses – as such clauses are known – clearly represent limitations on an insured's protection, and where such clauses appear on a policy, the insured should understand what they mean and the limitation that exists in his cover.

'. . . bodily injury loss or damage arising directly or indirectly from the design plan formula or specification of any Goods or instruction advice or information on the characteristics use storage or application of any Goods'

In the earlier days of product liability insurance, before the great increase in technology, insurers took the view that they were covering claims arising out of defective products provided the defect arose during the manufacturing process. In many cases this was indeed the real risk. However, products need not necessarily be defective because of a manufacturing defect. The manufacturing process may be satisfactory and the real fault lie in the design or specification. Drugs are an obvious example.

There is a divergence of opinion among insurers as to whether these risks should be covered by insurance or not. Some insurers take the view that the risks should be treated as trade risks and covered by the insured himself, since insurers are not in business effectively to guarantee that the product will be designed correctly.

Other insurers take the view that the design risk is part and parcel of the product liability risk and are prepared to cover it. It is a risk, however, that requires careful consideration by the underwriter before he provides cover.

In reality the risk is that attaching to the manufacturer, since it is he who is normally responsible for the design, plan, formula or specification of the end product. Normally, therefore, it is the insurers' intention to apply the exclusion only to the manufacturer. Unfortunately not all policies make this clear and it is a matter for discussion with insurers. If, for example, the exclusion under consideration appeared on a retailer's policy, it would, strictly interpreted, deny the retailer cover for injury caused by a defective product arising from a design mistake by the manufacturer. Some policies do clarify this situation by making it clear that the exclusion only applies where the defect in the goods arises because of a defective design, plan, formula or specification *by the insured* of any goods sold or supplied.

The second part of the exclusion deals with instruction, advice or information on the characteristics, use, storage or application of any goods. Again market practice varies on this aspect. Some insurers are prepared to modify the exclusion, others are not. However, since advice and instruction are normally an inherent part of any sales activity, the ideal situation would be to have the exclusion removed.

One thing is important. The insurance market is normally prepared to cover liability arising out of wrong advice or information, provided that advice or information is part and parcel of a contract for the sale of a product. Product liability insurers, however, do not normally intend to cover liability arising out of advice or information on its own, not connected with the sale of a product. The reason for this is that most product liability insurers would regard this type of risk as a professional negligence risk rather than a product liability risk and as such insurable in the professional negligence market.

Although the point is an important one, it is often an area which is imprecisely defined in product liability insurance policies and an area where many persons may be uninsured. For example, the insured may be asked to advise a customer on the best type of boiler; the customer may accept the advice and commission the insured to manufacture, supply and install the boiler. There may be an explosion because the insured's advice was bad in recommending the wrong type of boiler. Most insurers would deal with this as a product liability claim, provided the exclusion under consideration had been deleted. But a change in the circumstances may result in a different interpretation. The customer may ask the insured's advice as to the type of boiler required but commission another firm to manufacture, supply and erect the boiler. While the insured may be responsible because his advice was bad, since the advice was not part and parcel of a contract where the insured supplied the goods themselves, many insurers would argue that this was not a risk they intended to cover – despite what a literal interpretation of the policy may say.

Where an insured is giving or selling advice or technical know-how which is not connected with the sale of a product, it is an issue to be discussed with the insurers, or the insured's professional advisers, since there is an area of risk which is probably not covered by the product liability policy.

The answer may be to provide some form of professional negligence insurance similar to the policies taken out by lawyers, accountants and other professional people. However, it is not a popular form of insurance with insurers at the time of writing (1987) because of large underwriting losses.

'... loss of or damage to or the repair alteration or the replacement of any Goods'

The object of the policy is to protect the insured against his legal liability for injury to third parties or damage to their property *caused* by the defective goods themselves. It is not the intention of the policy to pay for the costs of repairing, altering or replacing the faulty goods. Most insurers regard the repair or replacement of faulty products as a trade risk to be carried by the insured himself.

A retailer may sell a television set to a customer. The television set may be defective, causing damage to the house and its contents. Insurers will protect the retailer against his legal liability for damage but will not pay for the cost of repairing or replacing the television set.

In some policies the exception is expressed in such a way as probably not to convey the insurers' true intention. For example, the television set mentioned above may not be defective, it remains in the customer's house for many years, and the customer buys from the same shop another piece of equipment, perhaps a radio. In delivering it the employees of the retailer accidentally drop it on to the television set, causing damage to it. Strictly speaking, this claim would not be recoverable under the policy, since the policy excludes damage to any goods sold or supplied by the insured. It is unlikely, however, that insurers would refuse to deal with the claim for this reason. What they really intend to exclude is damage to products sold or supplied by the insured because of *defects* in those products, for example defective valves in the television set. One policy wording makes this clear by excluding liability in respect of damage to any product supplied by the insured if such damage is attributable to any defect therein or the harmful nature or unsuitability thereof.

Where the insured sells a relatively simple product, for example, a bath, a pair of shoes or a bookcase, there are no problems. Damage to the article sold is not covered. Where the insured supplies a much more complex product, which may itself be made up from many component parts, difficulties can arise. The insured may manufacture and supply a very complex piece of electrical equipment worth many millions of pounds. It may be damaged by fire or explosion because of a defect in a component part. Generally it is the intention of the exclusion to exclude liability for the total product, not just the part that was defective. Another difficult point often arises regarding the interpretation of this exception. Costs incurred in getting to the defective product to take it out or to replace it are also excluded. Thus a steel girder giving support to a building may be defective, causing cracks to appear. The cost of shoring up the building and taking out the steel girder would not be covered.

USA risks

Where there are exports to the USA or Canada or the policy covers companies domiciled in the USA or Canada, various limitations may apply. This is due to the litigious nature of people in America, the very high awards of damages – partly caused by lawyers operating on a contingency fee basis, that is, they make no charge if the claim is lost but take a percentage of the damages if the claim is won – the systems of strict liability and that awards are made by juries.

Typically the restrictions placed on policies by insurers include:

(1) the policy becomes a 'claims made' policy;
(2) legal costs incurred in the defence or settlement of the claim are included in the limit of indemnity, not an addition to it;
(3) punitive damages may be excluded;
(4) where the product may give rise to the risk of pollution or impairment of the environment this may be excluded;
(5) disease risks such as asbestosis may be excluded.

Ionizing, radiation and war risks

The following exclusion deals with risks not insurable in the commercial insurance market:

(a) any legal liability of whatsoever nature directly or indirectly caused by or contributed to by or arising from:
  (i) ionizing radiations or contamination by radioactivity from any nuclear fuel or from any nuclear waste from the combustion of nuclear fuel;
  (ii) the radioactive toxic explosive or other hazardous properties of any explosion nuclear assembly or nuclear component thereof;
(b) any consequence whether direct or indirect of war invasion act of foreign enemy hostilities (whether war be declared or not) civil war rebellion revolution insurrection or military or usurped power.

Other exceptions

The insurance market divides itself into compartments. Thus, specialized markets may exist to insure the product liability risk of aircraft component manufacturers or firms supplying products to the oil and gas industry. There may therefore be specific exclusions of liability arising out of products supplied *with the knowledge of the insured* to these industries.

The words in italics are important. If products finish up in these industries in circumstances where the insured never intended them to, the policy protects him.

31 Policy conditions

Why conditions appear

Conditions appear in most insurance policies. They set out certain matters that have to be complied with before insurers become obliged to deal with any claim under the policy. Most conditions are expressly set out in the policy for clarification, but some conditions may be implied into the policy by law, for example a duty to act in good faith.

Conditions precedent and subsequent

Conditions may be broadly classified into three groups. A breach of the condition will affect the validity of the policy or a claim under the policy in different ways, depending on the group into which the condition falls.

Conditions precedent to the policy

These are conditions which must be observed before the policy comes into legal effect. A breach of one of these conditions will render the policy void from inception. An obvious example of such a condition is that concerned with the duty of utmost good faith. The proposer is under a duty to disclose to the insurer any material fact which may affect the insurer's assessment of acceptance of the risk. Breach of the condition of good faith will thus make the policy void from inception.

Conditions subsequent to the policy

An example of such a condition is condition 3 in the specimen policy – the insured shall give notice to the insurer of any alteration or change in risk. A breach of this type of condition renders the policy voidable from the date of the breach.

Conditions precedent to liability

An example of such a condition is condition 4a in the specimen policy, regarding reporting of claims to insurers. A failure to comply with the terms of the condition gives insurers the right to refuse to deal with the claim. Thus the claim is not recoverable, but a breach of the condition does not affect the validity of the policy for future claims.

Condition 1: Interpretation

Any word or expression to which a specific meaning has been attached in any part of this Policy or Schedule shall bear such meaning wherever it may appear.

Strictly speaking, this is not a condition but is there merely for clarification. The modern method of preparing policies is to reduce all typewritten matter to one section of the policy, namely the policy schedule. To avoid constant reference and to aid interpretation the condition stipulates that where a word or expression has been given a specific meaning, it shall have that specific meaning wherever the word or expression is repeated in the policy.

Condition 2: Duty to take care

The Insured shall take and cause to be taken all reasonable precautions to

(a) prevent bodily injury and loss and damage to property and the sale or supply of goods which are defective in any way

(b) comply with all statutory obligations and regulations imposed by any authority.

Reasonable businessmen conduct their affairs in such a way as to prevent as far as possible the risk of accidents. Although taking out product liability cover is a sensible precaution, it is not a licence for the insured to run his business in a less careful manner. The insured is expected to take as many precautions to prevent accidents after taking out insurance as he would have done before taking it out.

The condition appears to be out of place in a liability policy which is intended to protect the insured against claims where he has not exercised all reasonable precautions. It is when the insured has not taken all reasonable precautions, that is, has been negligent, that he requires the protection of the policy. If insurers were entitled to place too literal an interpretation on this condition, the value of the policy to the insured would be very much reduced. In fact, insurers may only plead a breach of this condition if they can show that the insured has acted recklessly in disregard for the safety of life or property. Moreover, the condition is imposed upon the insured, not employees.

Condition 3: Duty to notify risk changes

The Insured shall give immediate notice to the Company of any alteration which materially affects the risk.

Matters which affect the insurers' assessment of the risk must be disclosed to them by virtue of this condition. It is a condition which is frequently overlooked when a policyholder launches into a new line of products. In addition, policyholders will often unwisely risk being in breach of this condition by failing to disclose to insurers a change of risk which they fear will increase the premium, for example modifications to an existing product which the insured knows enhance the risk of danger.

Condition 4: Duty to notify injury or damage

(a) The Insured shall give written notice to the Company of any bodily injury loss or damage or claim or proceeding immediately the same shall have come to the knowledge of the Insured or his representative.

(b) The Insured shall not admit liability for or negotiate the settlement of any claim without the written consent of the Company which shall be entitled to conduct in the name of the Insured the defence or settlement of any claim or to prosecute for its own benefit any claim for indemnity or damages or otherwise and shall have full discretion in the conduct of any proceedings and in the settlement of any claim and the Insured shall give all such information and assistance as the Company may require.

Clauses similar to this appear in all liability insurance policies. Since the cost of any claim payment will ultimately be made by the insurers on behalf of the insured, the sooner they are notified of any occurrence likely to give rise to a claim the better. A failure to notify claims for injury or damage may result in late investigation, with the consequent problems associated with absence of witnesses, failure to recall events which may be important and other matters. Moreover, the insured must not prejudice his insurers' position by any admission or denial of liability. Generally the insured will not be familiar with the legal position, and though admissions or denials of liability may be made with the best motives, they may complicate subsequent legal procedures.

The condition stipulates that the handling of the claim will be undertaken by the insurers, although in the insured's name.

Condition 5: Cancellation of policy

The company may cancel this Policy by sending thirty days' notice by registered letter to the Insured at his last known address and shall return to the Insured the Premium less the pro rata portion thereof for the period the Policy has been in force subject to adjustment under Condition (6).

This is a common condition found in many insurance policies. It is a condition often criticized for its unfairness, since it is the insurer only who has the right to cancel the policy, not the insured. Insurers justify their position by pointing out that they exercise the right only in infrequent circumstances where they have reason to suspect the morals of the insured.

Strict compliance with the condition is necessary. Notice of cancellation, for example, must be sent by registered letter, not by ordinary post. If it is not sent to the insured's last known address, again the notification is ineffective.

Condition 6: Information to adjust premium

If any part of the Premium is calculated on estimates the Insured shall within one month from the expiry of each Period of Insurance furnish such details as the Company may require and the premium for such period shall be adjusted subject to any Minimum Premium.

It is normal to regulate the premium as a rate per £1000 of turnover. The estimated turnover for the forthcoming twelve months of the policy is estimated in the first month and premium levied on this amount. Twelve months later the insured declares his actual turnover for the policy year. If his turnover exceeds the estimate, an additional premium is payable. If his turnover is less than the estimate, he is entitled to a refund.

Condition 7: More than one policy

If an indemnity is or would but for the existence of this insurance be granted by any other insurance the Company shall not provide indemnity except in respect of any excess beyond the amount which is or would but for the existence of this insurance be payable.

This is a technical condition, dealing with the position which applies when more than one policy may be in force to cover a claim. This frequently happens in practice.

Condition 8: Condition of liability

The liability of the Company shall be conditional on the observance by the Insured of the terms provisions conditions and endorsements of this Policy.

This is a general sweeping-up condition, requiring the insured to comply with any terms and conditions of the policy before he is entitled to indemnity. In practice policy conditions are broken frequently. Insurers do not attempt to evade responsibility under their policies for minor breaches, but they do reserve their rights where they feel that there has been a major breach of one of the conditions and their position has thus been prejudiced. An example would be a breach of condition 4(b), where the insured has attempted to deal with a claim himself, made damaging admissions of liability, become threatened with legal proceedings and then passes the matter to his insurers.

32   Extensions to the policy

Liability under agreement

As one of the terms of doing business one person may quite frequently have to give an indemnity to another person against certain risks. Since such indemnities very often extend the normal common law position, they are treated by the insurer as underwriting considerations requiring close examination and thus are excluded from the terms of the basic policy being discussed by means of the exclusion of liability assumed under agreement. The risks can be covered, provided full details are given to the insurer to enable him to assess the risk and premium.

In practice one person may have to give an indemnity to another person and therefore requires an amendment to the contractual liability exclusion. For example, a food manufacturer may find that because a high percentage of his turnover goes to one large department store, that store can extract from him an indemnity to the effect that he indemnifies the store in respect of any claim against the store for injury to persons or damage to property arising out of the food manufactured. The terms of the indemnity may be wide enough to make the manufacturer liable even though injury or damage is really the negligence of the store not the manufacturer, for example overlong storage resulting in the food deteriorating. In effect, therefore, an insurer who opens up his policy to cover this assumed liability is also picking up part of the liability of the department store.

Although insurance officials talk loosely of extending the policy 'to include liability assumed under agreement', it is necessary to remember that not all aspects of the liability assumed under contract are covered by the policy. Other terms, limitations and exclusions of the policy still apply. For example, the policy will still not pay for the cost of repairing or replacing the faulty product. It is not every aspect of liability assumed under the agreement which is picked up by the policy but only the manufacturer's liability for injury to third parties or accidental loss of or damage to third party property.

Adding another party as a named insured

This often flows from the point discussed above. The department store, while taking a written indemnity from the manufacturer, may realize that the indemnity is worthless if the manufacturer does not have sufficient funds to back it up. Therefore, as one of the terms of his contract, in addition to requiring a written indemnity from the manufacturer the store may go on to say that the manufacturer's policy must be extended to indemnify the store in like manner to the manufacturer. Thus the store gets protection against third party claims under the manufacturer's policy.

By becoming a named insured the department store is subject to the terms, exceptions and conditions of the policy in just the same way as the original insured.

Financial loss

As has been explained, the policy protects the insured against his legal liability for accidental bodily injury to third parties or accidental damage to third party property. Provided there is this direct injury or damage, the financial losses or consequential losses flowing from that injury or damage are also protected by the policy.

Circumstances may arise where the claim made against the

insured is not dependent upon injury to third parties or damage to property. The claim may be a claim for a purely financial or economic loss. In that case no protection is afforded by the policy.

Some insurers are prepared to provide this cover. An example of a situation where it may be required has already been given. A manufacturer may supply a machine to provide power to a factory. The machine may be defective, as a result of which the factory is deprived of power. It therefore sustains a loss of production and makes a claim against the manufacturer for the lost production.

An example of wording providing this sort of cover is:

This policy extends to include liability for financial loss (even if not accompanied by loss of or damage to property) sustained by a customer or user of any goods supplied by the insured if such loss is a direct result of a defective or harmful condition of such goods or their failure to perform a function for which they were supplied by the insured.

Provided that this extension shall not apply to liability in respect of:
(a) The cost of repairing replacing or recalling such goods.
(b) The first 20 per cent of the loss, which amount shall be retained by the insured as his own liability and uninsured.

The 20 per cent of the claim borne by the insured is a variable factor, depending upon the degree of risk, or the underwriters' assessment of the risk. It should be noted that the cost of repairing, replacing or recalling defective goods is still an excluded risk.

There are many other different wordings in use. Some of them are on a 'claims made' basis. The wordings have to be studied carefully to make sure they give the insured what he wants. Often there will be specific areas of risk excluded, for example professional negligence, the cost of repairing or replacing defective products and claims for infringement of patents, trade names or other intellectual property.

Products guarantee

Two major limitations in a product liability policy are the exclusion of the cost of repairing or replacing the defective product and the limitation to physical injury to third parties or physical damage to third party property. A market exists to pick up these deficiencies by means of the issue of a separate policy known in the insurance market as a 'products guarantee policy'. It is necessary to point out that such risks are underwritten in only a small section of the market and the cover is not universally available.

The aim of a products guarantee policy is to protect the insured against his legal liability arising out of the failure of his products to fulfil their intended function. It will thus pay for the cost of repairing or replacing a faulty product and also for financial losses flowing from such defective products where there is no injury to third parties or damage to third party property.

Thus, in the example of a machine failing to supply power to a factory the products guarantee policy will protect the insured against his legal liability to repair or replace the faulty machine and also for the consequential losses sustained by the claimant. It may also be possible to extend such a policy to protect the insured against the cost of recalling defective products.

An extension to a products guarantee policy is one of the few ways in which product-recall cover can be obtained. Generally it is not a form of cover which insurers are prepared to grant.

There is often some confusion over the difference between a products guarantee policy and a financial loss extension to a product liability policy. In fact there is much similarity between them. The only difference is that the products guarantee policy extends to include the repair or replacement of the defective product itself – something which the financial loss extension does not do.

Directors and employees

The policy indemnifies the insured, normally a partnership or company. It is normally the partnership or company which is sued, not individual employees. Nevertheless most policies do grant a personal indemnity to partners, directors, managers and other employees so that they obtain protection under the policy in like manner to the insured.

Cost and expenses of criminal proceedings

The policy provides protection against civil liability to pay damages to third parties plus the legal costs and expenses of the defence or settlement of a claim. Criminal charges or prosecutions are not within its scope.

It is nevertheless possible to arrange insurance to indemnify the insured (or directors, managers or employees of the insured) against the legal costs and expenses incurred in the defence of criminal charges or proceedings arising out of infringement of various statutes, for example the Health and Safety At Work Act, the Consumer Protection Act 1987 or any appeal. The policy will not pay for any fines or penalties imposed.

Cross-liabilities

Where there is more than one party named as the insured, for example parent or subsidiaries or suppliers or agent, since each technically becomes the insured the cover may unwittingly be reduced in the sense that the policy does not provide protection if one party insured by the policy sues another party insured by the policy. This matter may be put right by incorporating a cross-liabilities clause which states that where there is more than one party named as the insured the policy shall apply separately to each party so that in reality the policy is construed as though a separate policy had been issued to each insured. However, the insurers' limit of liability is not increased beyond that stated in the policy, for example if the limit is £1 million, that is £1 million for all the parties not £1 million for each insured party.

Retrospective cover

As was explained earlier, the policy protects the insured against his liability for injury or damage occurring during the period of insurance. Injury or damage may occur without the insured being aware of it. The products may be causing a risk and the injury may be progressive. The litigation arising out of asbestosis is an example. The problem for the insured is that he may have had no insurance cover at the time the injury or damage 'occurred'. Even if he had cover it may have been for an inadequate amount (in the early 1960s many manufacturers did not buy product liability insurance or bought it for low limits of indemnity such as £100 000). In addition, the policies issued in the early 1960s were often restricted, for example by exclusions of liability arising out of design, plan, specification or formula. The insured may, therefore, run the risk that he may be sued today for injury or damage which occurred many years ago.

Provided he can trace the policies that applied many years previously he will be covered by them for injury or damage occurring during their period of cover (subject to their limitations and conditions), but those policies may be inadequate or – what is more to the point – the insured may not be able to trace them. It may, therefore, be possible to extend the current policy to indemnify the insured in respect of claims made against him during the currency of the policy for injury or damage which preceded its inception date. Of course, such an extension requires careful underwriting information and the policies are issued on the basis that the insured is not aware of any circumstance which might give rise to a claim against him. Insurers are intending to insure against some fortuitous or accidental event – not certainties.

Excess of loss policies

Where the insured requires a high limit of indemnity, say £25 million or over, it is necessary to have the policies 'layered'. In other words, a series of policies are arranged so that one sits on top of the other, for example £1 million first policy, £4 million second policy, £10 million third policy and so on. Each policy constitutes a separate contract with the insurers and each is subject to the insured disclosing all material information to the insurers. What is important is that each policy should follow the first policy word for word so that the cover is common throughout. In the difficult market conditions which apply in the late 1980s it may not be possible to achieve this since some of the insurers on the top layers may not be prepared to give the cover granted by the lower layers, particularly if there is a USA exposure.

Residual product liability

It has been emphasized more than once that the policy applies only
to the business described in the policy. It is important to describe
the business correctly. However, over the years the business may
have changed. The insured may be a paint manufacturer now but
years ago he may have been a chemical manufacturer. Those
chemicals, even though sold many years ago, are still capable of
causing injury or damage or claims against the insured during the
currency of his present policy. They would not be covered,
however, since they would not relate to the business of paint
manufacture. The policy may be extended to cover claims arising
out of products sold previously but not directly related to the
insured's current description of occupation.

In conclusion

So we have woven together all the strands of liability for defective products – contractual and tortious, by agreement and in negligence, in civil and in criminal law. Strict liability, in reasonable harmony with other EEC legal jurisdictions, has descended upon the UK scene. The hideous tragedies of Thalidomide sparked off bitter anger which, many years later, has led to new protection for consumers against death, injury or damage due to defective products.

Like all statutes, especially those of recent creation, the Consumer Protection Act enjoys enough obscurity in its phrasing to keep lawyers and judges happily at work. Sufficient unto the test cases be the interpretations thereof. Where possible, we have indicated our view of the likely (or at least, of the intended, parliamentary) meaning of the language used. But those concerned with product liability law must watch for change.

Neither is the Act beyond controversy. Like Lord Pearson, chairman and father of the Royal Commission on Civil Liability, I do not believe that the 'state of the art' defence should have been included. I hope that it will not take the anger and anguish of some future Thalidomide misery to remove it by amendment. Meanwhile, it exists; it will be interpreted, misinterpreted and reinterpreted; and 'producers', as well as importers into the EEC and

223

'own-branders', should at least know the basis and basics of product liability law – and should certainly look to their insurance cover.

We hope that you will have found this book approachable, understandable and readable – with the details accessible through the index. To understand the new product liability law, you must set it into the context and reality of the entire legal scene, civil and criminal, affecting liability for defective products.

With the law at your side, what you now need is good fortune to keep as far away from it as knowledge, cunning, care, concern and (above all) good luck can achieve.

Good luck, then!

Greville Janner

APPENDICES

APPENDICES

Appendix A   Specimen product liability policy

Whereas the Insured carrying on the business described in the Schedule and no other for the purposes of this insurance by a proposal and declaration which shall be the basis of this contract and is deemed to be incorporated herein has applied to the company (hereinafter called 'the Company') for the insurance hereinafter contained and has paid or agreed to pay the Premium as consideration for such insurance.

The Company will subject to the terms exceptions and conditions of this Policy indemnify the Insured against all sums which the Insured shall become legally liable to pay as damages in respect of

(1) accidental bodily injury (including death or disease) to any person
(2) accidental loss of or damage to property

happening anywhere in the world elsewhere than at premises owned or occupied by the Insured during the Period of Insurance and caused by any Goods sold supplied repaired altered treated or serviced from or in Great Britain, Northern Ireland, the Channel Islands and the Isle of Man in connection with the Business.

The Company will also pay legal costs and expenses recoverable by any claimant and all costs and expenses incurred with the written consent of the Company plus solicitor's fees incurred with the written consent of the Company for representation of the Insured at any coroner's inquest or fatal enquiry arising from any death proceedings in any court of summary jurisdiction arising out of any alleged breach of a statutory duty resulting in bodily injury or loss of or damage to property which may be the subject of a claim under this insurance.

Limit of indemnity

The liability of the Company for all damages in respect of all bodily injury loss or damage happening in any one Period of Insurance shall not in the aggregate exceed the Limit of Indemnity.

Exceptions

The Company will not indemnify the Insured against liability arising from

(1) bodily injury sustained by an employee and arising out of and in the course of his employment by the Insured
(2) loss of or damage to property belonging to or in the custody or control of the Insured
(3) liability assumed by the Insured under agreement unless such liability would have attached in the absence of such an agreement
(4) any action for damages brought in the courts of law of any territory outside Great Britain, Northern Ireland, the Channel Islands and the Isle of Man in which the Insured has a branch or is represented by an employee domiciled in such territory or by a party holding the Insured's power of attorney
(5) bodily injury loss or damage arising directly or indirectly from the design plan formula or specification of any Goods or instruction advice or information on the characteristics use storage or application of any Goods
(6) loss of or damage to or the repair alteration or the replacement of any Goods
(7) the Company will not indemnify the Insured in respect of
  (a) any legal liability of whatsoever nature directly or indirectly caused by or contributed to by or arising from

(i) ionizing radiations or contamination by radioactivity from any nuclear fuel or from any nuclear waste from the combustion of nuclear fuel

(ii) the radioactive toxic explosive or other hazardous properties of any explosion nuclear assembly or nuclear component thereof

(b) any consequence whether direct or indirect of war invasion act of foreign enemy hostilities (whether war be declared or not) civil war rebellion revolution insurrection or military or usurped power.

Conditions

(1) Any word or expression to which a specific meaning has been attached in any part of this Policy or Schedule shall bear such meaning wherever it may appear.

(2) The insured shall take and cause to be taken all reasonable precautions to

(a) prevent bodily injury and loss and damage to property and the sale or supply of goods which are defective in any way

(b) comply with all statutory obligations and regulations imposed by any authority.

(3) The Insured shall give immediate notice to the Company of any alteration which materially affects the risk.

(4) (a) The Insured shall give written notice to the Company of any bodily injury loss or damage or claim or proceeding immediately the same shall have come to the knowledge of the Insured or his representative.

(b) The Insured shall not admit liability for or negotiate the settlement of any claim without the written consent of the Company which shall be entitled to conduct in the name of the Insured the defence or settlement of any claim or to prosecute for its own benefit any claim for indemnity or damages or otherwise and shall have full discretion in the conduct of any proceedings and in the settlement of any claim and the Insured shall give all such information and assistance as the Company may require.

(5) The Company may cancel this Policy by sending thirty days' notice by registered letter to the Insured at his last known

address and shall return to the Insured the Premium less the pro rata portion thereof for the period the Policy has been in force subject to adjustment under Condition (6).

(6) If any part of the Premium is calculated on estimates the Insured shall within one month from the expiry of each Period of Insurance furnish such details as the Company may require and the premium for such period shall be adjusted subject to any Minimum Premium.

(7) If an indemnity is or would but for the existence of this insurance be granted by any other insurance the Company shall not provide indemnity except in respect of any excess beyond the amount which is or would but for the existence of this insurance be payable.

(8) The liability of the Company shall be conditional on the observance by the Insured of the terms provisions conditions and endorsements of this Policy.

Policy no.   *Branch*
Renewal date

The Schedule

The Insured: Name
                      Address

The Business:

Period of Insurance: (a) From the   to the
                                      (b) Any subsequent period for which the Insured shall pay and the Company shall agree to accept a renewal premium.

Premium: £
Subject to adjustment in terms of Condition 6

Renewal Premium: £   £
Subject to adjustment in terms of Condition 6

Signed this   day of   19   Checked

Appendix B   Specimen product liability proposal form

1 Name of proposer and address   . . . .
. . . .
2 How long established   . . . .

3 Give full description of goods manufactured, sold, supplied, repaired, serviced, tested or processed and estimated turnover.
(a) Manufactured by you: . . . .
. . . .
Estimated turnover: £. . . . . . .
(b) Sold or supplied but not   . . . .
manufactured by you: . . . .
Estimated turnover: £. . . . . . .
(c) Repaired, serviced, tested   . . . .
or processed by you: . . . .
Estimated turnover: £. . . . . . .

4 Do you supply goods for use   . . . .
in nuclear, aircraft or marine
industries?
5 (a) Do you import any   . . . .
goods?   . . . .
If so give details.   . . . .

(b) Do you export any   ....
goods?   ....
If so give details.

(c) If you give any indemnity to importers or exporters please supply details:

Imported		Exported	
Country	Turnover	Country	Turnover
....	....	....	....
....	....	....	....
....	....	....	....
....	....	....	....
....	....	....	....
....	....	....	....

6 Give full details of any claims made against you during the past five years:

Year	Total No. of claims	Settled		Outstanding	
		Number	Cost	Number	Cost
19 ...	....	....	....	....	....
19 ...	....	....	....	....	....
19 ...	....	....	....	....	....
19 ...	....	....	....	....	....
19 ...	....	....	....	....	....

7 Please state limit of indemnity   ....
required

8 Please attach copies of any instruction manuals, labels or other literature supplied with your goods or services.

9 (a) Have you previously been
insured for product liability   ....
risks? If so please give   ....
details.

(b) Has any insurer refused to
insure you or imposed
special terms and
conditions. If so please   ....
give details.   ....

I/We the undersigned desire to effect an insurance in terms of the policy to be issued by the insurance company.

I/We hereby declare that all the statements and particulars given by me/us in this proposal are correct and that no material fact has been omitted misrepresented or misstated, and I am/we are not aware of any other circumstance likely to affect the risk. I/We agree that the statements in the proposal shall form the basis of the contract between the company and me/us.

Date .... 19...   Signature ....

Appendix C Extracts from the Consumer Protection Act 1987

Sections 1–9, 45, 46 and 50 and Schedules 1 and 3

PRODUCT LIABILITY

Purpose and
construction of
Part I.

1.—(1) This Part shall have effect for the purpose of making such provision as is necessary in order to comply with the product liability Directive and shall be construed accordingly.

(2) In this Part, except in so far as the context otherwise requires—

'agricultural produce' means any produce of the soil, of stockfarming or of fisheries;

1976 c. 30.
1976 c. 13.

'dependant' and 'relative' have the same meaning as they have in, respectively, the Fatal Accidents Act 1976 and the Damages (Scotland) Act 1976;

'producer', in relation to a product, means—

(a) the person who manufactured it;

(b) in the case of a substance which has not been manufactured but has been won or abstracted, the person who won or abstracted it;

(c) in the case of a product which has not Part I been manufactured, won or abstracted but essential characteristics of which are attributable to an industrial or other process having been carried out (for example, in relation to agricultural produce), the person who carried out that process;

'product' means any goods or electricity and (subject to subsection (3) below) includes a product which is comprised in another product, whether by virtue of being a component part or raw material or otherwise; and

'the product liability Directive' means the Directive of the Council of the European Communities, dated 25th July 1985, (No. 85/374/EEC) on the approximation of the laws, regulations and administrative provisions of the member States concerning liability for defective products.

(3) For the purposes of this Part a person who supplies any product in which products are comprised, whether by virtue of being component parts or raw materials or otherwise, shall not be treated by reason only of his supply of that product as supplying any of the products so comprised.

2.—(1) Subject to the following provisions of this Part, Liability for where any damage is caused wholly or partly by a defect in defective products. a product, every person to whom subsection (2) below applies shall be liable for the damage.

(2) This subsection applies to—
  (a) the producer of the product;
  (b) any person who, by putting his name on the product or using a trade mark or other distinguishing mark in relation to the product, has held himself out to be the producer of the product;
  (c) any person who has imported the product into a member State from a place outside the member States in order, in the course of any business of his, to supply it to another.

(3) Subject as aforesaid, where any damage is caused wholly or partly by a defect in a product, any person who supplied the product (whether to the person who suffered the damage, to the producer of any product in which the product in question is comprised or to any other person) shall be liable for the damage if—

   (a) the person who suffered the damage requests the supplier to identify one or more of the persons (whether still in existence or not) to whom subsection (2) above applies in relation to the product;

   (b) that request is made within a reasonable period after the damage occurs and at a time when it is not reasonably practicable for the person making the request to identify all those persons; and

   (c) the supplier fails, within a reasonable period after receiving the request, either to comply with the request or to identify the person who supplied the product to him.

(4) Neither subsection (2) nor subsection (3) above shall apply to a person in respect of any defect in any game or agricultural produce if the only supply of the game or produce by that person to another was at a time when it had not undergone an industrial process.

(5) Where two or more persons are liable by virtue of this Part for the same damage, their liability shall be joint and several.

(6) This section shall be without prejudice to any liability arising otherwise than by virtue of this Part.

Meaning of 'defect'.

3.—(1)Subject to the following provisions of this section, there is a defect in a product for the purposes of this Part if the safety of the product is not such as persons generally are entitled to expect; and for those purposes 'safety', in relation to a product, shall include safety with respect to products comprised in that product and safety in the context of risks of damage to property, as well as in the context of risks of death or personal injury.

(2) In determining for the purposes of subsection (1) above what persons generally are entitled to expect in relation to a product all the circumstances shall be taken into account, including—

(a) the manner in which, and purposes for which, the product has been marketed, its get-up, the use of any mark in relation to the product and any instructions for, or warnings with respect to, doing or refraining from doing anything with or in relation to the product;

(b) what might reasonably be expected to be done with or in relation to the product; and

(c) the time when the product was supplied by its producer to another;

and nothing in this section shall require a defect to be inferred from the fact alone that the safety of a product which is supplied after that time is greater than the safety of the product in question.

4.—(1) In any civil proceedings by virtue of this Part Defences. against any person ('the person proceeded against') in respect of a defect in a product it shall be a defence for him to show—

(a) that the defect is attributable to compliance with any requirement imposed by or under any enactment or with any Community obligation; or

(b) that the person proceeded against did not at any time supply the product to another; or

(c) that the following conditions are satisfied, that is to say—

(i) that the only supply of the product to another by the person proceeded against was otherwise than in the course of a business of that person's; and

(ii) that section 2(2) above does not apply to that person or applies to him by virtue only of things done otherwise than with a view to profit; or

(d) that the defect did not exist in the product at the relevant time; or

    (e) that the state of scientific and technical knowledge at the relevant time was not such that a producer of products of the same description as the product in question might be expected to have discovered the defect if it had existed in his products while they were under his control; or

    (f) that the defect—

        (i) constituted a defect in a product('the subsequent product') in which the product in question had been comprised; and

        (ii) was wholly attributable to the design of the subsequent product or to compliance by the producer of the product in question with instructions given by the producer of the subsequent product.

(2) In this section 'the relevant time', in relation to electricity, means the time at which it was generated, being a time before it was transmitted or distributed, and in relation to any other product, means—

    (a) if the person proceeded against is a person to whom subsection (2) of section 2 above applies in relation to the product, the time when he supplied the product to another;

    (b) if that subsection does not apply to that person in relation to the product, the time when the product was last supplied by a person to whom that subsection does apply in relation to the product.

5.—(1) Subject to the following provisions of this section, in this Part 'damage' means death or personal injury or any loss of or damage to any property (including land).

(2) A person shall not be liable under section 2 above in respect of any defect in a product for the loss of or any damage to the product itself or for the loss of or any damage to the whole or any part of any product which has been supplied with the product in question comprised in it.

(3) A person shall not be liable under section 2 above for any loss of or damage to any property which, at the time it is lost or damaged, is not—

    (a) of a description of property ordinarily intended for private use, occupation or consumption; and

(b) intended by the person suffering the loss or Part I damage mainly for his own private use, occupation or consumption.

(4) No damages shall be awarded to any person by virtue of this Part in respect of any loss of or damage to any property if the amount which would fall to be so awarded to that person, apart from this subsection and any liability for interest, does not exceed £275.

(5) In determining for the purposes of this Part who has suffered any loss of or damage to property and when any such loss or damage occurred, the loss or damage shall be regarded as having occurred at the earliest time at which a person with an interest in the property had knowledge of the material facts about the loss or damage.

(6) For the purposes of subsection (5) above the material facts about any loss of or damage to any property are such facts about the loss or damage as would lead a reasonable person with an interest in the property to consider the loss or damage sufficiently serious to justify his instituting proceedings for damages against a defendant who did not dispute liability and was able to satisfy a judgment.

(7) For the purposes of subsection (5) above a person's knowledge includes knowledge which he might reasonably have been expected to acquire—

(a) from facts observable or ascertainable by him; or
(b) from facts ascertainable by him with the help of appropriate expert advice which it is reasonable for him to seek;

but a person shall not be taken by virtue of this subsection to have knowledge of a fact ascertainable by him only with the help of expert advice unless he has failed to take all reasonable steps to obtain (and, where appropriate, to act on) that advice.

(8) Subsections (5) to (7) above shall not extend to Scotland.

Application of
certain enactments
etc.
1976 c. 30.

1940 c. 42.

1976 c. 13.

1982 c. 53.

6.—(1) Any damage for which a person is liable under section 2 above shall be deemed to have been caused—

(a) for the purposes of the Fatal Accidents Act 1976, by that person's wrongful act, neglect or default;

(b) for the purposes of section 3 of the Law Reform (Miscellaneous Provisions) (Scotland) Act 1940 (contribution among joint wrongdoers), by that person's wrongful act or negligent act or omission;

(c) for the purposes of section 1 of the Damages (Scotland) Act 1976 (rights of relatives of a deceased), by that person's act or omission; and

(d) for the purposes of Part II of the Administration of Justice Act 1982 (damages for personal injuries, etc. – Scotland), by an act or omission giving rise to liability in that person to pay damages.

(2) Where—

(a) a person's death is caused wholly or partly by a defect in a product, or a person dies after suffering damage which has been so caused;

(b) a request such as mentioned in paragraph (a) of subsection (3) of section 2 above is made to a supplier of the product by that person's personal representatives or, in the case of a person whose death is caused wholly or partly by the defect, by any dependant or relative of that person; and

(c) the conditions specified in paragraphs (b) and (c) of that subsection are satisfied in relation to that request,

1934 c. 41.

this Part shall have effect for the purposes of the Law Reform (Miscellaneous Provisions) Act 1934, the Fatal Accidents Act 1976 and the Damages (Scotland) Act 1976 as if liability of the supplier to that person under that subsection did not depend on that person having requested the supplier to identify certain persons or on the said conditions having been satisfied in relation to a request made by that person.

(3) Section 1 of the Congenital Disabilities (Civil Liability) Act 1976 shall have effect for the purposes of this Part as if—

(a) a person were answerable to a child in respect of an occurrence caused wholly or partly by a defect in a product if he is or has been liable under section 2 above in respect of any effect of the ocurrence on a parent of the child, or would be so liable if the occurrence caused a parent of the child to suffer damage;

(b) the provisions of this Part relating to liability under section 2 above applied in relation to liability by virtue of paragraph (a) above under the said section 1; and

(c) subsection (6) of the said section 1 (exclusion of liability) were omitted.

(4) Where any damage is caused partly by a defect in a product and partly by the fault of the person suffering the damage, the Law Reform (Contributory Negligence) Act 1945 and section 5 of the Fatal Accidents Act 1976 (contributory negligence) shall have effect as if the defect were the fault of every person liable by virtue of this Part for the damage caused by the defect.

(5) In subsection (4) above 'fault' has the same meaning as in the said Act of 1945.

(6) Schedule 1 to this Act shall have effect for the purpose of amending the Limitation Act 1980 and the Prescription and Limitation (Scotland) Act 1973 in their application in relation to the bringing of actions by virtue of this Part.

(7) It is hereby declared that liability by virtue of this Part is to be treated as liability in tort for the purposes of any enactment conferring jurisdiction on any court with respect to any matter.

(8) Nothing in this Part shall prejudice the operation of section 12 of the Nuclear Installations Act 1965 (rights to compensation for certain breaches of duties confined to rights under that Act).

Prohibition on
exclusions from
liability.

7. The liability of a person by virtue of this Part to a person who has suffered damage caused wholly or partly by a defect in a product, or to a dependant or relative of such a person, shall not be limited or excluded by any contract term, by any notice or by any other provision.

Power to modify
Part I.

8.—(1) Her Majesty may by Order in Council make such modifications of this Part and of any other enactment (including an enactment contained in the following Parts of this Act, or in an Act passed after this Act) as appear to Her Majesty in Council to be necessary or expedient in consequence of any modification of the product liability Directive which is made at any time after the passing of this Act.

(2) An Order in Council under subsection (1) above shall not be submitted to Her Majesty in Council unless a draft of the Order has been laid before, and approved by a resolution of, each House of Parliament.

Application of
Part I to Crown.

9.—(1) Subject to subsection (2) below, this Part shall bind the Crown.

(2) The Crown shall not, as regards the Crown's liability by virtue of this Part, be bound by this Part further than the Crown is made liable in tort or in reparation under the Crown Proceedings Act 1947, as that Act has effect from time to time.

1947 c. 44.

Interpretation.

45.—(1) In this Act, except in so far as the context otherwise requires—

'aircraft' includes gliders, balloons and hovercraft;

'business' includes a trade or profession and the activities of a professional or trade association or of a local authority or other public authority;

'conditional sale agreement', 'credit-sale agreement' and 'hire-purchase agreement' have the same meanings as in the Consumer Credit Act 1974 but as if in the definitions in that Act 'goods' had the same meaning as in this Act;

1974 c. 39.

'contravention' includes a failure to comply and cognate expressions shall be construed accordingly;

'enforcement authority' means the Secretary of State, any other Minister of the Crown in charge of a Government department, any such department and any authority, council or other person on whom functions under this Act are conferred by or under section 27 above;

'gas' has the same meaning as in Part I of the Gas Act 1986;

'goods' includes substances, growing crops and things comprised in land by virtue of being attached to it and any ship, aircraft or vehicle;

'information' includes accounts, estimates and returns;

'magistrates' court', in relation to Northern Ireland, means a court of summary jurisdiction;

'mark' and 'trade mark' have the same meanings as in the Trade Marks Act 1938;

'modifications' includes additions, alterations and omissions, and cognate expressions shall be construed accordingly;

'motor vehicle' has the same meaning as in the Road Traffic Act 1972;

'notice' means a notice in writing;

'notice to warn' means a notice under section 13(1)(b) above;

'officer', in relation to an enforcement authority, means a person authorised in writing to assist the authority in carrying out its functions under or for the purposes of the enforcement of any of the safety provisions or of any of the provisions made by or under Part III of this Act;

'personal injury' includes any disease and any other impairment of a person's physical or mental condition;

'premises' includes any place and any ship, aircraft or vehicle;

'prohibition notice' means a notice under section 13(1)(a) above;

'records' includes any books or documents and any records in non-documentary form;

'safety provision' means the general safety requirement in section 10 above or any provision of safety regulations, a prohibition notice or a suspension notice;

'safety regulations' means regulations under section 11 above;

'ship' includes any boat and any other description of vessel used in navigation;

'subordinate legislation' has the same meaning as in the Interpretation Act 1978;

'substance' means any natural or artificial substance, whether in solid, liquid or gaseous form or in the form of a vapour, and includes substances that are comprised in or mixed with other goods;

'supply' and cognate expressions shall be construed in accordance with section 46 below;

'suspension notice' means a notice under section 14 above.

(2) Except in so far as the context otherwise requires, references in this Act to a contravention of a safety provision shall, in relation to any goods, include references to anything which would constitute such a contravention if the goods were supplied to any person.

(3) References in this Act to any goods in relation to which any safety provision has been or may have been contravened shall include references to any goods which it is not reasonably practicable to separate from any such goods.

(4) Section 68(2) of the Trade Marks Act 1938 (construction of references to use of a mark) shall apply for the purposes of this Act as it applies for the purposes of that Act.

(5) In Scotland, any reference in this Act to things comprised in land by virtue of being attached to it is a reference to moveables which have become heritable by accession to heritable property.

46.—(1) Subject to the following provisions of this section, references in this Act to supplying goods shall be

construed as references to doing any of the following, PART V
whether as principal or agent, that is to say—

(a) selling, hiring out or lending the goods;
(b) entering into a hire-purchase agreement to furnish the goods;
(c) the performance of any contract for work and materials to furnish the goods;
(d) providing the goods in exchange for any consideration (including trading stamps) other than money;
(e) providing the goods in or in connection with the performance of any statutory function; or
(f) giving the goods as a prize or otherwise making a gift of the goods;

and, in relation to gas or water, those references shall be construed as including references to providing the service by which the gas or water is made available for use.

(2) For the purposes of any reference in this Act to supplying goods, where a person ('the ostensible supplier') supplies goods to another person ('the customer') under a hire-purchase agreement, conditional sale agreement or credit-sale agreement or under an agreement for the hiring of goods (other than a hire-purchase agreement) and the ostensible supplier—

(a) carries on the business of financing the provision of goods for others by means of such agreements; and
(b) in the course of that business acquired his interest in the goods supplied to the customer as a means of financing the provision of them for the customer by a further person ('the effective supplier'),

the effective supplier and not the ostensible supplier shall be treated as supplying the goods to the customer.

(3) Subject to subsection (4) below, the performance of any contract by the erection of any building or structure on any land or by the carrying out of any other building works shall be treated for the purposes of this Act as a supply of goods in so far as, but only in so far as, it involves the provision of any goods to any person by means of their incorporation into the building, structure or works.

(4) Except for the purposes of, and in relation to, notices to warn or any provision made by or under Part III of this Act, references in this Act to supplying goods shall not include references to supplying goods comprised in land where the supply is effected by the creation or disposal of an interest in the land.

(5) Except in Part I of this Act references in this Act to a person's supplying goods shall be confined to references to that person's supplying goods in the course of a business of his, but for the purposes of this subsection it shall be immaterial whether the business is a business of dealing in the goods.

(6) For the purposes of subsection (5) above goods shall not be treated as supplied in the course of a business if they are supplied, in pursuance of an obligation arising under or in connection with the insurance of the goods, to the person with whom they were insured.

(7) Except for the purposes of, and in relation to, prohibition notices or suspension notices, references in Parts II to IV of this Act to supplying goods shall not include—

  (a) references to supplying goods where the person supplied carries on a business of buying goods of the same description as those goods and repairing or reconditioning them:

  (b) references to supplying goods by a sale of articles as scrap (that is to say, for the value of materials included in the articles rather than for the value of the articles themselves).

(8) Where any goods have at any time been supplied by being hired out or lent to any person, neither a continuation or renewal of the hire or loan (whether on the same or different terms) nor any transaction for the transfer after that time of any interest in the goods to the person to whom they were hired or lent shall be treated for the purposes of this Act as a further supply of the goods to that person.

(9) A ship, aircraft or motor vehicle shall not be treated for the purposes of this Act as supplied to any person by reason only that services consisting in the carriage of goods

or passengers in that ship, aircraft or vehicle, or in its use
for any other purpose, are provided to that person in
pursuance of an agreement relating to the use of the ship,
aircraft or vehicle for a particular period or for particular
voyages, flights or journeys.

PART V

50.—(1) This Act may be cited as the Consumer
Protection Act 1987.

Short title,
commencement
and transitional
provision.

(2) This Act shall come into force on such day as the
Secretary of State may by order made by statutory instrument appoint, and different days may be so appointed for
different provisions or for different purposes.

(3) The Secretary of State shall not make an order
under subsection (2) above bringing into force the repeal
of the Trade Descriptions Act 1972, a repeal of any
provision of that Act or a repeal of that Act or of any
provision of it for any purposes, unless a draft of the order
has been laid before, and approved by a resolution of,
each House of Parliament.

1972 c. 34.

(4) An order under subsection (2) above bringing a
provision into force may contain such transitional provision in connection with the coming into force of that
provision as the Secretary of State considers appropriate.

(5) Without prejudice to the generality of the power
conferred by subsection (4) above, the Secretary of State
may by order provide for any regulations made under the
Consumer Protection Act 1961 or the Consumer Protection
Act (Northern Ireland) 1965 to have effect as if made
under section 11 above and for any such regulations to
have effect with such modifications as he considers appropriate for that purpose.

1961 c. 40.
1965 c. 14 (N.I.).

(6) The power of the Secretary of State by order to
make such provision as is mentioned in subsection (5)
above, shall, in so far as it is not exercised by an order
under subsection (2) above, be exercisable by statutory
instrument subject to annulment in pursuance of a resolution of either House of Parliament.

(7) Nothing in this Act or in any order under subsection
(2) above shall make any person liable by virtue of Part I
of this Act for any damage caused wholly or partly by a

defect in a product which was supplied to any person by its producer before the coming into force of Part I of this Act.

(8) Expressions used in subsection (7) above and in Part I of this Act have the same meanings in that subsection as in that Part.

SCHEDULES

SCHEDULE 1

LIMITATION OF ACTIONS UNDER PART I

PART I

ENGLAND AND WALES

1. After section 11 of the Limitation Act 1980 (actions 1980 c. 58. in respect of personal injuries) there shall be inserted the following section—

Actions in respect of defective products. 11A.—(1) This section shall apply to an action for damages by virtue of any provision of Part I of the Consumer Protection Act 1987.

(2) None of the time limits given in the preceding provisions of this Act shall apply to an action to which this section applies.

(3) An action to which this section applies shall not be brought after the expiration of the period of ten years from the relevant time, within the meaning of section 4 of the said Act of 1987; and this subsection shall operate to extinguish a right of action and shall do so whether or not that right of action had accrued, or time under the following provisions of this Act had begun to run, at the end of the said period of ten years.

(4) Subject to subsection (5) below, an action to which this section applies in which the damages claimed by the plaintiff consist of or include damages in respect of personal injuries to the plaintiff or any other person or loss of or damage to any property, shall not be brought after the expiration of the period of three years from whichever is the later of—

(a) the date on which the cause of action accrued; and

249

(b) the date of knowledge of the injured person or, in the case of loss of or damage to property, the date of knowledge of the plaintiff or (if earlier) of any person in whom his cause of action was previously vested.

(5) If in a case where the damages claimed by the plaintiff consist of or include damages in respect of personal injuries to the plaintiff or any other person the injured person died before the expiration of the period mentioned in subsection (4) above, that subsection shall have effect as respects the cause of action surviving for the benefit of his estate by virtue of section 1 of the Law Reform (Miscellaneous Provisions) Act 1934 as if for the reference to that period there were substituted a reference to the period of three years from whichever is the later of—

(a) the date of death; and
(b) the date of the personal representative's knowledge.

(6) For the purposes of this section 'personal representative' includes any person who is or has been a personal representative of the deceased, including an executor who has not proved the will (whether or not he has renounced probate) but not anyone appointed only as a special personal representative in relation to settled land; and regard shall be had to any knowledge acquired by any such person while a personal representative or previously.

(7) If there is more than one personal representative and their dates of knowledge are different, subsection (5)(b) above shall be read as referring to the earliest of those dates.

(8) Expressions used in this section or section 14 of this Act and in Part I of the Consumer Protection Act 1987 have the same meanings in this section or that section as in that Part; and section 1(1) of that Act (Part I to be construed as enacted for the purpose of complying with the product liability Directive) shall apply for the purpose of construing this section and the following provisions of this Act so far as they relate to an action by

virtue of any provision of that Part as it applies for the Sch. 1
purpose of construing that Part.'

2. In section 12(1) of the said Act of 1980 (actions under 1976 c. 30.
the Fatal Accidents Act 1976), after the words 'section 11'
there shall be inserted the words 'or 11A'.

3. In section 14 of the said Act of 1980 (definition of
date of knowledge), in subsection (1), at the beginning
there shall be inserted the words 'Subject to subsection
(1A) below,' and after that subsection there shall be
inserted the following subsection—

'(1A) In section 11A of this Act and in section 12 of
this Act so far as that section applies to an action by
virtue of section 6(1)(a) of the Consumer Protection
Act 1987 (death caused by defective product) references to a person's date of knowledge are references
to the date on which he first had knowledge of the
following facts—

(a) such facts about the damage caused by the
defect as would lead a reasonable person
who had suffered such damage to consider it
sufficiently serious to justify his instituting
proceedings for damages against a defendant
who did not dispute liability and was able to
satisfy a judgment; and

(b) that the damage was wholly or partly attributable to the facts and circumstances alleged
to constitute the defect; and

(c) the identity of the defendant;

but, in determining the date on which a person first
had such knowledge there shall be disregarded both
the extent (if any) of that person's knowledge on any
date of whether particular facts or circumstances
would or would not, as a matter of law, constitute a
defect and, in a case relating to loss of or damage to
property, any knowledge which that person had on a
date on which he had no right of action by virtue of
Part I of that Act in respect of the loss or damage.'

4. In section 28 of the said Act of 1980 (extension of
limitation period in case of disability), after subsection (6)
there shall be inserted the following subsection—

'(7) If the action is one to which section 11A of this Act applies or one by virtue of section 6(1)(a) of the Consumer Protection Act 1987 (death caused by defective product), subsection (1) above—

    (a) shall not apply to the time limit prescribed by subsection (3) of the said section 11A or to that time limit as applied by virtue of section 12(1) of this Act; and

    (b) in relation to any other time limit prescribed by this Act shall have effect as if for the words, "six years" there were substituted the words "three years".'

5. In section 32 of the said Act of 1980 (postponement of limitation period in case of fraud, concealment or mistake)—

    (a) in subsection (1), for the words 'subsection (3)' there shall be substituted the words 'subsections (3) and (4A)'; and

    (b) after subsection (4) there shall be inserted the following subsection—

        '(4A) Subsection (1) above shall not apply in relation to the time limit prescribed by section 11A(3) of this Act or in relation to that time limit as applied by virtue of section 12(1) of this Act.'

6. In section 33 of the said Act of 1980 (discretionary exclusion of time limit)—

    (a) in subsection (1), after the words 'section 11' there shall be inserted the words 'or 11A';

    (b) after the said subsection (1) there shall be inserted the following subsection—

        '(1A) The court shall not under this section disapply—

        (a) subsection (3) of section 11A; or

        (b) where damages claimed by the plaintiff are confined to damages for loss of or damage to any property, any other provision in its application to an action by virtue of Part I of the Consumer Protection Act 1987.';

(c) in subsections (2) and (4), after the words 'section Sᴄʜ. 1
11' there shall be inserted the words 'or subsection (4) of section 11A';
(d) in subsection (3)(b), after the words 'section 11' there shall be inserted the words 'by section 11A'; and
(e) in subsection (8), after the words 'section 11' there shall be inserted the words 'or 11A'.

Part II

Scotland

7. The Prescription and Limitation (Scotland) Act 1973 1973 c. 52. shall be amended as follows.

8. In section 7(2), after the words 'not being an obligation' there shall be inserted the words 'to which section 22A of this Act applies or an obligation'.

9. In Part II, before section 17, there shall be inserted the following section—

'Part II not 16A.—This Part of this Act does not apply to
to extend to any action to which section 22B or 22C of this
product Act applies.'
liability.

10. After section 22, there shall be inserted the following new Part—

'Part IIA

Prescription of Obligations and Limitation of Actions under Part I of the Consumer Protection Act 1987

Prescription of Obligations

Ten years' 22A.—(1) An obligation arising from liability
prescription under section 2 of the 1987 Act (to make repara-
of tion for damage caused wholly or partly by a
obligations. defect in a product) shall be extinguished if a

period of 10 years has expired from the relevant time, unless a relevant claim was made within that period and has not been finally disposed of, and no such obligation shall come into existence after the expiration of the said period.

(2) If, at the expiration of the period of 10 years mentioned in subsection (1) above, a relevant claim has been made but has not been finally disposed of, the obligation to which the claim relates shall be extinguished when the claim is finally disposed of.

(3) In this section—

    (a) a decision disposing of the claim has been made against which no appeal is competent;

    (b) an appeal against such a decision is competent with leave, and the time limit for leave has expired and no application has been made or leave has been refused;

    (c) leave to appeal against such a decision is granted or is not required, and no appeal is made within the time limit for appeal; or

    (d) the claim is abandoned;

a claim is finally disposed of when 'relevant claim' in relation to an obligation means a claim made by or on behalf of the creditor for implement or part implement of the obligation, being a claim made—

    (a) in appropriate proceedings within the meaning of section 4(2) of this Act; or

    (b) by the presentation of, or the concurring in, a petition for sequestration or by the submission of a claim under section 22 or 48 of the Bankruptcy (Scotland) Act 1985; or

    (c) by the presentation of, or the concurring in, a petition for the winding up of a company or by the submission of a claim in a liquidation in accordance with the rules made under section 411 of the Insolvency Act 1986;

1985 c. 66.

1986 c. 45.

'relevant time' has the meaning given in section Sᴄʜ. 1
4(2) of the 1987 Act.

(4) Where a relevant claim is made in an arbitration,
and the nature of the claim has been stated in a
preliminary notice (within the meaning of section 4(4) of
this Act) relating to that arbitration, the date when the
notice is served shall be taken for those purposes to be
the date of the making of the claim.

Limitation of actions

3 year   22B—(1) This section shall apply to an action
limitation of to enforce an obligation arising from liability
actions.   under section 2 of the 1987 Act (to make reparation for damage caused wholly or partly by a
defect in a product), except where section 22C of
this Act applies.

(2) Subject to subsection (4) below, an action to
which this section applies shall not be competent unless
it is commenced within the period of 3 years after the
earliest date on which the person seeking to bring (or a
person who could at an earlier date have brought) the
action was aware, or on which, in the opinion of the
court, it was reasonably practicable for him in all the
circumstances to become aware, of all the facts mentioned in subsection (3) below.

(3) The facts referred to in subsection (2) above are—

(a) that there was a defect in a product;
(b) that the damage was caused or partly caused
by the defect;
(c) that the damage was sufficiently serious to
justify the pursuer (or other person referred
to in subsection (2) above) in bringing an
action to which this section applies on the
assumption that the defender did not dispute
liability and was able to satisfy a decree;
(d) that the defender was a person liable for the
damage under the said section 2.

(4) In the computation of the period of 3 years mentioned in subsection (2) above, there shall be disregarded
any period during which the person seeking to bring the

action was under legal disability by reason of nonage or unsoundness of mind.

(5) The facts mentioned in subsection (3) above do not include knowledge of whether particular facts and circumstances would or would not, as a matter of law, result in liability for damage under the said section 2.

(6) Where a person would be entitled, but for this section, to bring an action for reparation other than one in which the damages claimed are confined to damages for loss of or damage to property, the court may, if it seems to it equitable to do so, allow him to bring the action notwithstanding this section.

Actions under the 1987 Act where death has resulted from personal injuries.   22C.—(1) This section shall apply to an action to enforce an obligation arising from liability under section 2 of the 1987 Act (to make reparation for damage caused wholly or partly by a defect in a product) where a person has died from personal injuries and the damages claimed include damages for those personal injuries or that death.

(2) Subject to subsection (4) below, an action to which this section applies shall not be competent unless it is commenced within the period of 3 years after the later of—

    (a) the date of death of the injured person;
      (b) the earliest date on which the person seeking to make (or a person who could at an earlier date have made) the claim was aware, or on which, in the opinion of the court, it was reasonably practicable for him in all the circumstances to become aware—
        (i) that there was a defect in the product;
      (ii) that the injuries of the deceased were caused (or partly caused) by the defect; and
     (iii) that the defender was a person liable for the damage under the said section 2.

(3) Where the person seeking to make the claim is a relative of the deceased, there shall be disregarded in the computation of the period mentioned in subsection (2) above any period during which that relative was under

legal disability by reason of nonage or unsoundness of Sch. 1 mind.

(4) Where an action to which section 22B of this Act applies has not been brought within the period mentioned in subsection (2) of that section and the person subsequently dies in consequence of his injuries, an action to which this section applies shall not be competent in respect of those injuries or that death.

(5) Where a person would be entitled, but for this section, to bring an action for reparation other than one in which the damages claimed are confined to damages for loss of or damage to property, the court may, if it seems to it equitable to do so, allow him to bring the action notwithstanding this section.

(6) In this section 'relative' has the same meaning as in the Damages (Scotland) Act 1976.

1976 c. 13.

(7) For the purposes of subsection (2)(b) above there shall be disregarded knowledge of whether particular facts and circumstances would or would not, as a matter of law, result in liability for damage under the said section 2.

Supplementary

Interpretation of this Part. 22D.—(1) Expressions used in this Part and in Part I of the 1987 Act shall have the same meanings in this Part as in the said Part I.

(2) For the purposes of section 1(1) of the 1987 Act, this Part shall have effect and be construed as if it were contained in Part I of that Act.

(3) In this Part, 'the 1987 Act' means the Consumer Protection Act 1987.'

11. Section 23 shall cease to have effect, but for the avoidance of doubt it is declared that the amendments in Part II of Schedule 4 shall continue to have effect.

12. In paragraph 2 of Schedule 1, after sub-paragraph (gg) there shall be inserted the following sub-paragraph—

'(ggg) to any obligation arising from liability under section 2 of the Consumer Protection Act 1987 (to make reparation for damage caused wholly or partly by a defect in a product);'.

SCHEDULE 3

Section 36. AMENDMENTS OF PART I OF THE HEALTH AND SAFETY AT WORK ETC. ACT 1974

1.—(1) Section 6 (general duties of manufacturers etc. as regard articles and substances for use at work) shall be amended as follows.

(2) For subsection (1) (general duties of designers, manufacturers, importers and suppliers of articles for use at work) there shall be substituted the following subsections—

'(1) It shall be the duty of any person who designs, manufactures, imports or supplies any article for use at work or any article of fairground equipment—

  (a) to ensure, so far as is reasonably practicable, that the article is so designed and constructed that it will be safe and without risks to health at all times when it is being set, used, cleaned or maintained by a person at work;

  (b) to carry out or arrange for the carrying out of such testing and examination as may be necessary for the performance of the duty imposed on him by the preceding paragraph;

  (c) to take such steps as are necessary to secure that persons supplied by that person with the article are provided with adequate information about the use for which the article is designed or has been tested and about any conditions necessary to ensure that it will be safe and without risks to health at all such times as are mentioned in paragraph (a) above and when it is being dismantled or disposed of; and

  (d) to take such steps as are necessary to secure, so far as is reasonably practicable, that persons so supplied are provided with all

258

such revisions of information provided to   Sch. 3
them by virtue of the preceding paragraph as
are necessary by reason of its becoming
known that anything gives rise to a serious
risk to health or safety.

(1A) It shall be the duty of any person who designs,
manufactures, imports or supplies any article of fairground equipment—

(a) to ensure, so far as is reasonably practicable,
that the article is so designed and constructed
that it will be safe and without risks to health
at all times when it is being used for or in
connection with the entertainment of members of the public;

(b) to carry out or arrange for the carrying out of
such testing and examination as may be
necessary for the performance of the duty
imposed on him by the preceding paragraph;

(c) to take such steps as are necessary to secure
that persons supplied by that person with the
article are provided with adequate information about the use for which the article is
designed or has been tested and about any
conditions necessary to ensure that it will be
safe and without risks to health at all times
when it is being used for or in connection
with the entertainment of members of the
public; and

(d) to take such steps as are necessary to secure,
so far as is reasonably practicable, that persons so supplied are provided with all such
revisions of information provided to them by
virtue of the preceding paragraph as are
necessary by reason of its becoming known
that anything gives rise to a serious risk to
health or safety.'

(3) In subsection (2) (duty of person who undertakes
the design or manufacture of an article for use at work
to carry out research), after the word 'work' there shall
be inserted the words 'or of any article of fairground
equipment'.

(4) In subsection (3) (duty of persons who erect or
install articles for use at work)—

SCH. 3

(a) after the words 'persons at work' there shall be inserted the words 'or who erects or installs any article of fairground equipment'; and

(b) for the words from 'it is' onwards there shall be substituted the words 'the article is erected or installed makes it unsafe or a risk to health at any such time as is mentioned in paragraph (a) of subsection (1) or, as the case may be, in paragraph (a) of subsection (1) or (1A) above.'

(5) For subsection (4) (general duties of manufacturers, importers and suppliers of substances for use at work) there shall be substituted the following subsection—

'(4) It shall be the duty of any person who manufactures, imports or supplies any substance–

(a) to ensure, so far as is reasonably practicable, that the substance will be safe and without risks to health at all times when it is being used, handled, processed, stored or transported by a person at work or in premises to which section 4 above applies;

(b) to carry out or arrange for the carrying out of such testing and examination as may be necessary for the performance of the duty imposed on him by the preceding paragraph;

(c) to take such steps as are necessary to secure that persons supplied by that person with the substance are provided with adequate information about any risks to health or safety to which the inherent properties of the substance may give rise, about the results of any relevant tests which have been carried out on or in connection with the substance and about any conditions necessary to ensure that the substance will be safe and without risks to health at all such times as are mentioned in paragraph (a) above and when the substance is being disposed of; and

(d) to take such steps as are necessary to secure, so far as is reasonably practicable, that persons so supplied are provided with all such revisions of information provided to them by virtue of the preceding paragraph as are

necessary by reason of its becoming known Sch. 3
that anything gives rise to a serious risk to
health or safety.'

(6) In subsection (5) (duty of person who undertakes
the manufacture of a substance for use at work to carry
out research)—

    (a) for the words 'substance for use at work' there
        shall be substituted the word 'substance'; and
    (b) at the end there shall be inserted the words 'at
        all such times as are mentioned in paragraph
        (a) of subsection (4) above'.

(7) In subsection (8) (relief from duties for persons
relying on undertakings by others)—

    (a) for the words 'for or to another' there shall be
        substituted the words 'for use at work or an
        article of fairground equipment and does so for
        or to another';
    (b) for the words 'when properly used' there shall
        be substituted the words 'at all such times as
        are mentioned in paragraph (a) of subsection
        (1) or, as the case may be, in paragraph (a) of
        subsection (1) or (1A) above'; and
    (c) for the words 'by subsection (1)(a) above' there
        shall be substituted the words 'by virtue of that
        paragraph'.

(8) After the said subsection (8) there shall be inserted the following subsection—

    '(8A) Nothing in subsection (7) or (8) above
shall relieve any person who imports any article or
substance from any duty in respect of anything
which—

    (a) in the case of an article designed outside the
        United Kingdom, was done by and in the
        course of any trade, profession or other
        undertaking carried on by, or was within the
        control of, the person who designed the
        article; or
    (b) in the case of an article or substance manu-
        factured outside the United Kingdom, was
        done by and in the course of any trade,

SCH. 3

profession or other undertaking carried on
by, or was within the control of, the person
who manufactured the article or substance.'

(9) In subsection (9) (definition of supplier in certain
cases of supply under a hire-purchase agreement), for
the words 'article for use at work or substance for use at
work' there shall be substituted the words 'article or
substance'.

(10) For subsection (10) (meaning of 'properly used')
there shall be substituted the following subsection—

'(10) For the purposes of this section an absence of
safety or a risk to health shall be disregarded in so far
as the case in or in relation to which it would arise is
shown to be one the occurrence of which could not
reasonably be foreseen; and in determining whether
any duty imposed by virtue of paragraph (a) of
subsection (1), (1A) or (4) above has been performed
regard shall be had to any relevant information or
advice which has been provided to any person by the
person by whom the article has been designed, manufactured, imported or supplied or, as the case may be,
by the person by whom the substance has been
manufactured, imported or supplied.'

2. In section 22 (prohibition notices)—

(a) in subsections (1) and (2) (notices in respect of
activities which are or are about to be carried on
and involve a risk of serious personal injury), for
the word 'about', in each place where it occurs,
there shall be substituted the word 'likely';

(b) for subsection (4) (notice to have immediate
effect only if the risk is imminent) there shall be
substituted the following subsection—

'(4) A direction contained in a prohibition notice in pursuance of subsection
(3)(d) above shall take effect—

(a) at the end of the period specified in
the notice; or

(b) if the notice so declares, immediately.'

3. After section 25 there shall be inserted the following
section—

'Power of   25A.—(1) A customs officer may, for the pur- Sch. 3
customs   pose of facilitating the exercise or performance
officer to   by any enforcing authority or inspector of any of
detain
articles and the powers or duties of the authority or inspector
substances. under any of the relevant statutory provisions,
             seize any imported article or imported substance
             and detain it for not more than two working days.

(2) Anything seized and detained under this section shall be dealt with during the period of its detention in such manner as the Commissioners of Customs and Excise may direct.

(3) In subsection (1) above the reference to two working days is a reference to a period of forty-eight hours calculated from the time when the goods in question are seized but disregarding so much of any period as falls on a Saturday or Sunday or on Christmas Day, Good Friday or a day which is a bank holiday under the Banking and Financial Dealings Act 1971 in   1974 c. 37. the part of Great Britain where the goods are seized.'

4. After section 27 (power to obtain information) there shall be inserted the following section—

'Information   27A.—(1) If they think it appropriate to do
communi-   so for the purpose of facilitating the exercise or
cated by the performance by any person to whom subsection
Commis-
sioners of   (2) below applies of any of that person's powers
Customs and   or duties under any of the relevant statutory
Excise.   provisions, the Commissioners of Customs and
              Excise may authorise the disclosure to that per-
              son of any information obtained for the pur-
              poses of the exercise by the Commissioners of
              their functions in relation to imports.

(2) This subsection applies to an enforcing authority and to an inspector.

(3) A disclosure of information made to any person under subsection (1) above shall be made in such manner as may be directed by the Commissioners of Customs and Excise and may be made through such persons acting on behalf of that person as may be so directed.

(4) Information may be disclosed to a person under subsection (1) above whether or not the disclosure of the information has been requested by or on behalf of that person.'

5. In section 28 (restrictions on disclosure of information), in subsection (1)(a), after the words 'furnished to any person' there shall be inserted the words 'under section 27A above or'.

6. In section 33(1)(h) (offence of obstructing an inspector), after the word 'duties' there shall be inserted the words 'or to obstruct a customs officer in the exercise of his powers under section 25A'.

7. In section 53(1) (general interpretation of Part I)—

(a) after the definition of 'article for use at work' there shall be inserted the following definition—
'"article of fairground equipment" means any fairground equipment or any article designed for use as a component in any such equipment;'

(b) after the definition of 'credit-sale agreement' there shall be inserted the following definition—
1979 c. 2.
'"customs officer" means an officer within the meaning of the Customs and Excise Management Act 1979;'

(c) before the definition of 'the general purposes of this Part' there shall be inserted the following definition—
'"fairground equipment" means any fairground ride, any similar plant which is designed to be in motion for entertainment purposes with members of the public on or inside it or any plant which is designed to be used by members of the public for entertainment purposes either as a slide or for bouncing upon, and in this definition the reference to plant which is designed to be in motion with members of the public on or inside it includes a reference to swings, dodgems and other plant which is designed to be in motion wholly or

partly under the control of, or to be put in Sᴄʜ. 3
motion by, a member of the public;'
(d) after the definition of 'local authority' there shall
be inserted the following definition—
'"micro-organism" includes any microscopic
biological entity which is capable of replication;'
(e) in the definition of 'substance', after the words
'natural or artificial substance' there shall be
inserted the words '(including micro-organisms)'.

Published by Her Majesty's Stationery Office, London,
ISBN 0 10 544387 5

Appendix D Extracts from the Sale of Goods Act 1979

Sections 2–20, 27–37, 49–53 and 55

FORMATION OF THE CONTRACT

Contract of sale

2.—(1) A contract of sale of goods is a contract by which the seller transfers or agrees to transfer the property in goods to the buyer for a money consideration, called the price.

(2) There may be a contract of sale between one part owner and another.

(3) A contract of sale may be absolute or conditional.

(4) Where under a contract of sale the property in the goods is transferred from the seller to the buyer the contract is called a sale.

(5) Where under a contract of sale the transfer of the property in the goods is to take place at a future time or subject to some condition later to be fulfilled the contract is called an agreement to sell.

(6) An agreement to sell becomes a sale when the time elapses or the conditions are fulfilled subject to which the property in the goods is to be transferred.

3.—(1) Capacity to buy and sell is regulated by the general law concerning capacity to contract and to transfer and acquire property.

(2) Where necessaries are sold and delivered to a minor or to a person who by reason of mental incapacity or drunkenness is incompetent to contract, he must pay a reasonable price for them.

(3) In subsection (2) above 'necessaries' means goods suitable to the condition in life of the minor or other person concerned and to his actual requirements at the time of the sale and delivery.

Formalities of contract

4.—(1) Subject to this and any other Act, a contract of sale may be made in writing (either with or without seal), or by word of mouth, or partly in writing and partly by word of mouth, or may be implied from the conduct of the parties.

(2) Nothing in this section affects the law relating to corporations.

Subject matter of contract

5.—(1) The goods which form the subject of a contract of sale may be either existing goods, owned or possessed by the seller, or goods to be manufactured or acquired by him after the making of the contract of sale, in this Act called future goods.

(2) There may be a contract for the sale of goods the acquisition of which by the seller depends on a contingency which may or may not happen.

(3) Where by a contract of sale the seller purports to effect a present sale of future goods, the contract operates as an agreement to sell the goods.

6. Where there is a contract for the sale of specific goods, and the goods without the knowledge of the seller have perished at the time when the contract is made, the contract is void.

PART II
Goods
perishing
before sale
but after
agreement
to sell.

7. Where there is an agreement to sell specific goods and subsequently the goods, without any fault on the part of the seller or buyer, perish before the risk passes to the buyer, the agreement is avoided.

The price

Ascertainment
of price.

8.—(1) The price in a contract of sale may be fixed by the contract, or may be left to be fixed in a manner agreed by the contract, or may be determined by the course of dealing between the parties.

(2) Where the price is not determined as mentioned in subsection (1) above the buyer must pay a reasonable price.

(3) What is a reasonable price is a question of fact dependent on the circumstances of each particular case.

Agreement
to sell at
valuation.

9.—(1) Where there is an agreement to sell goods on the terms that the price is to be fixed by the valuation of a third party, and he cannot or does not make the valuation, the agreement is avoided; but if the goods or any part of them have been delivered to and appropriated by the buyer he must pay a reasonable price for them.

(2) Where the third party is prevented from making the valuation by the fault of the seller or buyer, the party not at fault may maintain an action for damages against the party at fault.

Conditions and warranties

Stipulations
about time.

10.—(1) Unless a different intention appears from the terms of the contract, stipulations as to time of payment are not of the essence of a contract of sale.

(2) Whether any other stipulation as to time is or is not of the essence of the contract depends on the terms of the contract.

(3) In a contract of sale 'month' prima facie means calendar month.

11.—(1) Subsections (2) to (4) and (7) below do not apply to Scotland and subsection (5) below applies only to Scotland.

(2) Where a contract of sale is subject to a condition to be fulfilled by the seller, the buyer may waive the condition, or may elect to treat the breach of the condition as a breach of warranty and not as a ground for treating the contract as repudiated.

(3) Whether a stipulation in a contract of sale is a condition, the breach of which may give rise to a right to treat the contract as repudiated, or a warranty, the breach of which may give rise to a claim for damages but not to a right to reject the goods and treat the contract as repudiated, depends in each case on the construction of the contract; and a stipulation may be a condition, though called a warranty in the contract.

(4) Where a contract of sale is not severable and the buyer has accepted the goods or part of them, the breach of a condition to be fulfilled by the seller can only be treated as a breach of warranty, and not as a ground for rejecting the goods and treating the contract as repudiated, unless there is an express or implied term of the contract to that effect.

(5) In Scotland, failure by the seller to perform any material part of a contract of sale is a breach of contract, which entitles the buyer either within a reasonable time after delivery to reject the goods and treat the contract as repudiated, or to retain the goods and treat the failure to perform such material part as a breach which may give rise to a claim for compensation or damages.

(6) Nothing in this section affects a condition or warranty whose fulfilment is excused by law by reason of impossibility or otherwise.

(7) Paragraph 2 of Schedule 1 below applies in relation to a contract made before 22 April 1967 or (in the application of this Act to Northern Ireland) 28 July 1967.

12.—(1)In a contract of sale, other than one to which subsection (3) below applies, there is an implied condition on the part of the seller that in the case of a sale he has a

PART II
When condition to be treated as warranty.

Implied terms about title, etc.

right to sell the goods, and in the case of an agreement to sell he will have such a right at the time when the property is to pass.

(2) In a contract of sale, other than one to which subsection (3) below applies, there is also an implied warranty that—

    (a) the goods are free, and will remain free until the time when the property is to pass, from any charge or encumbrance not disclosed or known to the buyer before the contract is made, and

    (b) the buyer will enjoy quiet possession of the goods except so far as it may be disturbed by the owner or other person entitled to the benefit of any charge or encumbrance so disclosed or known.

(3) This subsection applies to a contract of sale in the case of which there appears from the contract or is to be inferred from its circumstances an intention that the seller should transfer only such title as he or a third person may have.

(4) In a contract to which subsection (3) above applies there is an implied warranty that all charges or encumbrances known to the seller and not known to the buyer have been disclosed to the buyer before the contract is made.

(5) In a contract to which subsection (3) above applies there is also an implied warranty that none of the following will disturb the buyer's quiet possession of the goods, namely—

    (a) the seller;

    (b) in a case where the parties to the contract intend that the seller should transfer only such title as a third person may have, that person;

    (c) anyone claiming through or under the seller or that third person otherwise than under a charge or encumbrance disclosed or known to the buyer before the contract is made.

(6) Paragraph 3 of Schedule 1 below applies in relation to a contract made before 18 May 1973.

13.—(1) Where there is a contract for the sale of goods by description, there is an implied condition that the goods will correspond with the description.

(2) If the sale is by sample as well as by description it is not sufficient that the bulk of the goods corresponds with the sample if the goods do not also correspond with the description.

(3) A sale of goods is not prevented from being a sale by description by reason only that, being exposed for sale or hire, they are selected by the buyer.

(4) Paragraph 4 of Schedule 1 below applies in relation to a contract made before 18 May 1973.

14.—(1) Except as provided by this section and section 15 below and subject to any other enactment, there is no implied condition or warranty about the quality or fitness for any particular purpose of goods supplied under a contract of sale.

(2) Where the seller sells goods in the course of a business, there is an implied condition that the goods supplied under the contract are of merchantable quality, except that there is no such condition—

    (a) as regards defects specifically drawn to the buyer's attention before the contract is made; or

    (b) if the buyer examines the goods before the contract is made, as regards defects which that examination ought to reveal.

(3) Where the seller sells goods in the course of a business and the buyer, expressly or by implication, makes known—

    (a) to the seller, or

    (b) where the purchase price or part of it is payable by instalments and the goods were previously sold by a credit-broker to the seller, to that credit-broker,

any particular purpose for which the goods are being bought, there is an implied condition that the goods supplied under the contract are reasonably fit for that purpose, whether or not that is a purpose for which such goods are commonly supplied, except where the circumstances show that the buyer does not rely, or that it is unreasonable for him to rely, on the skill or judgment of the seller or credit-broker.

(4) An implied condition or warranty about quality or fitness for a particular purpose may be annexed to a contract of sale by usage.

(5) The preceding provisions of this section apply to a sale by a person who in the course of a business is acting as agent for another as they apply to a sale by a principal in the course of a business, except where that other is not selling in the course of a business and either the buyer knows that fact or reasonable steps are taken to bring it to the notice of the buyer before the contract is made.

(6) Goods of any kind are of merchantable quality within the meaning of subsection (2) above if they are as fit for the purpose or purposes for which goods of that kind are commonly bought as it is reasonable to expect having regard to any description applied to them, the price (if relevant) and all the other relevant circumstances.

(7) Paragraph 5 of Schedule 1 below applies in relation to a contract made on or after 18 May 1973 and before the appointed day, and paragraph 6 in relation to one made before 18 May 1973.

(8) In subsection (7) above and paragraph 5 of Schedule 1 below references to the appointed day are to the day appointed for the purposes of those provisions by an order of the Secretary of State made by statutory instrument.

Sale by sample

Sale by
sample.

15.—(1) A contract of sale is a contract for sale by sample where there is an express or implied term to that effect in the contract.

(2) In the case of a contract for sale by sample there is an implied condition—

(a) that the bulk will correspond with the sample PART II
in quality;

(b) that the buyer will have a reasonable opportunity of comparing the bulk with the sample;

(c) that the goods will be free from any defect, rendering them unmerchantable, which would not be apparent on reasonable examination of the sample.

(3) In subsection (2)(c) above 'unmerchantable' is to be construed in accordance with section 14(6) above.

(4) Paragraph 7 of Schedule 1 below applies in relation to a contract made before 18 May 1973.

PART III

EFFECTS OF THE CONTRACT

Transfer of property as between seller and buyer

16. Where there is a contract for the sale of unascertained goods no property in the goods is transferred to the buyer unless and until the goods are ascertained.

Goods must be ascertained.

17.—(1) Where there is a contract for the sale of specific or ascertained goods the property in them is transferred to the buyer at such time as the parties to the contract intend it to be transferred.

Property passes when intended to pass.

(2) For the purpose of ascertaining the intention of the parties regard shall be had to the terms of the contract, the conduct of the parties and the circumstances of the case.

18. Unless a different intention appears, the following are rules for ascertaining the intention of the parties as to the time at which the property in the goods is to pass to the buyer.

Rules for ascertaining intention.

Rule 1.—Where there is an unconditional contract for the sale of specific goods in a deliverable state the property in the goods passes to the buyer when the contract is made, and it is immaterial whether the time of payment or the time of delivery, or both, be postponed.

Rule 2.—Where there is a contract for the sale of specific goods and the seller is bound to do something to the goods for the purpose of putting them into a deliverable state, the property does not pass until the thing is done and the buyer has notice that it has been done.

Rule 3.—Where there is a contract for the sale of specific goods in a deliverable state but the seller is bound to weigh, measure, test, or do some other act or thing with reference to the goods for the purpose of ascertaining the price, the property does not pass until the act or thing is done and the buyer has notice that it has been done.

Rule 4.—When goods are delivered to the buyer on approval or on sale or return or other similar terms the property in the goods passes to the buyer:—

(a) when he signifies his approval or acceptance to the seller or does any other act adopting the transaction;

(b) if he does not signify his approval or acceptance to the seller but retains the goods without giving notice of rejection, then, if a time has been fixed for the return of the goods, on the expiration of that time, and, if no time has been fixed, on the expiration of a reasonable time.

Rule 5.—(1) Where there is a contract for the sale of unascertained or future goods by description, and goods of that description and in a deliverable state are unconditionally appropriated to the contract, either by the seller with the assent of the buyer or by the buyer with the assent of the seller, the property in the goods then passes to the buyer; and the assent may be express or implied, and may be given either before or after the appropriation is made.

(2) Where, in pursuance of the contract, the seller delivers the goods to the buyer or to a carrier or other bailee or custodier (whether named by the buyer or not) for the purpose of transmission to the buyer, and does not reserve the right of disposal, he is to be taken to have

unconditionally appropriated the goods to the PART III contract.

19.—(1) Where there is a contract for the sale of Reservation specific goods or where goods are subsequently appropri- of right of ated to the contract, the seller may, by the terms of the disposal. contract or appropriation, reserve the right of disposal of the goods until certain conditions are fulfilled; and in such a case, notwithstanding the delivery of the goods to the buyer, or to a carrier or other bailee or custodier for the purpose of transmission to the buyer, the property in the goods does not pass to the buyer until the conditions imposed by the seller are fulfilled.

(2) Where goods are shipped, and by the bill of lading the goods are deliverable to the order of the seller or his agent, the seller is prima facie to be taken to reserve the right of disposal.

(3) Where the seller of goods draws on the buyer for the price, and transmits the bill of exchange and bill of lading to the buyer together to secure acceptance or payment of the bill of exchange, the buyer is bound to return the bill of lading if he does not honour the bill of exchange, and if he wrongfully retains the bill of lading the property in the goods does not pass to him.

20.—(1) Unless otherwise agreed, the goods remain at Risk prima the seller's risk until the property in them is transferred to facie passes the buyer, but when the property in them is transferred to with property. the buyer the goods are at the buyer's risk whether delivery has been made or not.

(2) But where delivery has been delayed through the fault of either buyer or seller the goods are at the risk of the party at fault as regards any loss which might not have occurred but for such fault.

(3) Nothing in this section affects the duties or liabilities of either seller or buyer as a bailee or custodier of the goods of the other party.

PART IV

PERFORMANCE OF THE CONTRACT

Duties of
seller and
buyer.

27. It is the duty of the seller to deliver the goods, and of the buyer to accept and pay for them, in accordance with the terms of the contract of sale.

Payment and
delivery are
concurrent
conditions.

28. Unless otherwise agreed, delivery of the goods and payment of the price are concurrent conditions, that is to say, the seller must be ready and willing to give possession of the goods to the buyer in exchange for the price and the buyer must be ready and willing to pay the price in exchange for possession of the goods.

Rules about
delivery.

29.—(1) Whether it is for the buyer to take possession of the goods or for the seller to send them to the buyer is a question depending in each case on the contract, express or implied, between the parties.

(2) Apart from any such contract, express or implied, the place of delivery is the seller's place of business if he has one, and if not, his residence; except that, if the contract is for the sale of specific goods, which to the knowledge of the parties when the contract is made are in some other place, then that place is the place of delivery.

(3) Where under the contract of sale the seller is bound to send the goods to the buyer, but no time for sending them is fixed, the seller is bound to send them within a reasonable time.

(4) Where the goods at the time of sale are in the possession of a third person, there is no delivery by seller to buyer unless and until the third person acknowledges to the buyer that he holds the goods on his behalf; but nothing in this section affects the operation of the issue or transfer of any document of title to goods.

(5) Demand or tender of delivery may be treated as ineffectual unless made at a reasonable hour; and what is a reasonable hour is a question of fact.

(6) Unless otherwise agreed, the expenses of and incidental to putting the goods into a deliverable state must be borne by the seller.

30.—(1) Where the seller delivers to the buyer a quantity of goods less than he contracted to sell, the buyer may reject them, but if the buyer accepts the goods so delivered he must pay for them at the contract rate.

(2) Where the seller delivers to the buyer a quantity of goods larger than he contracted to sell, the buyer may accept the goods included in the contract and reject the rest, or he may reject the whole.

(3) Where the seller delivers to the buyer a quantity of goods larger than he contracted to sell and the buyer accepts the whole of the goods so delivered he must pay for them at the contract rate.

(4) Where the seller delivers to the buyer the goods he contracted to sell mixed with goods of a different description not included in the contract, the buyer may accept the goods which are in accordance with the contract and reject the rest, or he may reject the whole.

(5) This section is subject to any usage of trade, special agreement, or course of dealing between the parties.

31.—(1) Unless otherwise agreed, the buyer of goods is not bound to accept delivery of them by instalments.

(2) Where there is a contract for the sale of goods to be delivered by stated instalments, which are to be separately paid for, and the seller makes defective deliveries in respect of one or more instalments, or the buyer neglects or refuses to take delivery of or pay for one or more instalments, it is a question in each case depending on the terms of the contract and the circumstances of the case whether the breach of contract is a repudiation of the whole contract or whether it is a severable breach giving rise to a claim for compensation but not to a right to treat the whole contract as repudiated.

32.—(1) Where, in pursuance of a contract of sale, the seller is authorised or required to send the goods to the buyer, delivery of the goods to a carrier (whether named by the buyer or not) for the purpose of transmission to the buyer is prima facie deemed to be a delivery of the goods to the buyer.

(2) Unless otherwise authorised by the buyer, the seller must make such contract with the carrier on behalf of the buyer as may be reasonable having regard to the nature of the goods and the other circumstances of the case; and if the seller omits to do so, and the goods are lost or damaged in course of transit, the buyer may decline to treat the delivery to the carrier as a delivery to himself or may hold the seller responsible in damages.

(3) Unless otherwise agreed, where goods are sent by the seller to the buyer by a route involving sea transit, under circumstances in which it is usual to insure, the seller must give such notice to the buyer as may enable him to insure them during their sea transit; and if the seller fails to do so, the goods are at his risk during such sea transit.

Risk where goods are delivered at distant place.

33. Where the seller of goods agrees to deliver them at his own risk at a place other than that where they are when sold, the buyer must nevertheless (unless otherwise agreed) take any risk of deterioration in the goods necessarily incident to the course of transit.

Buyer's right of examining the goods.

34.—(1) Where goods are delivered to the buyer, and he has not previously examined them, he is not deemed to have accepted them until he has had a reasonable opportunity of examining them for the purpose of ascertaining whether they are in conformity with the contract.

(2) Unless otherwise agreed, when the seller tenders delivery of goods to the buyer, he is bound on request to afford the buyer a reasonable opportunity of examining the goods for the purpose of ascertaining whether they are in conformity with the contract.

Acceptance.

35.—(1) The buyer is deemed to have accepted the goods when he intimates to the seller that he has accepted them, or (except where section 34 above otherwise provides) when the goods have been delivered to him and he does any act in relation to them which is inconsistent with the ownership of the seller, or when after the lapse of a reasonable time he retains the goods without intimating to the seller that he has rejected them.

(2) Paragraph 10 of Schedule 1 below applies in relation to a contract made before 22 April 1967 or (in

the application of this Act to Northern Ireland) 28 July PART IV
1967.

36. Unless otherwise agreed, where goods are delivered Buyer not
to the buyer, and he refuses to accept them, having the bound to
right to do so, he is not bound to return them to the seller, return rejected
but it is sufficient if he intimates to the seller that he goods.
refuses to accept them.

37.—(1) When the seller is ready and willing to deliver Buyer's
the goods, and requests the buyer to take delivery, and the liability for
buyer does not within a reasonable time after such request not taking
take delivery of the goods, he is liable to the seller for any delivery of
loss occasioned by his neglect or refusal to take delivery, goods.
and also for a reasonable charge for the care and custody
of the goods.

(2) Nothing in this section affects the rights of the
seller where the neglect or refusal of the buyer to take
delivery amounts to a repudiation of the contract.

PART VI

ACTIONS FOR BREACH OF THE CONTRACT

Seller's remedies

49.—(1) Where, under a contract of sale, the property
in the goods has passed to the buyer and he wrongfully
neglects or refuses to pay for the goods according to the
terms of the contract, the seller may maintain an action
against him for the price of the goods.

(2) Where, under a contract of sale, the price is
payable on a day certain irrespective of delivery and the
buyer wrongfully neglects or refuses to pay such price,
the seller may maintain an action for the price, although
the property in the goods has not passed and the goods
have not been appropriated to the contract.

(3) Nothing in this section prejudices the right of the
seller in Scotland to recover interest on the price from
the date of tender of the goods, or from the date on
which the price was payable, as the case may be.

PART VI
Damages
for non-
acceptance.

50.—(1) Where the buyer wrongfully neglects or re-fuses to accept and pay for the goods, the seller may maintain an action against him for damages for non-acceptance.

(2) The measure of damages is the estimated loss directly and naturally resulting, in the ordinary course of events, from the buyer's breach of contract.

(3) Where there is an available market for the goods in question the measure of damages is prima facie to be ascertained by the difference between the contract price and the market or current price at the time or times when the goods ought to have been accepted or (if no time was fixed for acceptance) at the time of the refusal to accept.

Buyer's remedies

Damages
for non-
delivery.

51.—(1) Where the seller wrongfully neglects or refuses to deliver the goods to the buyer, the buyer may maintain an action against the seller for damages for non-delivery.

(2) The measure of damages is the estimated loss directly and naturally resulting, in the ordinary course of events, from the seller's breach of contract.

(3) Where there is an available market for the goods in question the measure of damages is prima facie to be ascertained by the difference between the contract price and the market or current price of the goods at the time or times when they ought to have been delivered or (if no time was fixed) at the time of the refusal to deliver.

Specific
performance.

52.—(1) In any action for breach of contract to deliver specific or ascertained goods the court may, if it thinks fit, on the plaintiff's application, by its judgment or decree direct that the contract shall be performed specifically, without giving the defendant the option of retaining the goods on payment of damages.

(2) The plaintiff's application may be made at any time before judgment or decree.

(3) The judgment or decree may be unconditional, or on such terms and conditions as to damages, payment of the price and otherwise as seem just to the court.

(4) The provisions of this section shall be deemed to PART VI
be supplementary to, and not in derogation of, the right
of specific implement in Scotland.

53.—(1) Where there is a breach of warranty by the Remedy for
seller, or where the buyer elects (or is compelled) to treat breach of
any breach of a condition on the part of the seller as a warranty.
breach of warranty, the buyer is not by reason only of such
breach of warranty entitled to reject the goods; but he
may—

    (a) set up against the seller the breach of warranty in
        diminution or extinction of the price, or

    (b) maintain an action against the seller for damages
        for the breach of warranty.

(2) The measure of damages for breach of warranty is
the estimated loss directly and naturally resulting, in the
ordinary course of events, from the breach of warranty.

(3) In the case of breach of warranty of quality such
loss is prima facie the difference between the value of
the goods at the time of delivery to the buyer and the
value they would have had if they had fulfilled the
warranty.

(4) The fact that the buyer has set up the breach of
warranty in diminution or extinction of the price does
not prevent him from maintaining an action for the same
breach of warranty if he has suffered further damage.

(5) Nothing in this section prejudices or affects the
buyer's right of rejection in Scotland as declared by this
Act.

PART VII

SUPPLEMENTARY

55.—(1) Where a right, duty or liability would arise Exclusion of
under a contract of sale of goods by implication of law, it implied terms
may (subject to the Unfair Contract Terms Act 1977) be 1977 c. 50.
negatived or varied by express agreement, or by the course
of dealing between the parties, or by such usage as binds
both parties to the contract.

PART VII

(2) An express condition or warranty does not negative a condition or warranty implied by this Act unless inconsistent with it.

(3) Paragraph 11 of Schedule 1 below applies in relation to a contract made on or after 18 May 1973 and before 1 February 1978, and paragraph 12 in relation to one made before 18 May 1973.

Published by Her Majesty's Stationery Office, London,
ISBN 0 10 545479 6

Appendix E   Extracts from the Unfair Contract Terms Act 1977

Sections 2–6, 8, 11, Schedule 2 and section 12

Avoidance of liability for negligence, breach of contract, etc.

2.—(1) A person cannot by reference to any contract term or to a notice given to persons generally or to particular persons exclude or restrict his liability for death or personal injury resulting from negligence.

Negligence liability.

(2) In the case of other loss or damage, a person cannot so exclude or restrict his liability for negligence except in so far as the term or notice satisfies the requirement of reasonableness.

(3) Where a contract term or notice purports to exclude or restrict liability for negligence a person's agreement to or awareness of it is not of itself to be taken as indicating his voluntary acceptance of any risk.

3.—(1) This section applies as between contracting parties where one of them deals as consumer or on the other's written standard terms of business.

Liability arising in contract.

(2) As against that party, the other cannot by reference to any contract term—

283

(a) when himself in breach of contract, exclude or restrict any liability of his in respect of the breach; or

(b) claim to be entitled—

    (i) to render a contractual performance substantially different from that which was reasonably expected of him, or

    (ii) in respect of the whole or any part of his contractual obligation, to render no performance at all,

except in so far as (in any of the cases mentioned above in this subsection) the contract term satisfies the requirement of reasonableness.

Unreasonable
indemnity
clauses.

4.—(1) A person dealing as consumer cannot by reference to any contract term be made to indemnify another person (whether a party to the contract or not) in respect of liability that may be incurred by the other for negligence or breach of contract, except in so far as the contract term satisfies the requirement of reasonableness.

(2) This section applies whether the liability in question—

(a) is directly that of the person to be indemnified or is incurred by him vicariously;

(b) is to the person dealing as consumer or to someone else.

Liability arising from sale or supply of goods

'Guarantee'
of consumer
goods.

5.—(1) In the case of goods of a type ordinarily supplied for private use or consumption, where loss or damage—

(a) arises from the goods proving defective while in consumer use; and

(b) results from the negligence of a person concerned in the manufacture or distribution of the goods,

liability for the loss or damage cannot be excluded or restricted by reference to any contract term or notice contained in or operating by reference to a guarantee of the goods.

(2) For these purposes—

    (a) goods are to be regarded as 'in consumer use' when a person is using them, or has them in his possession for use, otherwise than exclusively for the purposes of a business; and

    (b) anything in writing is a guarantee if it contains or purports to contain some promise or assurance (however worded or presented) that defects will be made good by complete or partial replacement, or by repair, monetary compensation or otherwise.

(3) This section does not apply as between the parties to a contract under or in pursuance of which possession or ownership of the goods passed.

6.—(1) Liability for breach of the obligations arising from— Sale and hire-purchase

56 & 57 Vict.

    (a) section 12 of the Sale of Goods Act 1893 (seller's implied undertakings as to title, etc.); c. 71.

    (b) section 8 of the Supply of Goods (Implied Terms) Act 1973 (the corresponding thing in relation to hire-purchase), 1973 c. 13.

cannot be excluded or restricted by reference to any contract term.

(2) As against a person dealing as consumer, liability for breach of the obligations arising from—

    (a) section 13, 14 or 15 of the 1893 Act (seller's implied undertakings as to conformity of goods with description or sample, or as to their quality or fitness for a particular purpose);

    (b) section 9, 10 or 11 of the 1973 Act (the corresponding things in relation to hire-purchase),

cannot be excluded or restricted by reference to any contract term.

(3) As against a person dealing otherwise than as consumer, the liability specified in subsection(2) above can be excluded or restricted by reference to a contract

PART I

term, but only in so far as the term satisfies the requirement of reasonableness.

(4) The liabilities referred to in this section are not only the business liabilities defined by section 1(3), but include those arising under any contract of sale of goods or hire-purchase agreement.

Other provisions about contracts

Misrepre-
sentation.

8.—(1) In the Misrepresentation Act 1967, the following is substituted for section 3—

1967 c. 7

'Avoidance
of provision
excluding
liability for
misrepre-
sentation.

3. If a contract contains a term which would exclude or restrict—

(a) any liability to which a party to a contract may be subject by reason of any misrepresentation made by him before the contract was made; or

(b) any remedy available to another party to the contract by reason of such a misrepresentation,

that term shall be of no effect except in so far as it satisfies the requirement of reasonableness as stated in section 11(1) of the Unfair Contract Terms Act 1977; and it is for those claiming that the term satisfies that requirement to show that it does.'

1967 c. 14 (N.I.).

(2) The same section is substituted for section 3 of the Misrepresentation Act (Northern Ireland) 1967.

Explanatory provisions

The 'reason-
ableness'
test.
1967 c. 7.
1967 c. 14. (N.I.).

11.—(1) In relation to a contract term, the requirement of reasonableness for the purposes of this Part of this Act, section 3 of the Misrepresentation Act 1967 and section 3 of the Misrepresentation Act (Northern Ireland) 1967 is that the term shall have been a fair and reasonable one to be included having regard to the circumstances which were, or ought reasonably to have been, known to or in the contemplation of the parties when the contract was made.

(2) In determining for the purposes of section 6 or 7 Part I above whether a contract term satisfies the requirement of reasonableness, regard shall be had in particular to the matters specified in Schedule 2 to this Act; but this subsection does not prevent the court or arbitrator from holding, in accordance with any rule of law, that a term which purports to exclude or restrict any relevant liability is not a term of the contract.

(3) In relation to a notice (not being a notice having contractual effect), the requirement of reasonableness under this Act is that it should be fair and reasonable to allow reliance on it, having regard to all the circumstances obtaining when the liability arose or (but for the notice) would have arisen.

(4) Where by reference to a contract term or notice a person seeks to restrict liability to a specified sum of money, and the question arises (under this or any other Act) whether the term or notice satisfies the requirement of reasonableness, regard shall be had in particular (but without prejudice to subsection (2) above in the case of contract terms) to—

    (a) the resources which he could expect to be available to him for the purpose of meeting the liability should it arise; and

    (b) how far it was open to him to cover himself by insurance.

(5) It is for those claiming that a contract term or notice satisfies the requirement of reasonableness to show that it does.

SCHEDULE 2

'GUIDELINES' FOR APPLICATION OF REASONABLENESS TEST

Sections 11(2) and 24(2).

The matters to which regard is to be had in particular for the purposes of sections 6(3), 7(3) and (4), 20 and 21 are any of the following which appear to be relevant—

    (a) the strength of the bargaining positions of the parties relative to each other, taking into account (among other things) alternative means by which

SCH. 2

the customer's requirements could have been met;

(b) whether the customer received an inducement to agree to the term, or in accepting it had an opportunity of entering into a similar contract with other persons, but without having to accept a similar term;

(c) whether the customer knew or ought reasonably to have known of the existence and extent of the term (having regard, among other things, to any custom of the trade and any previous course of dealing between the parties);

(d) where the term excludes or restricts any relevant liability if some condition is not complied with, whether it was reasonable at the time of the contract to expect that compliance with that condition would be practicable;

(e) whether the goods were manufactured, processed or adapted to the special order of the customer.

'Dealing as consumer'.

12.—(1) A party to a contract 'deals as consumer' in relation to another party if—

(a) he neither makes the contract in the course of a business nor holds himself out as doing so; and

(b) the other party does make the contract in the course of a business; and

(c) in the case of a contract governed by the law of sale of goods or hire-purchase, or by section 7 of this Act, the goods passing under or in pursuance of the contract are of a type ordinarily supplied for private use or consumption.

(2) But on a sale by auction or by competitive tender the buyer is not in any circumstances to be regarded as dealing as consumer.

(3) Subject to this, it is for those claiming that a party does not deal as consumer to show that he does not.

Published by Her Majesty's Stationery Office, London,
ISBN 0 10 545077 4

Appendix F Extracts from the Supply of Goods and Services Act 1982

Sections 1–5 and 11

PART I

SUPPLY OF GOODS

Contracts for the transfer of property in goods

1.—(1) In this Act a 'contract for the transfer of goods' means a contract under which one person transfers or agrees to transfer to another the property in goods, other than an excepted contract. The contracts concerned.

(2) For the purposes of this section an excepted contract means any of the following:—

  (a) a contract of sale of goods;
  (b) a hire-purchase agreement;
  (c) a contract under which the property in goods is (or is to be) transferred in exchange for trading stamps on their redemption;
  (d) a transfer or agreement to transfer which is made by deed and for which there is no consideration other than the presumed consideration imported by the deed;
  (e) a contract intended to operate by way of mortgage, pledge, charge or other security.

(3) For the purposes of this Act a contract is a contract for the transfer of goods whether or not services are also provided or to be provided under the contract, and (subject to subsection (2) above) whatever is the nature of the consideration for the transfer or agreement to transfer.

Implied terms about title, etc.

2.—(1) In a contract for the transfer of goods, other than one to which subsection (3) below applies, there is an implied condition on the part of the transferor that in the case of a transfer of the property in the goods he has a right to transfer the property and in the case of an agreement to transfer the property in the goods he will have such a right at the time when the property is to be transferred.

(2) In a contract for the transfer of goods, other than one to which subsection (3) below applies, there is also an implied warranty that—

(a) the goods are free, and will remain free until the time when the property is to be transferred, from any charge or encumbrance not disclosed or known to the transferee before the contract is made, and

(b) the transferee will enjoy quiet possession of the goods except so far as it may be disturbed by the owner or other person entitled to the benefit of any charge or encumbrance so disclosed or known.

(3) This subsection applies to a contract for the transfer of goods in the case of which there appears from the contract or is to be inferred from its circumstances an intention that the transferor should transfer only such title as he or a third person may have.

(4) In a contract to which subsection(3) above applies there is an implied warranty that all charges or encumbrances known to the transferor and not known to the transferee have been disclosed to the transferee before the contract is made.

(5) In a contract to which subsection (3) above applies there is also an implied warranty that none of the following will disturb the transferee's quiet possession of the goods, namely—

(a) the transferor;

(b) in a case where the parties to the contract intend that the transferor should transfer only such title as a third person may have, that person;

(c) anyone claiming through or under the transferor or that third person otherwise than under a charge or encumbrance disclosed or known to the transferee before the contract is made.

PART I

3.—(1) This section applies where, under a contract for the transfer of goods, the transferor transfers or agrees to transfer the property in the goods by description.

Implied terms where transfer is by description.

(2) In such a case there is an implied condition that the goods will correspond with the description.

(3) If the transferor transfers or agrees to transfer the property in the goods by sample as well as by description it is not sufficient that the bulk of the goods corresponds with the sample if the goods do not also correspond with the description.

(4) A contract is not prevented from falling within subsection (1) above by reason only that, being exposed for supply, the goods are selected by the transferee.

4.—(1) Except as provided by this section and section 5 below and subject to the provisions of any other enactment, there is no implied condition or warranty about the quality or fitness for any particular purpose of goods supplied under a contract for the transfer of goods.

Implied terms about quality or fitness.

(2) Where, under such a contract, the transferor transfers the property in goods in the course of a business, there is (subject to subsection (3) below) an implied condition that the goods supplied under the contract are of merchantable quality.

(3) There is no such condition as is mentioned in subsection (2) above—

(a) as regards defects specifically drawn to the transferee's attention before the contract is made; or

(b) if the transferee examines the goods before the contract is made, as regards defects which that examination ought to reveal.

PART I

(4) Subsection (5) below applies where, under a contract for the transfer of goods, the transferor transfers the property in goods in the course of a business and the transferee, expressly or by implication, makes known—

(a) to the transferor, or

(b) where the consideration or part of the consideration for the transfer is a sum payable by instalments and the goods were previously sold by a credit-broker to the transferor, to that credit-broker,

any particular purpose for which the goods are being acquired.

(5) In that case there is (subject to subsection (6) below) an implied condition that the goods supplied under the contract are reasonably fit for that purpose, whether or not that is a purpose for which such goods are commonly supplied.

(6) Subsection (5) above does not apply where the circumstances show that the transferee does not rely, or that it is unreasonable for him to rely, on the skill or judgment of the transferor or credit-broker.

(7) An implied condition or warranty about quality or fitness for a particular purpose may be annexed by usage to a contract for the transfer of goods.

(8) The preceding provisions of this section apply to a transfer by a person who in the course of a business is acting as agent for another as they apply to a transfer by a principal in the course of a business, except where that other is not transferring in the course of a business and either the transferee knows that fact or reasonable steps are taken to bring it to the transferee's notice before the contract concerned is made.

(9) Goods of any kind are of merchantable quality within the meaning of subsection (2) above if they are as fit for the purpose or purposes for which goods of that kind are commonly supplied as it is reasonable to expect having regard to any description applied to them, the price (if relevant) and all the other relevant circumstances.

5.—(1) This section applies where, under a contract for the transfer of goods, the transferor transfers or agrees to transfer the property in the goods by reference to a sample.

(2) In such a case there is an implied condition—

(a) that the bulk will correspond with the sample in quality; and

(b) that the transferee will have a reasonable opportunity of comparing the bulk with the sample; and

(c) that the goods will be free from any defect, rendering them unmerchantable, which would not be apparent on reasonable examination of the sample.

(3) In subsection (2)(c) above 'unmerchantable' is to be construed in accordance with section 4(9) above.

(4) For the purposes of this section a transferor transfers or agrees to transfer the property in goods by reference to a sample where there is an express or implied term to that effect in the contract concerned.

Exclusion of implied terms, etc.

11.—(1) Where a right, duty or liability would arise under a contract for the transfer of goods or a contract for the hire of goods by implication of law, it may (subject to subsection (2) below and the 1977 Act) be negatived or varied by express agreement, or by the course of dealing between the parties, or by such usage as binds both parties to the contract.

(2) An express condition or warranty does not negative a condition or warranty implied by the preceding provisions of this Act unless inconsistent with it.

(3) Nothing in the preceding provisions of this Act prejudices the operation of any other enactment or any rule of law whereby any condition or warranty (other than one relating to quality or fitness) is to be implied in a contract for the transfer of goods or a contract for the hire of goods.

Published by Her Majesty's Stationery Office, London, ISBN 0 10 542982 1

Index

295